THE BATTLE FOR YEMEN

Al-Qaeda and the Struggle for Stability

Edited By Ramzy Mardini

The Jamestown Foundation
Washington, DC

THE JAMESTOWN FOUNDATION

Published in the United States by
The Jamestown Foundation
1111 16th Street NW
Suite 320
Washington, DC 20036
http://www.jamestown.org

For more information on this book of the Jamestown Foundation, email pubs@jamestown.org

ISBN 978-0-615-36666-1

Cover art provided by Peggy Archambault of Peggy Archambault Design

Jamestown's Mission

The Jamestown Foundation's mission is to inform and educate policy makers and the broader policy community about events and trends in those societies which are strategically or tactically important to the United States and which frequently restrict access to such information. Utilizing indigenous and primary sources, Jamestown's material is delivered without political bias, filter or agenda. It is often the only source of information which should be, but is not always, available through official or intelligence channels, especially in regard to Eurasia and terrorism.

Origins

Launched in 1984 after Jamestown's late president and founder William Geimer's work with Arkady Shevchenko, the highest-ranking Soviet official ever to defect when he left his position as undersecretary general of the United Nations, The Jamestown Foundation rapidly became the leading source of information about the inner workings of closed totalitarian societies.

Over the past two decades, Jamestown has developed an extensive global network of experts – from the Black Sea to Siberia, from the Persian Gulf to the Pacific. This core of intellectual talent includes scientists, journalists, scholars and economists. Their insight contributes significantly to policy makers engaged in addressing today's new and emerging global threats, including that from international terrorists.

The Battle For Yemen
Al-Qaeda and the Struggle for Stability

Table of Contents

Acknowledgements
Timeline of Key Events

Chapter Two
Yemen's War on Terrorism

Chapter Three
The Radical Faces of Yemen

Chapter Four
The Houthi Rebellions

Chapter Five
U.S.-Yemen Relations

Chapter Six
Economic Challenges to Stability

Appendix
Conference Speeches

Acknowledgements

The list of those who have contributed to this volume of writings about Yemen is quite extensive. Given that many of the contributors to this compilation of Jamestown's writings on Yemen are the analysts themselves, we owe our gratitude for their research and analysis without which this volume would not be possible. Many of these experts have spent a decade or more covering developments in this important country which has become a major focus of U.S. attention following the attempted 2009 Christmas Day bombing by Omar al-Farooq Abdulmutallab.

Yemen is an endlessly fascinating country that has occupied the attention of American policymakers before and after 9/11. Ironically the number of works on al-Qaeda and other militant groups operating in the Arabian Peninsula remain quite scarce in spite of the international attention Yemen has received. Toward this goal, Jamestown has sought to fill this void by providing a timely fact-based research and analysis on *The Battle for Yemen* and the role played by al-Qaeda and other militant groups in undermining regional stability.

As with most books published by The Jamestown Foundation, this volume is designed to be a reference volume for the policymaking community and is not designed to be the final word on militant movements in Yemen. What it does offer its readers is a reference tool to read about the key actors and groups making up al-Qaeda and other militant movements in Yemen. No organization in the world is better suited to address this issue than the analysts who write for The Jamestown Foundation and its flagship publication *Terrorism Monitor*. This group represents a truly global network of analysts and experts that extends to over fifty different countries. It is their insight that makes our analysis on terrorism unique and a key source of timely information to the U.S. policymaking community. We owe a deep debt of gratitude to these writers who have helped Jamestown continue to offer a diverse array of perspectives on conflict and instability which remains sorely lacking in the mainstream Western media.

This book would not be possible without the assistance of Ramzy Mardini. We owe him a special note of thanks for the endless hours he spent in editing the articles that make up this book. He has played a critical role in the past several months liaising with analysts around the world and in making this compilation of Jamestown writings on Yemen come together. A special note of thanks also is due to Julianne Opet of Jamestown staff who assisted in this project and played, as always, a crucial role in all the various logistical aspects in the publishing of this book.

I would like to thank the Jamestown Board of Directors, in particular, our Chairman, Willem de Vogel, for his support, guidance, and boundless energy. Under his leadership, Jamestown continued to expand and regenerate in this age of uncertainty enabling this foundation to fulfill its role of providing timely indigenous sourced information to policymakers around the globe.

Finally, The Jamestown Foundation owes its gratitude to our generous donors who support our activities. Without their support, our research would simply not be possible. And lastly we would like to thank the readers of Jamestown's publications for their continuing support, feedback and encouragement.

Glen E. Howard
President
The Jamestown Foundation

Yemen: Timeline of Key Events [1]

1500s: Ottomans absorb part of Yemen into their empire but are expelled in the 1600s.

1839: Aden comes under British rule, and when the Suez Canal opens in 1869, it serves as a major refueling port.

1849: Ottomans return to north, but later face revolt.

1918: Ottoman Empire dissolves; North Yemen gains independence and is ruled by Imam Yahya.

1948: Imam Yahya is assassinated, but his son Imam Ahmad beats off opponents of feudal rule and succeeds his father.

1962: Imam Ahmad dies and is succeeded by his son, but army officers seize power and set up the Yemen Arab Republic, sparking civil war between royalists supported by Saudi Arabia and republicans backed by Egypt.

1967: Formation of South Yemen, comprising Aden and former Protectorate of South Arabia. Country is later officially known as the People's Democratic Republic of Yemen. Program of nationalization begins.

1971: Thousands flee to north following crackdown on dissidents. Armed groups formed in bid to overthrow government.

1972: Border clashes between Yemen Arab Republic and the People's Democratic Republic of Yemen. A ceasefire is brokered by the Arab League.

1978: Ali Abdullah Saleh named President of Yemen Arab Republic.

1979: Fresh fighting between Yemen Arab Republic and People's Democratic Republic of Yemen.

---

[1] Timeline is compiled by BBC News: "Yemen Timeline: A Chronology of Key Events," BBC News, March 17, 2010 (last updated): http://news.bbc.co.uk/2/hi/middle_east/country_profiles/1706450.stm. Also, additions to timeline were made independently.

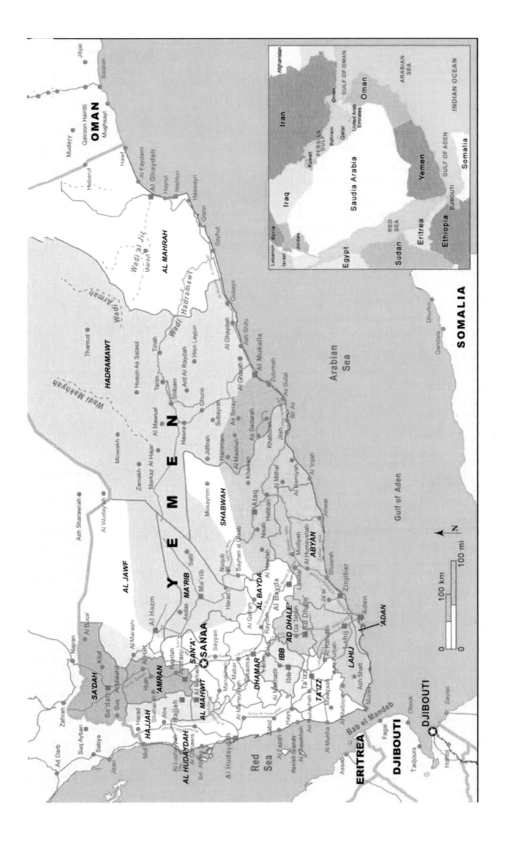

1986: Thousands die in South Yemen in political rivalry. President Ali Nasser Muhammad flees the country and is later sentenced to death for treason. New government formed.

1990: Unified Republic of Yemen proclaimed, with Ali Abdullah Saleh as president.

1991: Yemen opposes U.S.-led action against Iraq in Gulf War.

1992: Food price riots in major towns.

1993 April: Coalition government formed, made up of ruling parties of former north and south.

1993 August: Vice President Ali Salem al-Beedh withdraws to Aden, alleging that south is being marginalized and that southerners are being attacked by northerners.

1994: Armies of former north and south, which have failed to integrate, gather on former frontier as relations between southern and northern leaders deteriorate.

1994 May: President Ali Abdullah Saleh declares state of emergency and dismisses Vice President Ali Salim al-Baid and other southern government members following political deadlock and sporadic fighting. Foreigners flee escalating fighting.

1994 May 21: Vice President Ali Salem al-Beedh declares independence of Democratic Republic of Yemen. President Saleh rejects secession as illegal.

1994 July: Northern forces take control of Aden, secessionist leaders flee abroad and are sentenced to death in absentia.

1995: Yemen and Eritrea clash over disputed island territory.

2000 October 12: U.S. naval vessel, the USS Cole, is damaged in a suicide attack in Aden, which was subsequently blamed on al-Qaeda. Seventeen U.S. personnel are killed.

2000 October: Bomb explodes at British Embassy in Yemen. Four Yemenis who are jailed say they carried out attack in solidarity with Palestinians.

2001 February: Violence in run-up to municipal polls and referendum, in which voters show support for constitutional reform extending presidential term and powers.

2001 November: President Ali Abdullah Saleh visits U.S. and tells President George W. Bush that Yemen is a partner in the fight against terrorism.

2002 February: Yemen expels more than 100 foreign Islamic scholars, including British and French nationals, in crackdown on terror and suspected al-Qaeda members.

2002 October: Supertanker Limburg badly damaged in attack off the Yemeni coast. The attack is blamed on al-Qaeda.

2002 November: Leader of al-Qaeda in Yemen, Sinan Qa'id al-Harthi (a.k.a. Abu Ali al-Harthi) is assassinated. His replacement is Muhammad al-Ahdal.

2003 April: The 10 chief suspects in the bombing of the USS Cole escape from custody in Aden.

2003 November: Yemeni forces arrest Muhammad al-Ahdal, the replacement of the late al-Qaeda in Yemen leader Sinan Qa'id al-Harthi (aka Abu Ali al-Harthi).

2004 March: Two militants, suspected of masterminding bombing of USS Cole, are re-arrested.

2004 June-August: The outbreak of a Houthi rebellion begins on June 18, as government troops battle supporters of dissident cleric Hussein al-Houthi in the north.

2004 August: Court sentences 15 men on terror charges, including bombing of Limburg tanker in 2002.

2004 September: Government says its forces have killed dissident cleric Hussein al-Houthi, the leader of a revolt in the north.

2005 March-April: More than 200 people are killed in a resurgence of fighting between government forces and supporters of the slain rebel cleric Hussein al-Houthi.

2005 May: President Ali Abdullah Saleh says the leader of the rebellion in the north has agreed to renounce the campaign in return for a pardon. Minor clashes continue.

2005 July: Police and witnesses say at least 36 people are killed across the country in clashes between police and demonstrators protesting about a cut in fuel subsidies.

2005 December: More than 60 people are killed when a landslide destroys a mountain village around 20km from Sanaa.

2006 February 3: In a major setback in Yemen's fight against terrorism, twenty-three prisoners escape from a high-security prison at the headquarters of the Political Security Organization in the capital city of Sana'a. Over half of the escapees had been highly valued al-Qaeda suspects involved in the attacks on the USS Cole and the Limburg tanker. The event is often referred to as the "Great Escape," and is said to have paved the way for the reorganization of al-Qaeda in the Arabian Peninsula.

2006 March: More than 600 followers of slain Shiite cleric Hussein al-Houthi who were captured following a rebellion he led in 2004 are released under an amnesty.

2006 September: President Ali Abdullah Saleh wins another term in elections.

2007 January-March: Scores are killed or wounded in clashes between security forces and al-Houthi rebels in the north.

2007 June: Houthi rebel leader Abdul Malik al-Houthi accepts a ceasefire.

2007 July: Suicide bomber attacks a tourist convoy killing eight Spaniards and two Yemenis in the province of Marib.

2007 August: Citizens banned from carrying firearms in Sana'a. Demonstrations without a permit are outlawed.

2007 October: Volcano erupts on the Red Sea island of Jabal al-Tair where Yemen has a military base.

2007 November: Clashes between Yemeni tribesmen and army personnel protecting a Ukrainian oil company leave 16 people dead in the south-eastern Shabwa province.

2008 January: Renewed clashes between security forces and rebels loyal to Abdul Malik al-Houthi.

2008 January 13: Al-Qaeda in Yemen issues its first publication of its online journal, *Sada al-Malahim*.

2008 April: Clashes with troops as southern Yemenis protest against alleged northern bias in state job allocation. One man killed.

2008 March-April: Series of bomb attacks on police, official, diplomatic, foreign business and tourism targets. U.S. Embassy evacuates all non-essential personnel.

2008 September: Attack on U.S. Embassy in Yemeni capital Sana'a kills 18 people, including six assailants. Six suspects arrested.

2008 October: President Ali Abdullah Saleh announces arrest of suspected Islamist militants allegedly linked to Israeli intelligence.

2008 November: Police fire warning shots at Common Forum opposition rally in Sana'a. Demonstrators demand electoral reform and fresh polls. At least five protestors and two police officers injured.

2009 February: Government announces release of 176 al-Qaeda suspects on condition of good behavior.

2009 June: Yemen announces the arrest of Hassan bin Hussein Alwan in the province of Marib, claiming him the largest financier of al-Qaeda in Yemen; Nine foreigners are abducted in remote Saada region. The bodies of three are later found. The fate of the remaining six hostages remains unclear, though local rebels deny responsibility.

2009 August: The Yemeni army launches a fresh offensive against Shiite rebels in the northern Saada province. Tens of thousands of people are displaced by the fighting.

2009 October: Clashes break out between the northern rebels and Saudi security forces along the two countries' common border. The rebels accuse Saudi Arabia of supporting the Yemeni government in attacks against them. The Saudi government denies this.

2009 November: Saudi Arabia says it has regained control of territory seized by Yemeni rebels in a cross-border incursion.

2009 December: Yemen-based branch of al-Qaeda claims it was behind failed attack on U.S. airliner on Christmas Day. The Yemeni government calls on the West for more support to help it combat the al-Qaeda threat.

2010 January: President Ali Abdullah Saleh says government open to talks with al-Qaeda militants, provided that they renounce violence.

2010 February: Government signs ceasefire with northern Houthi rebels.

2010 March: Northern rebels release 178 captives after the government accuses the Shiite Houthi group of failing to comply with the terms of the truce reached in February 2010.

Introduction: Yemen, al-Qaeda and America's Challenge

By Bruce Riedel

Well before the failed al-Qaeda attack on a passenger jet landing at Detroit on Christmas day 2009 President Barack Obama's administration had made defeating al-Qaeda's franchise in Yemen, al-Qaeda in the Arabian Peninsula (AQAP), a top priority. It will be a very difficult mission to accomplish because Yemen has always been one of the world's least governable spaces, it is deeply divided on complex and confusing sectarian and regional grounds, and its ruling government is a weak partner in the fight. To make matters worse, several decades of bad U.S.-Yemeni relations have soured many Yemenis on America and made some sympathetic to al-Qaeda. This new volume of articles from the Jamestown Foundation helps to put all of these issues in perspective. As the United States embarks on developing a new relationship with Yemen, this volume provides important insights into the challenges we will face.

Al-Qaeda has long been active in Yemen, the original home land of Osama bin Laden's family, and one of its first major terror attacks was conducted in Aden in 2000 when an al-Qaeda cell nearly sank the U.S.S. Cole. Bin Laden married a Yemeni girl just before 9/11 to further cement his ties to the country. A year ago the al-Qaeda franchises in Saudi Arabia and Yemen merged after the Saudi branch had been effectively destroyed by the Saudi authorities under the leadership of Deputy Interior Minister Prince Muhammad bin Nayif. The new AQAP showed its claws when it almost assassinated the Prince last August with a suicide bomber.

The same bomb makers who produced that devise probably made the bomb that Omar al-Farooq Abdulmutallab used on Northwest flight 253. In claiming credit for the Detroit attack AQAP highlighted how they had built a bomb that "all the advanced, new machines and technologies and the security boundaries of the world's airports" had failed to detect. AQAP has also provided refugee for the Yemeni American cleric Sheikh Anwar al-Awlaki who was in contact with U.S. Army Major Nidal Hasan who killed 13 soldiers at Fort Hood in Texas on November 5, 2009. In claiming credit for the Christmas day airline attack AQAP also lauded the Fort Hood massacre and urged other American Muslims to emulate Nidal Hasan.

Nominally part of the Ottoman Empire from the 1520s north Yemen gained independence at the end of the First World War when the Ottoman Turks

1

collapsed. After 1918 the north was ruled by a regime dominated by the minority Zaidi Shiite, a uniquely Yemeni Shiite movement that is independent of the larger, mainstream Shiite sect that runs Iran. It lost a border war to Saudi Arabia in 1934 that has left Yemenis angry towards Riyadh ever since.

In 1962 Egyptian backed Arab nationalists overthrew the Zaidi Imam in a bloody coup. A long civil war followed with 70,000 Egyptian soldiers backing the republicans and Saudi Arabia, Jordan and even Israel covertly backing the royalists. The Egyptians could not suppress the tribes and left in defeat. A series of military dictators have ruled since. The Zaidi tribes in the north recently rebelled against the central government again under the leadership of the Houthis. There are several insightful articles here on the Houthi rebellion and its implications for Yemeni stability.

The southern part of Yemen became a colony of the British East India Company in 1839 and was ruled from Bombay for a century. The British only wanted to suppress piracy and use the port of Aden as a transit stop on the sail to India. They barely ruled the interior, leaving it in the hands of tribal sheikhs. In 1968, the British were ousted by Moscow-backed communist terrorists. When the Soviet Union collapsed in 1990 the abandoned and broke communist south had no choice but to merge with the north. The hero of unification was President Ali Abdullah Saleh who survived a Saudi backed southern rebellion in 1994 and has now been in office 32 years. The south still seeks to break away.

Saleh is himself a Zaidi Shiite but also a firm Arab nationalist. He has courted the jihadists in the past and keeps his ties to the clerics. He backed Saddam Hussein and Iraq in the first gulf war in 1990. In response the Saudis expelled a million Yemeni expatriate workers from the Kingdom and backed the anti-Saleh southern insurrection in 1994. Saleh has allowed parliamentary elections but the regime is in fact a police state. Saleh is a fascinating figure, a wily survivor and is profiled in this volume.

His government's battle against al-Qaeda illustrates its weaknesses. Again and again al-Qaeda operatives have been captured by the government only to escape from prison. The head of AQAP, Nasir al-Wuhayshi, broke out of the nation's number one prison in 2006 along with some twenty other terrorists. His number two, Sa'id al-Shihri, is a Saudi released by the Bush administration from Guantanamo to the Kingdom. Senior al-Qaeda operatives have been killed only to be replaced by others. This volume studies the prison breaks, the key al-Qaeda leaders and the clerical establishment that fosters jihad in Yemen.

INTRODUCTION

U.S.-Yemen relations have never really fully recovered from the 1990 Gulf War differences. All aid was cut off in 1991 and only slowly resumed. After al-Qaeda blew up the U.S.S. Cole in Aden harbor in October 2000 the investigation of the attack only further embittered both sides as each claimed the other was holding back key information. The Bush and Obama administrations have rightly refused to send Yemeni detainees back from Guantanamo given the history of prison breaks in the last decade. Yemenis rightly believe we treat them like a poor cousin of their traditional Saudi enemy. Again there is much to be learned in this volume about our troubled ties to Sana'a.

In November 2001, after 9/11, Saleh visited President George W. Bush in the Oval Office. As the President's senior adviser for the Near East, I took the notes of their conversation. Saleh began by saying he was there to mostly listen but then launched a 30-minute monologue, eloquently describing the multiple crises Yemen faces. Population growth, illiteracy, increasing water shortages, declining oil production, qat addiction, tribal unrest, and the al-Qaeda threat were all on his agenda. Ours was focused on al-Qaeda. The exchange symbolized the problem for America in Yemen. We wanted to fight al-Qaeda but we can only do so by dealing with a much larger range of problems that creates the environment al-Qaeda thrives in.

The Jamestown Foundation has earned a well-deserved reputation for publishing insightful analysis of the terrorist threats America faces today. Yemen, along with Pakistan and Afghanistan, is at the top of that agenda. This volume is a timely contribution to the development of an effective national security strategy to deal with the threat posed from al-Qaeda in Yemen.

Bruce Riedel is a Senior Fellow at the Saban Center for Middle East Policy at the Brookings Institution. He served thirty years in the CIA and has traveled extensively throughout Yemen. His 2008 book, The Search for Al Qaeda, came out in paperback last spring.

Chapter One

Yemen: Al-Qaeda's New Playground

Shifting Sands: Al-Qaeda and Tribal Gun-Running Along the Yemeni Frontier

By Stephen Ulph

For centuries, tribal politics in Yemen have been driven by one simple concept: loyalty is sold to the highest bidder. While both Saudi Arabia and the Yemeni government have used this principle to their advantage, it is al-Qaeda that has been the high bidder in recent years, seeking to ensure a regular transport for arms to its cells in Saudi Arabia and beyond. Under the new conditions created by the war on terror, however, Yemeni President Ali Abdullah Saleh is being forced to find resolution to this long-standing problem.

Al-Qaeda's presence in remote tribal areas is a subject of intense interest in the West given the porous frontier of the Saudi-Yemeni border and the arms trafficking that occurs within this zone. Tribal gun-running in this region is particularly important given the links between Yemen and al-Qaeda that date back to the mid-1990s when the bulk of al-Qaeda's foot soldiers in Afghanistan reportedly came from Yemen. In fact, Bin Laden was apparently so successful in attracting recruits from Yemen that the Yemeni component of his forces in Afghanistan once was believed to be as high as 4,000 men. Other accounts estimate that this number even went as high as 32,000, which alongside the Pakistanis would make the Yemenis the bulk of Bin Laden's forces in Afghanistan [1].

The tribal border areas of Yemen have long served as a conducive political environment for al-Qaeda. It is in this region that suspicion of – and opposition to – the central government is a constant inconstancy that has made the governing of Yemen more closely resemble that of a 'tribalocracy.' The abiding preoccupation of the tribal groups in rural and remote Yemen is autonomy, and what each perceives as its due share of national resources and funding. The inability of Sana'a to accommodate these competing interests, whether for economic or political reasons, spawns inevitable disaffection. When this is combined with Sana'a's attempts at expanding the reach of the central government, it morphs into antagonism.

A painful example of the strength of this antagonism was learnt in December 2001 when the Yemeni Government launched an operation in Marib designed to capture Abu Ali al-Harthi, a former bodyguard of Osama bin Laden, as part of the war on terrorism. The tribal leaderships viewed the action as an attack on their autonomy, irrespective of the al-Qaeda factor. Moreover, for Yemenis of whatever complexion al-Qaeda is a western preoccupation, not theirs. If anything, bin Laden scores over George W. Bush politically, culturally and ethnically. The mission, as it turned out, not only failed in its objective but also caused heavy government losses when soldiers met heavy resistance from well-armed tribesmen [2].

A Culture of Arms

The role of arms in tribal society represent a major problem for Yemeni authorities in exerting control over troublesome tribal regions where local sympathy for bin Laden often outweighs support for the central government. Al-Qaeda has been able to exploit this culture to funnel weapons and equipment to cells operating inside Saudi Arabia which has needless to say irritated relations with Riyadh. It is the level of this armament which complicates the issue in establishing enough governmental authority to eradicate the influence of militant Islamism.

Government officials themselves speak of 60 million weapons dispersed among a population of 18 million. That is, three firearms per capita. Outside the major cities the tradition of bearing arms is well ingrained. All males past puberty openly carry arms, which makes for an explicitness in arms trading that few countries can match. The town of Saada, for example, situated 25 miles south of the border with Saudi Arabia, boasts the biggest arms souk where, in addition to small firearms, an 85mm surface-to-surface missile can be purchased as well as, discreetly, surface-to-air missiles. Arm trafficking is strongly defended by the regional tribal leaders, who fear that the loss of the trade will spell their marginalization from political life. Consequently, President Saleh, who during the 1994 civil war purchased tribal support in his drive to consolidate power, is wary enough of their influence not to attempt radical intervention into tribal arms smuggling.

Saudi-Yemeni tensions focused acutely on the 1,500 km border. During the 1990s, particularly after Yemen voiced its support for Saddam Hussein during the 1991 Gulf War, border clashes claimed victims on both sides and, despite the long-awaited 2000 Jeddah border treaty, the resentment lingers on. One of the disastrous consequences of the period was Riyadh's policy of lending financial support to opponents of President Saleh, including religious radicals. When the border dispute was officially brought to an end in 2000 Saudi funding to the Yemeni Islamists dried up, which left them open to blandishments from al-Qaeda.

Escalations on the Border

When the earlier Saudi policy in due course backfired, the finger of suspicion pointed back at the Yemeni arms smugglers over the border. The trade has grown progressively more violent, with a total of 36 Saudi border guards killed at the Saudi frontier town of Jizan between March 2002 and February 2003. The explosives used in last year's bombings were claimed by official Saudi media to be of Yemeni origin, as were those used in earlier attacks on the American compound in 1995 and the mosque bombing in Bahah province in 1993. Since the May 2005 bombings, daily hauls of large quantities of weapons and explosives have already notched up figures in excess of 100,000 rounds of ammunition, grenades, over 2,000 sticks of dynamite, 100s of bazookas and more than 1,200 assorted firearms. By December 2004, as a result of the increased policing of the border, the number of persons arrested had topped 4,000.

By February 2005 of this year tensions between the two countries peaked. In early January 2005 the Saudis initiated construction of a security fence, part of a larger plan to erect what is to be an electronic surveillance system costing some $9 billion, along the entire length of the Kingdom's land and sea frontiers. The point of contention was a raised barrier section designed to close off a 20km stretch in a neutral no-man's land zone. Placing the barrier within the zone was taken by local Yemeni tribal figures as a breach of the Jeddah agreement. These last have already started to attack workers erecting demarcation posts and have issued threats of more concerted military action, claiming a force of 3,000 in place to defend Yemeni claims. While some swift diplomacy has to an extent calmed the issue, with talk of increased border security policing, the construction of the barrier is itself a sign of Saudi distrust of Yemeni commitment. Riyadh has stated that it intends to maintain the work carried out to date.

Balance of Risks

The central government's effort to crack down on arms trafficking creates a balance of risks for both the Yemeni government and al-Qaeda. Having galvanized international and now regional reaction, al-Qaeda appears to be gambling that President Salih will not be able to sustain domestic opposition to a security policy perceived as serving U.S. interests. But it is an unsafe gamble since al-Qaeda cannot rely on the unconditional protection of the tribes. As in Iraq, where U.S. pockets proved deeper than Saddam Hussein's, enough to secure his betrayal by former supporters, military support in the face of overwhelmingly superior technology and a concerted carrot-and-stick treatment from Sana'a will not come cheap.

For his part, the Yemeni President has had to weigh the options of buying loyalty away from the Islamist militants, which given the complexities of inter-tribal relations may prove difficult. Ultimately, President Saleh's political future may force him to give the tribes more autonomy if he cannot deliver more economic assistance. The traditional weak point in tribal politics in Yemen also applies here as well. If the centre at Sana'a cannot be maintained equidistant to all, then the pressure to make an accommodation for fear of losing out becomes all the more cogent.

Increasingly, there are signs that the sands may be shifting. More telling, perhaps, than the optimistic statement of Prime Minister Abdul Qadir Bajammal that payoffs to tribes had acted to dismantle 90 percent of al-Qaeda cells in the country, is the uncharacteristic call made earlier in January 2005 by al-Qaeda for a deal with the Yemeni government: that operations against western interests in Yemen be halted in return for safe passage for the mujahideen to join their fellows in Iraq, Afghanistan and Palestine. Consequently, Yemen and al-Qaeda might be reaching a new modus vivendi in the tribal areas. If permission is being sought from Sana'a, then it would appear that al-Qaeda's confidence in tribal protection has waned.

[Originally Publication: *Terrorism Monitor* 2 (7) - May 19, 2005]

Notes

1. An indication of the preponderance of Yemeni mujahideen in Afghanistan and how their numbers devalued their currency, may be gauged by a letter complaining of their treatment was published in the London-based Arabic political journal al-Majalla in December 2002. It featured what was a semi-mutinous complaint signed by 32 Yemeni fighters addressed to Commander Sayf al-'Adl, which began sarcastically: "From 'dervishes' and

tribesmen on the frontline..," and listed what they held was the incompetence of their commanders and their cavalier and hypocritical treatment of them, in particular from Sayf al-'Adl, whom they heard had referred to them disdainfully as 'tramps'. The letter was dated September 11, 2000.

2. The issue was resolved in November 2002 with the US Predator attack, which killed Al-Harithi. The action avoided the problem of an army itself composed of tribesman who cannot be relied on to fire on members of their own or allied tribes. Tribesmen have also been suspected of compromising operations by revealing information to protect relatives and allies.

Yemen's Al-Iman University: A Pipeline for Fundamentalists?

By Gregory D. Johnsen

The recent arrests of 23 men, including four Europeans and three Australians, have once again raised questions about Yemen's al-Iman University and its possible links to extremism. Initial reports suggested that the European and Australian suspects, who were accused of smuggling weapons to Islamist militias in Somalia, were students at al-Iman; this claim, however, was quickly denied by the university's president and founder Sheikh Abdul Majid al-Zindani (*Asharq al-Awsat*, November 1, 2006). Al-Zindani, who was listed as a "specially designated global terrorist" by both the United States and the United Nations in 2004, has often used this ploy to distance himself and the university from students suspected of terrorist activities [1]. This time, however, his claim was defended by Yemeni President Ali Abdullah Saleh, who paid a surprise visit to al-Iman on November 12, 2006 (Saba News, November 12, 2006). An analysis of the university itself displays how it is both an institution of higher learning and a pipeline for fundamentalist activity.

President Saleh's Defense of al-Iman

Saleh's recent comments marked the second time in three months that he has publicly defended the university against its critics. The first time was on August 21, 2006, when Saleh was the keynote speaker at the graduation ceremony of al-Iman's third group of graduates. He claimed on that occasion that Western governments had been sending students to the university in an attempt to ascertain the university's curriculum, but that they had "failed because the university taught only the Quran and Sunna" (*Asharq al-Awsat*, August 22, 2006). He said that this sort of behavior has caused the university's students to "live in a corner of fear" from Western security infiltration (*Asharq al-Awsat*, August 22, 2006). Saleh went further in his November defense of the university, not only claiming that al-Iman did not produce extremists, but also praising al-Zindani as a "leading soldier in the Yemeni Revolution and an enlightened academic soldier" (*al-Hayat*, November 13, 2006). Saleh flatly denied the allegation that al-Iman produced terrorists. "That is a lie," he said in his speech. "If this is a nest of terrorists, then what is the president of the country doing here?" (*al-Hayat*, November 13, 2006).

9

Saleh has defended al-Zindani before, most notably in March 2006 of this year, when he told U.S. Ambassador Thomas Krajeski: "Sheikh al-Zindani is a rational, balanced and moderate man and we know him well and the Yemeni government guarantees [his actions] and I guarantee his character" (*al-Quds al-Arabi*, March 12, 2006). His speech at al-Iman came only days before Saleh was scheduled to head a delegation to a donor's conference in London, signifying once again that Saleh is not willing to trade al-Zindani for economic aid.

Regardless of Saleh's defense, al-Iman University is not the terrorist producing institute that the United States thinks it is, but then neither is it the misunderstood religious college that Yemen claims it to be; the problem is that the university is a complex mix of the two, which is what makes it so difficult to define. The university, which sits on the outskirts of Sanaa, is best known in the United States as the place where American Taliban John Walker Lindh studied before leaving for Pakistan and later Afghanistan. In Yemen, it is famous for producing students such as Ali al-Jarallah and Abed Abdul al-Razak Kamal, who were responsible for the murder of an opposition politician and three Baptist missionaries in late 2002. Over the years, al-Zindani has issued separate statements claiming that none of these students, except for al-Jarallah, ever attended the university. In a 2005 interview with the Lebanese journalist Hazim al-Amin, al-Zindani said that al-Jarallah only studied at al-Iman for a year and a half before leaving out of frustration over the lack of religiosity at the university (*al-Hayat*, October 12, 2005). Nevertheless, like his carefully worded and ambiguous statements about the nature of his relationship with Osama bin Laden, al-Zindani's denials appear more contrived than concrete.

The Makeup of the University

Al-Zindani established the university in 1993, the same year that he took up a post on the five-man presidential council, although the university did not start classes until 1994. The university, which initially operated outside of government control, relied on donations and the support of wealthy benefactors. The Yemeni government, under Saleh's instructions, donated the land, while Saudi Arabia and a host of private groups from around the Islamic world contributed financial capital. It is often assumed that bin Laden was among these donors, as he was fairly close to al-Zindani during the 1980s when both men spent a great deal of time in Afghanistan and Pakistan. Musa al-Qarni, a Saudi scholar, told *al-Hayat* in March 2006 that the two, along with Abdullah Azzam, were the most prominent men at the absentia trial of Ahmad Shah Masoud (*al-Hayat*, March 8, 2006). Despite these ties, however, al-Zindani has denied that bin Laden was a source of funding for al-Iman (*Asharq al-Awsat*, June 3, 2001). Ever since al-Zindani was listed as a "specially designated global terrorist," he has become even more reticent to discuss the university's sources of funding. In his interview with al-Amin, al-Zindani said that if he revealed the university's donors, they would come under international pressure to end their support for al-Iman (*al-Hayat*, October 12, 2005).

Despite government support – Saleh laid the cornerstone for the university – al-Iman has not led a trouble-free existence. In the aftermath of the September 11 attacks, the university was closed down temporarily and scores of foreign students were deported. It has also been accused of fostering a military wing by the ruling General People's Congress' newspaper, *al-Mu'atammar*. Al-Zindani wasted little time in putting out a statement emphatically denying this, saying that the very claim was designed to help foreigners accuse al-Iman of supporting terrorism (al-Jazeera, January 6, 2005). This denial, like his many others, did little to convince al-Zindani's numerous critics within the government. Yet while al-Zindani's enemies maintain a significant amount of power, he has always been protected, when it mattered most, by President Saleh.

On a number of occasions, the United States has, in fact, made a similar claim that the university has a military wing, but the accusation is usually dismissed out of hand by the Yemeni government. In 2005, Mansur al-Zindani, Abdul Majid's brother and a member of parliament, laughed off the suggestion in his interview with al-Amin, saying that maybe the U.S. government could not read their own satellite pictures. "There is a military camp (the 1st Armored Division) next to the university, and maybe the Americans can't see the border, and maybe they think the soldiers are actually on university grounds" (*al-Hayat*, October 12, 2005).

Given al-Zindani's status and the rumors about al-Iman, it has always been extremely difficult to get inside the walls of the university. Nicholas Kristof, a columnist for the *New York Times*, was turned away at the gate by armed soldiers in 2002. Even the Arabic press has had difficulties getting access, but in the past two years al-Zindani has granted passes to two journalists, al-Amin for *al-Hayat* and Arafat Madabish, a Yemeni stringer writing for *Asharq al-Awsat*. Both men have published lengthy reports on the university, which represent a great deal of what outsiders know about the institution. Al-Amin describes the university center as a "town within a town," as it has an Internet café, restaurant, laundromat, grocery store, telephone center and other small shops. He divides the students at al-Iman into two categories according to their dress. Some of the students wear traditional Islamic clothes, while others wear normal street clothes (*al-Hayat*, March 12, 2005). This division of the students can also be seen in their political inclinations. The vast majority of them are quietists, but there is a significant group that tends toward extremism and violence.

The university currently has an enrollment of 4,650 students: 3,750 males and 800 females (*Asharq al-Awsat*, July 21, 2006). Like other universities, there are dorms available for the students, although no women live on campus and most Yemeni students live with their families or stay with friends in Sana'a. The vast majority of these students are serious-minded young scholars; they almost have to be, as a full course of study in one of al-Iman's four schools takes seven years, which is why the university has only graduated three groups of students since it started offering classes in 1994. Al-Iman offers degrees in the schools of Sharia (or Islamic jurisprudence), Arabic, Islamic Preaching and Human Sciences. There is a small contingent of students that veer away from the quietist trend of their colleagues. They tend to be foreign students that are drawn to al-Iman by al-Zindani's radical reputation, while the Yemeni students are attracted by the overt religiosity of the university. These categories are not, of course, concrete. Some Yemeni students are inclined toward political violence, while some foreigners are interested only in knowledge. Yet, generally speaking, the categories hold true.

Al-Iman's enrollment numbers and experience bear this out. While the university has students from more than 50 countries—including the United States, Somalia, Kosovo, Indonesia, Albania and most European countries—the actual number of these students is quite small, hovering around 150. These students are also inclined to be more interested in contemporary politics than in completing their studies, which is why al-Zindani has some wiggle room in refusing to call people like Lindh and Kamal students, as neither of them ever finished a degree. The foreign students also work as a convenient scapegoat for the Yemeni government. They can be expelled from the university at a much greater rate than the Yemeni students, partly out of their self-selecting nature as being more politically active, and partly because the government does not have to deal with the tribes and families of these students. This allows Yemen to look like it is being tough on potential terrorists at al-Iman, while not suffering domestically for its actions.

Conclusion

Al-Iman will continue to straddle this divide as a legitimate religious institution and as a fundamentalist pipeline for as long as it is given cover by the Yemeni government. Saleh's recent speeches at al-Iman suggest that this support will not end soon. Periodically, the government will be forced to crack down on extremists attending the university, but this will continue to be tempered by al-Zindani's denials, which will be supported by Saleh. Al-Iman's legitimate practices will allow the Yemeni government to defend it, which will provide the university with the political space to carry out its more nefarious actions.

[Original Publication: *Terrorism Monitor* 4 (22) – November 16, 2006]

Notes

1. For a detailed profile of Sheikh al-Zindani, see *Terrorism Monitor*, April 6, 2006.

Expansion of Yemen's Refining Capacity Raises Terrorism Concerns

By John Solomon

On May 16, 2007, the Yemeni-Gulf Oil Services Company (YGOSC) announced its intention to build a refinery in the Ras Essa area of Hodeidah Province on the Red Sea coast. Scheduled for completion in August 2009, YGOSC expects the project to increase its refining capacity by 35% over existing capacity (Yemen MOM; Saba News, May 16, 2007). The project represents a key part of the Yemeni government's optimistic plan to expand its hydrocarbon production and refining capacity. This development highlights the possibility of future terrorist attacks on Yemeni energy infrastructure, which could destabilize a key U.S. ally and probably cause an increase in oil prices. A historical trend of attacks on oil infrastructure has been ongoing in Yemen since October 2002. In addition, al-Qaeda has publicly and repeatedly issued directives and fatwas calling for strikes on oil-related targets in the Arabian Peninsula since 2004.

The Yemeni government derives 70% of its revenue from oil production (Yemen MOM; Saba News, May 16, 2007). According to the U.S. Energy Information Administration, in 2006 Yemen exported around 330,000 barrels per day (bpd) of oil mainly to Asian markets. Although this figure represents less than one-half of one percent of the world's total daily production, Yemen's oil sector is significant as the stability of President Ali Abdullah Saleh's regime appears closely tied to the state's dependence on export sales of its hydrocarbons. The dependence on oil exports comes with additional negative political exposure. Unlike much of the petroleum production in the Middle East region, Yemeni production is heavily reliant on private foreign firms, with American, French and British companies controlling majority shares in a considerable number of concessions.

In order to diversify its revenue stream and build its weak economy, the Yemeni government is turning to natural gas production and marketing through the Yemeni Liquid Natural Gas Company (YLNG) in which they hold a 21.73% stake, with the remainder held by French, American and Korean companies. Planned projects include a 320-kilometer pipeline from processing centers in Marib to a liquefaction plant at Balhaf Harbor (World Press, August 4, 2006). The pipeline could be an attractive target for al-Qaeda given its strategic importance coupled with the fact that attacks have been carried out against oil pipelines in the past.

Perhaps of wider interest to the region is Yemen's location at the entrance of the Bab el-Mandeb Strait, one of the world's most strategic shipping lanes, through which three million bpd of oil is moved in tankers originating in the Persian Gulf, and passing through the Suez Canal en route to Western markets. Disruption of this shipping lane could divert tanker traffic around the southern tip of Africa, which would add considerable transit time and cost, resulting in sharp price increases of a wide range of goods and services.

Historical patterns and recent information indicate that the Yemeni state is at significant risk of suffering terrorist attacks on its energy infrastructure. These factors suggest that jihadis in Yemen and the greater Arabian Peninsula have both an intention and justification for undertaking attacks against oil and gas targets within Yemeni territory. There is a clear historical pattern of al-Qaeda's targeting of energy infrastructure in Yemen, beginning with the October 2002 attack on the French Very Large Crude Carrier, the MV Limburg. The strike resulted in the spillage of 90,000 barrels into the Gulf of Aden and economic damage quantified as a $0.48/barrel price increase due to higher insurance premiums, which in turn caused an additional loss of $3.8 million in monthly port revenue (Maritime Transport Committee, "Security Transport: Risk Factors and Economic Impact," OECD 2003). In the wake of a failed attack on the U.S.S. The Sullivans in January 2000 and a successful attack on the U.S.S. Cole in October of the same year, al-Qaeda has demonstrated a maritime capability that threatens the Bab el-Mandeb passage in addition to Yemeni oil infrastructure located along the coast. (Albeit, since the Saudi mastermind of those attacks, Abdul al-Nashiri, was detained in November 2002, no significant maritime attack has taken place in Yemen).

In September 2006, days prior to President Saleh's reelection, Yemeni security forces stopped a group calling itself al-Qaeda in Yemen from detonating vehicle-borne IEDs on oil installations in Hadramaut and Marib provinces. The next day, security forces reportedly detained four individuals on suspicion of plotting attacks on the Yemeni government and Canadian Nexen oil company facilities. The investigations into the oil facility and Sana'a attacks continued, but no charges were filed. These were the first attempted attacks in Yemen against energy targets since the attack on the MV Limburg. The timing and scope of the attacks just after Ayman al-Zawahiri's September 11, 2006 denunciation of the theft of Arab oil revealed a degree of sophistication previously lacking on the part of al-Qaeda operatives in Yemen as the attacks occurred within 30 minutes of each other in different provinces.

In addition, sufficient justification exists for attacks on oil installations in Yemen. The 30th issue of the al-Qaeda-affiliated publication Sawt al-Jihad calls on jihadis to attack energy infrastructure as a means to both destabilize the hydrocarbon-dependent "apostate" regimes and to damage the economies of the West (*Terrorism Focus*, February 20, 2007). Although the publication is probably referring principally to the Saudi and Kuwaiti regimes, al-Qaeda and jihadis in Yemen view the Saleh regime as an apostate government. Its alliance with the United States and its reliance on oil revenue make its energy interests a desirable terrorist target.

The U.S.-aligned Saleh regime's dependence on oil exports underscores the relative prominence of the oil target in Yemen. Recent events and al-Qaeda directives are consistent with a continued threat against energy infrastructure. Moreover, the Saleh government is in a precarious position. A counter-terrorism policy that is perceived as too aggressive could further alienate considerable segments of the population. At the same time, however, failing to act boldly increases the odds for jihadis who wish to strike at the regime's only lifeblood. As a result, concern about the vulnerability of the planned Ras Essa refinery and Yemen's overall energy sector to targeting by jihadis is warranted.

[Original Publication: *Terrorism Focus* 4 (16) – May 29, 2007]

Is al-Qaeda in Yemen Regrouping?

By Gregory D. Johnsen

In November 2002, the United States dealt a devastating blow to al-Qaeda in Yemen when it assassinated Sinan Qa'id al-Harthi (a.k.a. Abu Ali al-Harthi) with a missile from a Predator drone. One year later, in November 2003, Yemeni forces arrested al-Harthi's replacement, Muhammad al-Ahdal, on a tip from an al-Qaeda member. The two operations effectively crippled the organization, removing its head of operations and its chief financial officer. Yet, more recently, the group has been reorganizing itself and, once again, appears capable of carrying out attacks. On May 1, 2007, al-Qaeda in Yemen told Yemeni correspondent Faysal Mukrim that it was preparing to strike certain officers within the country's security establishment, whom it accused of using torture against al-Qaeda suspects in Yemeni prisons (*al-Hayat*, May 1, 2007). As proof of the seriousness of its claims, Al-Qaeda in Yemen said that it was behind the March 29, 2007 assassination of Ali Mahmud Qasaylah, the chief criminal investigator in the central Yemeni governorate of Marib (*al-Hayat*, May 1, 2007). The unnamed source claimed that the assassination was in retaliation for Qasaylah's role in the attack on al-Harthi, which also occurred in Marib. Yemeni security forces denied that Qasaylah, who was transferred to Marib at the beginning of 2002, had anything to do with the operation that killed al-Harthi (*al-Hayat*, May 1, 2007).

Initially, al-Qaeda's claims were met with skepticism since they came more than a month after Qasaylah was killed and they were relayed through Mukrim, who is seen as close to the government and is not often the reporter of choice for militants in the country. They also followed calls by HOOD, a local human rights organization, and the Marib branch of the Islah party for an investigation into Qasaylah's death (al-Sawha.net, April 23, 2007; News Yemen, April 17, 2007). This led some to believe that Mukrim's sources were overreaching in an attempt to play on the unknown. Yet, in the weeks following the al-Qaeda claims, the Ministry of the Interior announced that it was looking for three men in connection with Qasaylah's death (almotamar.net, May 15, 2007).

Throughout mid-May 2007, the Ministry of the Interior took out half-page ads in official newspapers, offering a reward of five million Yemeni riyals, roughly $25,000, for information leading to the capture of the three suspects: Naji Ali Salih Jardan, Ali Ali Nasir Doha and Abd al-Aziz Said Muhammad Jardan. To make matters worse for the government, the latter two suspects had been in prison from 2004-2006 on suspicion of being involved in transporting Yemenis to Iraq to fight against U.S.-led forces (News Yemen, December 24, 2005; News Yemen, March 24, 2006). Both Doha and Abd al-Aziz Said Muhammad Jardan were arrested in Yemen upon their return from Syria, where they claimed they were seeking medical treatment. Their eventual release has, as the wanted posters indicate, proven premature.

Qasaylah's death and the subsequent claim of responsibility by al-Qaeda in Yemen suggest that the group is reforming with the help of members trained in Iraq and is returning to settle old scores. This could prove to be a dangerous revival of the security threat in Yemen.

[Original Publication: *Terrorism Focus* 4 (15) – May 30, 2007]

Yemen Attack Reveals Struggle Among al-Qaeda's Ranks

By Gregory D. Johnsen

Throughout the spring and early summer, a schism has emerged within the ranks of al-Qaeda in Yemen, pitting younger, more radicalized members against the moderate old guard. These strategic differences materialized on July 2, 2007, when a suicide bomber attacked a convoy of Spanish tourists in the governorate of Marib, killing nine people. The new generation of militants, many of whom were radicalized in Iraq, is determined to carry out attacks in Yemen. This represents a sharp break from the old guard, who have advised their younger members to have patience and allow for negotiations with the Yemeni government to continue. The old guard is also concerned that any attacks within Yemen will lead to a government crackdown on its leadership, much like what happened in the aftermath of the U.S.S. Cole attack in 2000 and the September 11 attacks in 2001 (*al-Ghad*, July 4, 2007).

Since 2003, the Yemeni government and al-Qaeda in Yemen have reached what could best be described as a tacit non-aggression pact. Through various programs and channels, Yemen has attempted to convince the militants not that their beliefs are incorrect, but rather that they would hurt their own cause and base of operations by acting violently within the borders of the state. For the new generation of al-Qaeda leaders, however, this is tantamount to a treasonous alliance with tyrants. On June 21, 2007, al-Qaeda in Yemen posted an audio-message on an Islamist website that announced that it had selected Nasir al-Wuhayshi – one of the 23 men who escaped from a Yemeni prison in February 2006 – to be its new leader. The message itself, however, seemed designed to convince the old guard that negotiations were a betrayal of their cause. The message was read by a man who identified himself as Abu Hurayra al-San'ani. He warned the old guard that jihad could not be paused in order to seek the release of prisoners. He insisted, "If they are killed, they end up as martyrs. Then, how can the jihad stop today for the sake of prisoners? Go back to your senses." This statement seemed to confirm the new tactics, which were first dramatically displayed with the March 29, 2007 assassination of Ali Mahmud Qasaylah, the chief criminal investigator in the Marib governorate. This murder was supposedly in retaliation for Qasaylah's role in the 2002 assassination of al-Qaeda leader Abu Ali al-Harthi (*Terrorism Focus*, May 22, 2007).

Six days after the audio statement, al-Qaeda in Yemen released another statement through the independent weekly *al-Shar'a*. This time the message was directed at the Yemeni government. The statement made four demands on the government: release al-Qaeda members in prison; lift restrictions on travel to Iraq; stop cooperating with the enemies of Islam, particularly the United States and its allies; and announce a return to Shari'a law (News Yemen, July 2, 2007). These two statements, directed at al-Qaeda's old guard and the Yemeni government, clearly articulate the philosophy of al-Qaeda in Yemen's new generation of leaders.

In a press conference the day after the attack in Marib, President Ali Abdullah Saleh offered a 15 million Yemeni rial (roughly $75,500) reward for information leading to the capture of those responsible. He also said that early evidence suggested that the attack was the work of a non-Yemeni Arab (*al-Hayat*, July 4, 2007). Security operations during the following days resulted in several arrests in the governorates of Aden, Sana'a and Abyan (*al-Hayat*, July 5, 2007). The man who Yemen charged as the mastermind of the attack, however, was, as Saleh suggested, a foreigner. Ahmad Basaywani Duwaydar, a 50 year-old Egyptian with a Yemeni wife, was killed on July 5, 2007 in a shootout with Yemeni security forces in western Sana'a. Duwaydar, who previously lived in Egypt in 1990, had been convicted in absentia during the 1999 "Albania Returnees" trial (*al-Hayat*, July 7, 2007). Regardless of Duwaydar's culpability for the July 2, 2007 attack, his death will likely have little bearing on the generational fissures that have erupted within al-Qaeda in Yemen.

Overall, the attack on the Spanish tourists was a symbol not just of the resurgence of al-Qaeda in Yemen, but also of the new power of younger, more dogmatic militants. Although the outcome of this internecine struggle for control is uncertain, it seems likely that Yemen's tense spring will turn into a dangerous summer.

[Original Publication: *Terrorism Focus* 4 (22) – July 10, 2007]

Yemen's Role in al-Qaeda's Strategy

By Michael Scheuer

Osama bin Laden has always had a very soft spot in his heart for Yemen, saying that it is "one of the best Arab and Muslim countries in terms of its adherence to tradition and the faith ... [its] topography is mountainous, and its people are tribal and armed, and allow one to breathe clean air unblemished by humiliation." Yemen is, of course, also the site of his family's origin and he has often praised the Kindah tribe of which his family is part. The bin Ladens hail from the village of al-Rubat in the Hadramaut region, and Osama took his fourth wife from there. Bin Laden also has referred often to the religious importance of Yemen, noting the Prophet Muhammad's high regard for Yemen because of its quick adoption of Islam after the faith's founding and because he believed that from Yemen "would come 12,000 [fighters] who would support God and His Prophet, and they are among the best of us" (al-Islah, September 2, 1996).

Abundant Manpower

But affection is always overruled by the requirements of war-fighting in bin Laden's mentality and Yemen has long figured prominently in the conduct of the defensive jihad in terms of manpower and geographic importance. Yemenis, for example, have had significant representation in al-Qaeda since its founding: Tariq al-Fahdli, from southern Yemen, fought alongside bin Laden against the Soviets and was on Yemeni President Saleh's senior council; Nasir Ahmad Nasir al-Bahri (Abu Jandal), who was the longtime chief of his bodyguard unit, is also from Yemen (al-Quds al-Arabi, August 3, 2004). After the Soviet withdrawal from Afghanistan, moreover, bin Laden and several of his colleagues sent guns, money and Arab veterans of Afghanistan into Yemen to fight alongside the Saleh-led insurgents who eventually defeated the communist regime of southern Yemen to reunify the country in 1990 (al-Qatan al-Arabi, December 27, 1996). Al-Qaeda's first anti-U.S. attack – against U.S. troops on the way to Somalia – was conducted in Aden, Yemen, in December 1992.

More recently, 80 percent of those involved in the October 2000 attack on the U.S.S. Cole were Saudis of Yemeni origin. The members of the al-Qaeda cell that the FBI dismantled in Lackawanna, New York in 2002 were all Yemenis. Furthermore, a significant number of the non-Iraqi mujahideen fighting U.S.

forces in Iraq are Yemenis. Indeed, in late 2007 the leader of al-Qaeda in Iraq, Abu Hamzah al-Muhajir, called specifically on the Yemeni Islamists to provide more fighters to support the Iraqi mujahideen. On November 29, 2007, al-Qaeda's chief in Yemen, Nasir al-Wuhayshi (a.k.a. Abu Basir), publicly answered that he would immediately send more fighters. "Oh Abu Hamzah, here we come, oh, Iraq, here we come," Abu Basir pledged (Message from the Amir of al-Qaeda in Yemen to Abu Hamza al-Muhajir, November 29, 2007).

Lasting Geographic Importance

Beyond "the extended manpower fighting for God in happy Yemen," bin Laden and al-Qaeda have always valued what they refer to as "the strategic depth" that Yemen affords (al-Islah, September 2, 1996; *al-Quds al-Arabi*, March 9, 1994). While bin Laden and his organization were based in Sudan from 1991 to 1996, for example, they established a sort of "naval bridge" that permitted the flow of guns and fighters between Yemen and Port Sudan in support of Hasan al-Turabi's Islamist regime in Khartoum. In the other direction, bin Laden sent al-Qaeda operatives from Port Sudan to Yemen and from there infiltrated them into Saudi Arabia across the imperfectly guarded Saudi-Yemeni border as well as into Oman. In Yemen, bin Laden also cultivated ties with President Saleh and prominent Islamist shaykhs – including Sheikh Abdul Majid al-Zindani, head of the Yemen Reform Party – and by doing so facilitated the growth of substantial al-Qaeda infrastructure across the country. Al-Qaeda's presence in Yemen also brought it into closer contact with the Egyptian Islamist groups based there: the Gama'a al-Islamiyah and Ayman al-Zawahiri's Egyptian Islamic Jihad, the latter of which later united with al-Qaeda. Finally, al-Qaeda has found that some of its Yemeni members are of great assistance in inserting al-Qaeda operatives into the states of East Arica, the Indian Ocean and the South Pacific, because of the Yemeni diaspora that was established centuries ago in those regions by Yemeni sailors and commercial traders.

Operational Key and Base of Last Resort

For al-Qaeda, Yemen provides a pivotal, central base that links its theaters of operation in Afghanistan, Iraq, East Africa and the Far East; it also provides a base for training Yemeni fighters and for the rest and refit of fighters from multiple Islamist groups after their tours in Afghanistan, Iraq and Somalia.

Today, it appears to be an especially important safe haven for Somali Islamist fighters and the leaders of the Union of Islamic Courts who fled their country after the late-2006 invasion of Ethiopian forces. Some of these Somali fighters – after having regrouped and rearmed – have returned to Mogadishu from Yemen and are contributing to the growth of the Islamist insurgency there (*Christian Science Monitor*, February 12, 2007).

Al-Qaeda's organization in Yemen seems to have stabilized after the period of turmoil and governmental suppression that followed the November 2002 death of its leader Sinan Qa'id al-Harthi (a.k.a. Abu Ali al-Harthi). Under the above-mentioned Abu Basir—who escaped from a Yemeni prison in early 2006 – al-Qaeda in Yemen clearly has found its legs and is becoming more active (*Yemen Times*, July 5, 2007). In late June 2007, for example, Abu Basir issued a warning that al-Qaeda would attack in Yemen if its members were not released from prison; on July 4, 2007, al-Qaeda attacked, using a suicide car bomb to kill seven Spanish tourists at an ancient pagan temple east of Sana'a (al-Jazeera, July 3, 2007). Then, on January 13, 2008, the Yemen wing again warned that it would attack if the Saleh regime did not release imprisoned al-Qaeda members; on January 19, 2008, al-Qaeda killed two Belgian tourists and their drivers in the Hadramaut area (Reuters, January 13, 2008; *Yemen Times*, January 26, 2008). Abu Basir's organization is thus showing some of the same sophistication demonstrated by al-Qaeda groups elsewhere: targeting the tourism industry that earns the country foreign exchange; establishing credibility by making threats and then making good on them; and improving intra-Yemen and international communications by using the internet. In regard to the latter, al-Qaeda in Yemen published the first issue of its internet journal *Sada al-Malahim* (The Echo of Battles) on January 13, 2008 (memriwmp.org, January 16, 2008).

Attacks by al-Qaeda in Yemen are likely to continue at a level that does not lead to an all-out confrontation with Saleh's regime. In all likelihood, al-Qaeda intends to cause just enough sporadic damage to persuade Saleh's regime that it is best to curtail its efforts to destroy al-Qaeda and to allow the group to operate relatively freely in and from Yemen as long as no major attacks are staged in the country. Indeed, such a modus vivendi may be in the works as Sana'a officials have experimented with putting imprisoned Islamists through a reeducation process that shows them the error of their ways and then releases them on the promise of good behavior (*Asharq al-Awsat*, May 21, 2006). This almost certainly equates to a license for the militants to do what they want, where they want, as long as it is not in Yemen. Possibly signaling a growing rapprochement between Saleh and the militants, al-Qaeda in Yemen spokesman Ahmad Mansur recently claimed that the government had solicited al-Qaeda's support in fighting Shiite rebels in the north in return for "easing the persecution of our members" (*al-Wasat*, January 31, 2008).

Finally, Yemen has long been regarded by Western and Muslim commentators as a possible refuge-of-last-resort if bin Laden ever has to flee South Asia—bin Laden also has stated such a possibility – and for this reason al-Qaeda must seek to maintain a viable presence in the country. Al-Qaeda in Yemen is particularly strong in the governorates of Marib and Hadramaut – the attacks described above and others have occurred there – and both share a remote, mountainous topography that is much like that of Afghanistan. The two provinces also are inhabited by a welter of deeply conservative Islamic tribes – Marib alone has four powerful tribes with over 70 clans. As in Afghanistan, the mores of these Yemeni tribes cause their members to "think they must do their duty to protect those who are in need for protection whatever they have done. This feeling becomes even stronger if those who need protection are religious people, because the tribesmen here are greatly affected by religious discourse" (*Yemen Observer*, November 11, 2007).

[Original Publication: *Terrorism Focus* 5 (5) – February 7, 2008]

Attacks on Oil Industry Are First Priority for al-Qaeda in Yemen

By Gregory D. Johnsen

Over the past six months, al-Qaeda in Yemen's strategy has become increasingly clear. It aims to strike at both Yemen and Western countries – particularly the United States – by attacking them at their most vital and vulnerable points: oil and tourism. For Yemen the danger is clear. Oil revenues account for roughly 75 percent of the nation's budget, while tourism remains one of the few legitimate areas of growth for an economy that is headed for failure. But this strategy is also calculated to hurt the West by targeting Western citizens and striking at oil production in the Arabian Peninsula. No longer is there a clear distinction, at least for al-Qaeda in Yemen, between attacking what is often referred to as the near enemy or the far enemy; instead it has devised an approach to simultaneously attack both. This strategy – which is more overarching than it is detailed – also allows for fighters to remain in Yemen instead of traveling to Iraq or Afghanistan, which is effectively decentralizing the front.

The January 18, 2008 attack on a tourist convoy in the eastern governorate of Hadramaut that resulted in the deaths of two Belgians and two Yemeni drivers is the most recent example of this strategy put into practice. Within days, al-Qaeda in Yemen claimed credit for the attack in a phone call to the independent weekly *al-Wasat* (*al-Wasat*, January 23, 2008). The Yemeni government has questioned al-Qaeda's involvement, claiming that the caller was a "well known fraud" (*News Yemen*, January 24, 2008). Even prior to the claim of responsibility, Yemen was suggesting that it might not be al-Qaeda (*al-Hayat*, January 23, 2008), but most Yemenis remain convinced that the attack was at least inspired by – if not the direct work of – al-Qaeda.

The attack came days after al-Qaeda in Yemen released the first issue of its online journal, *Sada al-Malahim* (The Echo of Battles) on January 13, 2008. An interview with Saudi fighter Abu Hamam al-Qahtani reveals that targeting oil supplies in the Arabian Peninsula is a priority for al-Qaeda as well as a reason for fighters to remain in the Arabian Peninsula instead of traveling to Iraq or Afghanistan.

The journal also demanded the release of al-Qaeda members being held in Yemeni prisons. According to an al-Qaeda in Yemen communications officer identified as Ahmad Mansur, there are roughly 220 fighters in Yemen's prisons (*al-Wasat*, January 30, 2008). Both the nature and tone of the statement resemble one that al-Qaeda in Yemen released on the eve of the July 2007 attack on a caravan of Spanish tourists in Marib (al-Jazeera, July 3, 2007). The practice of making a statement calling for the release of its colleagues followed by an attack is emerging as a pattern in the second phase of the war against al-Qaeda in Yemen.

This second phase began in February 2006, when 23 militants escaped from a political security prison in Sana'a. These militants – under the leadership of Nasir al-Wuhayshi, the head of al-Qaeda in Yemen – have formed the core of al-Qaeda in Yemen's second generation, which has made clear its opposition to the policy of negotiation and non-aggression favored by its older colleagues (see *Terrorism Focus*, August 14, 2007). Since then this younger, more radicalized group has attempted coordinated suicide attacks on oil and gas facilities in Marib and Hadramaut, assassinated a government official in Marib, attacked a tourist caravan in Marib and carried out this most recent attack in Hadramaut.

This history as well as the articles and interview in *Sada al-Malahim* make clear that the first priority for al-Qaeda in Yemen is oil, but when this proves too well protected to be feasible it moves on to the softer target of tourists. The third category of targets is those Yemeni officials it believes responsible for either the torture or death of al-Qaeda members (*al-Hayat*, May 1, 2007).

Effectively combating this strategy will require the same level of dedication and cooperation that Yemen and the United States demonstrated in the first phase of the war against al-Qaeda in Yemen from 2000 to 2003. In November 2002, the two allies were able to assassinate the then head of the organization, Ali Qaid al-Harithi, and arrest his replacement, Muhammad Hamdi al-Ahdal, a year later. If the al-Qaeda communications officer is to be believed, al-Qaeda in Yemen has grown significantly – from 80 fighters to roughly 300 – since the United States invaded Iraq (*al-Wasat*, January 30, 2008). Combating this renewed strength on the part of al-Qaeda in Yemen will require an effective alliance between the United States and Yemen.

[Original Publication: *Terrorism Focus* 5 (5) – February 8, 2008]

Soldier's Brigade of Yemen Continues Attacks

By Gregory D. Johnsen

One day after Yemen announced the arrest of an 11-man al-Qaeda cell in the spring of 2008, the organization attempted to strike back on May 30, 2008 with an attack on an oil refinery in the southern port city of Aden. The attack caused little damage, but called into question statements by Yemen's Interior Ministry that it was on the verge of dismantling the Soldier's Brigade of Yemen, an apparent al-Qaeda offshoot which has claimed credit for a series of attacks in recent months (*al-Hayat*, May 30, 2008).

The group claimed credit for the attack in a statement posted to the jihadi website al-ekhlaas.net on May 31, 2008 (al-ekhlaas.net, May 31, 2008). The statement was the group's eighth since it first announced its existence on February 24, 2008. Despite the group's rhetoric about expelling infidels from the Arabian Peninsula, its various attacks have not resulted in the deaths of any Westerners. Instead, it has only managed some structural damage and the deaths of a number of Yemenis.

This apparent ineptitude has not gone unnoticed in jihadi circles outside of Yemen. In a statement posted to al-ekhlaas.net on May 26, 2008, al-Qaeda called on its "brothers in Yemen to return to the days of attacks like those on the U.S.S. Cole and the Limburg and the like, as these attacks have an effect on people today" (News Yemen, May 26, 2008). The statement went on to say that neither "attacking [President] Ali Abdullah Saleh's house or killing Yemeni soldiers was useful at this time," referencing some of the group's previous targets. It also differentiated between Yemeni soldiers and policemen and those in Iraq. Only the latter, the statement claimed, are legitimate targets as they are in league with the United States (News Yemen, May 26, 2008).

Still Yemen seems confident that it is nearing a breakthrough in its struggle against terrorism. On the same day al-Qaeda issued its corrective to its Yemeni colleagues, the Interior Ministry announced that it would soon release the names and pictures of 70 "terrorists" (News Yemen, May 26, 2008). Included among the 70 are al-Qaeda operatives as well as members of the *Shabab al-Muminin* ("The Believing Youth"), or followers of Abdul Malik al-Houthi – Zaidi Shiites who have been waging war against the state since June 2004. Over the past few weeks, the periodic conflict between the two sides has once again erupted in heavy fighting.

The listing of both sets of suspects on one list seems a deliberate confusing of the two conflicts by Yemen in order to link its domestic worries to larger regional and Western concerns of a resurgent al-Qaeda threat. It later emerged from the reporting of Faysal Mukrim of the pan-Arab daily *al-Hayat* that 30 of the suspects are affiliated with al-Qaeda (*al-Hayat*, May 30, 2008). He also reported that the 11-man al-Qaeda cell consisted of six Saudis, three Chadians and two Yemenis, and that security sources within Yemen were confident that the information the suspects had provided would prove instrumental in rolling up the network (*al-Hayat*, May 30, 2008).

But so far this seems to have had little impact on the Soldier's Brigade of Yemen. The same user, Jund al-Iman, who has posted all of the group's statements on al-ekhlaas.net also posted the statement claiming credit for the attack on the Aden oil refinery. The network, at least for the moment, appears to be functioning without interruption.

[Original Publication: *Terrorism Focus* 5 (21) – June 4, 2008]

Attacks in Yemen Reflect al-Qaeda's Global Oil Strategy

By Chris Zambelis

Recent attacks by al-Qaeda's Yemeni branch, *Kataeb Jund al-Yemen* (Soldiers of Yemen Brigades), against oil facilities across Yemen indicate that al-Qaeda's larger strategy to strike oil targets remains a top priority. On June 30, 2008 the group took credit for rocket attacks against an oil refinery in Safir, located east of the capital Sana'a, in Marib province. The group later posted video footage of attack on a radical Islamist website [1]. The attack represented the latest in a series of strikes against oil infrastructure and personnel in Yemen over the last year by militants tied to al-Qaeda, including a May 30, 2008 attack against an oil refinery in the port city of Aden (see *Terrorism Focus*, June 3, 2008). In a related incident, the group threatened to escalate its campaign of violence against oil infrastructure and foreign interests in Yemen unless the state released members of its group currently detained by Yemeni authorities (*Yemen Post*, August 11, 2008).

Oil's significance figures prominently in Osama bin Laden's strategic thinking, especially as this summer's record-high oil prices continue to impact the U.S. and global economies. Although the primary factors that determine oil prices are market forces that reflect supply and demand, other intangibles also help dictate the price of oil. Geopolitical events such as war and political instability in and around oil-producing countries and regions can create uncertainty about the future availability of oil supplies. This uncertainty causes traders to add a security premium to oil prices that can range, depending on the circumstances, between $1 and $25 per barrel, or higher. Adverse weather that threatens oil infrastructure and transport routes can also drive the price of oil up. Steady global demand for oil – led by record-high demand from Asia – is also responsible for an increase in oil prices.

According to a recent essay titled "Al-Qaeda and the Battle for Oil" that has been circulating on radical Islamist websites since June, militants are well aware of the economics of oil. The author of the essay goes as far as to claim that al-Qaeda's strategy to defeat the United States rests on bankrupting America by driving up oil prices by any means necessary [2]. The author also mentions that the recent attacks against oil infrastructure in Yemen, along with attacks in Iraq and Saudi Arabia, have been critical to al-Qaeda's success so far.

Based on its actions and discourse, it is apparent that al-Qaeda operates a dynamic oil strategy that contains political, economic, and military aspects. While the recent attacks in Yemen reflect the military aspects of al-Qaeda's oil strategy, it is worth examining the evolution of al-Qaeda's oil strategy over the years.

Oil and Political Opposition

Any discussion of oil's significance for al-Qaeda must begin with Saudi Arabia and bin Laden's opposition to the Saudi monarchy. Bin Laden's criticism of the royal family dates back to the emergence of the Advice and Reform Committee (ARC), a London-based opposition group bin Laden helped found in 1994 that sought to unify Saudi opposition elements and to encourage the reform of the kingdom from within. The ARC illustrated the political aspects of al-Qaeda's oil strategy, with bin Laden accusing Saudi leaders of, among other things, corruption, mismanagement, and squandering oil revenues to maintain the ostentatious lifestyles of the royal family [3]. Bin Laden also accused Saudi Arabia of using its preeminent position within the Organization of the Petroleum Exporting Countries (OPEC) to provide the United States with oil at artificially low prices at the expense of Muslim interests. He condemned the royal family for using oil revenues to purchase expensive U.S. weapons systems that would prove useless in defending the kingdom. Instead, bin Laden saw Saudi purchases of U.S. arms as a move designed to curry favor with Washington [4]. Despite its support for the 1973 Arab oil embargo to protest U.S. support for Israel during the 1973 Yom Kippur/Ramadan War, Saudi Arabia secretly permitted the sale of oil to the United States military to sustain U.S. forces in Vietnam and elsewhere. Saudi Arabia also deposited billions of dollars of revenue earned during the oil crisis into the U.S. economy to mitigate the effects of the embargo.

Bin Laden's criticism of the Saudi royal family throughout the 1990s must be seen in the context of Saudi Arabia's self-declared role as the Guardian of the Two Holy Mosques of Mecca and Medina. The kingdom considers its oil wealth to be a gift from God, a gift it believes bestows a claim of special legitimacy upon the ruling family [5]. In this sense, bin Laden's direct criticism of the royal family challenged the monarchy's claim of religious legitimacy and its right to preside over Mecca and Medina. Despite its disdain for Saudi Arabia, however, al-Qaeda initially opposed attacks against oil targets in the kingdom and elsewhere in the region. The group's position is outlined in the following excerpt from bin Laden's

August 23, 1996, "Declaration of Jihad Against the Americans Occupying the Land of the Two Holy Places":

> *I would like here to alert my brothers, the mujahideen, the sons of the nation, to protect this [oil] wealth and not to include it in the battle, as it is a great Islamic wealth and a large economic power essential for the soon-to-be-established Islamic state, by God's permission and grace* [6].

It appears that al-Qaeda was concerned about the possibility that attacks against Saudi oil facilities - and oil targets elsewhere on Arab soil – would alienate Muslim opinion, even if that resource was being squandered by a corrupt dictatorship widely detested by its own people and Muslims throughout the Middle East.

Oil and Economic Warfare

Researchers tracking al-Qaeda tend to focus on assessing the group's ability to commit spectacular acts of violence. At the same time, al-Qaeda's ability to launch (or inspire) attacks must be seen in the context of the group's long-term strategy, a strategy which aims to bankrupt the United States by engaging it through an economic war of attrition. The following excerpt from bin Laden's October 29, 2004 public statement illustrates this aspect of al-Qaeda's strategy:

> *Al-Qaeda spent $500,000 on the September 11 attacks, while America lost more than $500 billion, at the lowest estimate, in the event and its aftermath. That makes a million American dollars for every al-Qaeda dollar, by the grace of God Almighty. This is in addition to the fact that it lost an enormous amount of jobs – and as for the federal deficit, it made record losses, estimated at over a trillion dollars. Still more serious for America was the fact that the mujahideen forced Bush to resort to an emergency budget in order to continue fighting in Afghanistan and Iraq. This shows the success of our plan to bleed America to the point of bankruptcy...* [7].

Here lies the economic aspect of al-Qaeda's oil strategy. While al-Qaeda had previously opposed targeting oil, bin Laden's December 16, 2004, statement would mark a major shift in the group's strategy:

Targeting America in Iraq in terms of economy and losses in life is a golden and unique opportunity. Do not waste it only to regret it later. One of the most important reasons that led our enemies to control our land is the theft of our oil. Do everything you can to stop the biggest plundering operation in history – the plundering of the resources of the present and future generations in collusion with the agents and the aliens... Be active and prevent them from reaching the oil, and mount your operations accordingly, particularly in Iraq and the Gulf [Saudi Arabia, Yemen, Gulf monarchies, etc.], for this is their fate (BBC, December 16, 2004).

It is difficult to discern the precise reason behind al-Qaeda's shift in strategy at this juncture. One likely possibility is that bin Laden was inspired by the Iraqi insurgency, especially its nationalist strain, which targeted oil infrastructure to great effect in order to undermine the U.S.-led Coalition's efforts to control the country. Although most of the damage against the Iraqi oil infrastructure, especially oil pipelines, was easily repairable, the ongoing violence and instability coupled with the deliberate targeting of oil-related sites by the insurgents undermined investor confidence and raised concerns about Iraq's potential to regain its place as a major oil producer. These factors, along with a host of others, contributed to a steady increase in oil prices during this volatile period. In keeping with al-Qaeda's long-term goal of bankrupting the United States, it is likely that bin Laden identified an opportunity to up the ante against the United States and its allies in the region by making oil fair game.

Oil and Military Operations

Bin Laden's explicit call for attacks against oil installations to harm the U.S. economy resulted in a spike in security premiums and raised concerns about a new round of terrorist attacks. For al-Qaeda's oil strategy to have any hopes of succeeding in the long-term, however, the group would have to back up its words with action. Al-Qaeda's Saudi affiliate, al-Qaeda in the Arabian Peninsula, rose to the occasion by mounting an ambitious attack against Saudi Arabia's Abqaiq oil facility on February 24, 2006 (*Middle East Online*, February 24, 2006; *Arab News*, February 26, 2006). Abqaiq is the world's largest oil complex. The attackers failed to breach the first cordon of the facility's security perimeter with their explosives-laden vehicles, resulting in a firefight between the militants and Saudi security forces outside the facility. The militants ultimately detonated their explosives prematurely in what proved to be a botched operation. Despite the operation's failure, oil prices immediately jumped $2 per barrel amid already record-high prices due to fear of future attacks on oil facilities in the kingdom and other parts of the region [8].

Even if the militants had succeeded in detonating their explosives inside Abqaiq, they did not have anywhere near the amount of explosives required to destroy the massive complex. The underlying message behind the attack was clear: the military aspect of al-Qaeda's oil strategy had become operational. Although from an operational perspective, an attack against a more accessible target may have yielded a better result, ultimately, the decision to strike Abqaiq was also meant to inspire al-Qaeda's sympathizers to attempt similar attacks in their own countries. Furthermore, in February 2007, al-Qaeda's *Sawt al-Jihad* magazine called for attacks against U.S. oil interests in the Western Hemisphere, specifically attacks against oil infrastructure in Canada, Mexico, and Venezuela (three key sources of U.S. energy) to further damage the U.S. economy (*Sawt al-Jihad*, January 2007).

Conclusion

Despite al-Qaeda's explicit call for attacks against oil infrastructure, radical Islamists and their sympathizers continue to debate the utility of such tactics. Members of a popular radical Islamist chat room forum recently debated the legitimacy of such attacks on a thread discussing the June 30, 2008 attacks on Yemen's Safir oil refinery, entitled "Is Attacking the Oil Fields of Marib in Yemen Considered Jihad or Sabotage?" The crux of the debate revolved around whether the oil derived from Safir benefits Yemen or the United States. One respondent expressed his opposition to the attacks, based on his belief that the oil was not destined for the West; "If the petroleum coming out of the wells is not going to the West and the nations of heresy, why should they be attacked?" (www.muslm.net, June 30-July 6, 2008).

In response, another forum member agreed in principle that oil facilities should not be targeted, presumably due to their role in sustaining regional economies. At the same time, he added that the recent attacks in Yemen were justified due to the Yemeni regime's close ties to the United States, especially in the military arena. Radical Islamists detest the Yemeni government, much like they do the Saudi royal family and other U.S.-backed autocracies in the region. These sentiments are illustrated in the author's response:

My dear brother, I'm with you. I see no need to bombard the oil refineries...but I believe the brothers in the Yemeni Qaeda when they said it, considering that these refineries are used by the tyrant of Yemen [Yemeni President Ali Abdullah Saleh] to provide fuel to the Crusaders in their war against Islam. Everyone knows that Yemen supplies the American navy with fuel, and this is what motivated the men of tawheed [declaring the oneness of God] to shed blood for the sake of "there is no god but God" by wrecking the American destroyer [U.S.S. Cole] in Aden (www.muslm.net, June 26-July 6, 2008).

Despite the apparent doubts expressed above about the utility of attacking oil installations, by all accounts, the experience of Abqaiq and the recent incidents in Yemen indicate that al-Qaeda's call for an all-out war against oil should remain cause for serious concern in the Middle East and beyond.

[Original Publication: *Terrorism Monitor* 6 (17) – September 4, 2008]

Notes

1. Video still shots of the footage released by Jund al-Yemen and related links can be accessed at clearinghouse.infovlad.net/showthread.php (accessed September 2008).
2. Zadi al-Taqwa, "Al-Qaeda and the Battle for Oil," www.alqimmah.net/showthread.php (accessed September 2008).
3. For more background on the Advice and Reform Committee (ARC), see Mamoun Fandy, Saudi Arabia and the Politics of Dissent (New York: St. Martin's Press, 1999), pp. 178-194. For details on the ARC and other domestic Saudi opposition groups operating at the time, see Daryl Champion, The Paradoxical Kingdom: Saudi Arabia and the Momentum of Reform (New York: Columbia University Press, 2003), pp. 216-308.
4. For more details, see As'ad Abukhalil, The Battle for Saudi Arabia: Royalty, Fundamentalism, and Global Power (New York: Seven Stories Press, 2004), p. 97.
5. Steve Coll, The Bin Ladens: An Arabian Family in the American Century (New York: The Penguin Press, 2008), p. 149.
6. For a full transcript of Osama bin Laden's August 23, 1996 "Declaration of Jihad Against the Americans Occupying the Land of the Two Holy Places," see Robert O. Marlin IV, What Does al-Qaeda Want?: Unedited Communiques (Berkeley: North Atlantic Books, 2004), pp. 1-17.
7. For a full transcript of Osama bin Laden's October 29, 2004 "Statement to the American People," see Bruce Lawrence, Messages to the World: The Statements of Osama bin Laden (New York: Verso, 2005), pp. 237-244.
8. For more background on the implications of the February 26, 2006 Abqaiq attacks, see "Saudi Arabian Oil Facilities: The Achilles Heel of the Western Economy," Jamestown Foundation, May 2006, www.jamestown.org/docs/Jamestown-SaudiOil.pdf.

Al-Qaeda in Yemen Supports Southern Secession

By Abdul Hameed Bakier

Exploiting ongoing unrest in Southern Yemen, al-Qaeda's leader in Yemen released an audio statement on May 13, 2009 entitled "To Our People in the South," in support of southern Yemeni efforts to secede from Yemen. The audiotape was released through the jihadi media outlet *al-Malahim* (shmo5alislam.net, May 14, 2009). Various jihadi forums debated al-Qaeda's call for a week afterwards (hanein.info, May 14, 2009).

As the Soviet bloc began to crumble in 1990, North and South Yemen (a socialist state supported by the Soviet Union) were hastily united despite a history of bitter enmity between the political structures in both parts of the country. Perhaps unsurprisingly, the Sana'a regime led by President Ali Abdullah Saleh waged a war in 1994 to eliminate South Yemen's socialists. Since that time, Yemen has witnessed waves of public unrest due to poor social and economic conditions in the south. The latest upheaval in the region was in March 2009, when Yemen's president Ali Abdullah Saleh ordered his defense minister to quell the unrest in Chanffar city in the Abyan governorate (al-Arabiya TV, May 24, 2009). Most of the protests against the Yemeni regime have been led by the Southern Mobility Movement (SMM), a popular opposition movement that incorporates "civil society organizations, political parties, societies, shaykhs, dignitaries, academics, politicians, independents and others," according to SMM leader Nasser al-Khabji (*Yemen Post*, March 12, 2009).

In light of this latest unrest in the south, al-Qaeda's leader in Yemen, Nasir al-Wuhayshi (a.k.a. Abu Basir), said in an audio statement that what the Yemeni government was doing in the southern districts of Lahij, al-Dhale, Abyan and Hadramaut was unacceptable and the people of the south have every right to defy the Yemen government's oppression, a right guaranteed by Islam. Al-Wuhayshi added, "We in al-Qaeda organization support what you are doing to reject oppression and support you against the government." Al-Wuhayshi reminded the southerners of South Yemen's defunct communist order and how it failed in the past, saying that only Islamic Shari'a renders justice and freedom. "A return to God's law is the only way out of this dilemma we're in... I warn you not to be manipulated again."

Al-Wuhayshi also appealed to the people of South Yemen to reject all forms of political parties, an implicit call not to join the Supreme Council for the

Liberation of Southern Yemen, which has been stirring up protests in the south under the leadership of the exiled former president of South Yemen, Ali Salem al-Beed. Al-Wuhayshi warns his fellow Salafists of the implications of allowing the regime of President Ali Abdallah Saleh, "an infidel apostate agent who has thrust aside the command of the Shari'a," to continue in its support of U.S. anti-terrorism efforts. "Even the rest of our brothers in Iraq and Palestine were not safe from this regime either, as it has provisioned the U.S. battleships to kill their children and women."

Al-Qaeda's incitement of Yemeni separatists was discussed extensively in jihadi forums by moderate Muslims, Arab nationalists and pro-al-Qaeda Salafi-Jihadis. The latter supported al-Qaeda's drive in southern Yemen on the pretext that the Yemeni government is arresting Salafis and preventing them from practicing their beliefs in mosques because Salafism is unacceptable to the United States.

Al-Qaeda claims Salafis are not supporting dissension, but are instead trying to help the oppressed southerners and prevent them from becoming communists again. According to al-Wuhayshi:

> *You have experienced the socialist regime, which imposed on you a lot of suffering - only God knows its amount. Yet here you are still drinking from the same glass at the hands of the gang of the [socialist] regime, which rules you today. It is about time that Islam rules so that you enjoy its justice and tolerance. Be cautious not to be deceived once again [by socialism], or the efforts you have exerted in fighting oppression and aggression will be credited to the immoral custodians of [political] parties. Such parties gave our umma [Islamic community] nothing but disunity, subordination and submission to the enemies.*

Another al-Qaeda leader, Ghalib al-Zayidi, told a pan-Arab daily that the "mujahideen" of Yemen would not repeat the mistake they made in 1994, when they joined the regime's campaign to destroy "the Socialist Party in defense of Yemeni unity after the government had promised them it would implement Islamic Shari'a" once the socialists had been eliminated. The regime broke its promise and "suddenly turned against the mujahideen and put them in jail. Some of them were killed and foreign mujahideen were expelled" (*al-Hayat*, May 23, 2009).

Observers believe al-Qaeda's religious argument is an excuse to destabilize southern Yemen because it does not recognize international borders between Islamic States. Stable countries are not suitable for al-Qaeda's sabotage activities. To strike at Yemen's strong points, al-Qaeda is constantly planning terror attacks on four major targets - oil facilities, foreign embassies, foreigners and security officials. Al-Qaeda can only grow and expand in countries burdened with sectarian and tribal conflicts similar to the situation in Somalia, just a short distance from Yemen. Setting up safe havens for military training and recruiting new cadres is only possible after weakening the Yemeni government. If all goes as al-Qaeda has planned, it would control the Bab al-Mandab strait from both sides through a presence in Yemen and Somalia, enabling it to hold maritime shipping hostage. Al-Wuhayshi's audio, ostensibly in support of the South Yemen opposition movement, is actually an attempt to exploit the situation and control the southern region because al-Qaeda would never ally itself with those who do not adhere to Salafi-Jihadism, let alone infidel communists. So far, it appears al-Qaeda efforts in Yemen are bearing fruit in the sense that it has made successful penetrations of the Yemeni security apparatus (al-Faloja.info, March 29, 2009).

[Original Publication: *Terrorism Monitor* 7 (16) – June 12, 2009]

Uncertainty Surrounds the Arrest of al-Qaeda Financier in Yemen

By Munir Mawari

Yemeni authorities announced in mid-June 2009 that they had arrested a Saudi citizen named Hassan bin Hussein Alwan in the province of Marib, saying that he is the biggest financier of al-Qaeda in Yemen and Saudi Arabia, as well as one of the most dangerous al-Qaeda elements in the Arabian Peninsula (26sep.net [Sana'a], June 14, 2009). Three days after this announcement, Yemen said that another Saudi al-Qaeda operative named Naif Dhess Yahia al-Harbi surrendered to Yemeni authorities (*Yemen Observer*, June 15, 2009; yemenembassy.org, June 18, 2009). The Saudi government confirmed the surrender of al-Harbi but denied having any information about the arrest of Alwan (*Asharq al-Awsat*, June 15, 2009; *al-Watan*, June 19, 2009). Al-Harbi is expected to be returned to Saudi Arabia according to bilateral security arrangements with Yemen. The Saudi and Yemeni branches of al-Qaeda were united last January to form al-Qaeda in the Arabian Peninsula (AQAP).

According to Yemeni sources, Alwan was moving between two provinces, Marib in the north and Abyan in the south. Yemeni security sources said that he was arrested after six months of surveillance and monitoring of his movements by the Yemeni National Security Agency (NSA), which is run by Ammar Saleh, a relative of Yemeni President Ali Abdallah Saleh (*Okaz* [Jeddah], June 16, 2009). The sources revealed that Alwan was collecting donations outside of Yemen under the guise of building mosques, schools, orphanages and charitable projects in Yemen, and that he has a distinct "ability to deceive the donors and convince them of the legitimacy of their donations" (*Saudi Gazette*, June 29, 2009). Alwan has been charged with forming a terrorist group in Yemen and financing its operations.

The NSA, which competes with Yemen's Political Security Organization (PSO), considers Alwan's arrest a big achievement and a remarkable example of Yemen's efforts to track down al-Qaeda elements, including Saudis who escaped to Yemen after Saudi security services defeated them inside the kingdom (*Okaz*, June 16, 2009). Yemeni authorities said the Alwan investigation had led to further arrests of al-Qaeda cells in Sana'a and Marib, some of which were allegedly preparing new terrorist attacks in Yemen (*Yemen Times*, June 15, 2009). More is expected; "[Alwan] is expected to be an intelligence goldmine for information, which will hopefully result in the capture or killing of al-Qaeda militants" (*Yemen Observer*, June 15, 2009).

The NSA points out that there are differences and divisions among the elements of the so-called al-Qaeda in the Arabian Peninsula, led by Nasir al-Wuhayshi. The agency refers to disagreements centered on the struggle for leadership of the organization and its strategy. It appears that the surrender of prominent AQAP member Abu Hareth Muhammad al-Awfi (a.k.a. Muhammad Atiq Awayd al-Harbi) to the Yemeni authorities, who in turn handed him over to the Kingdom in February 2009, was one sign of those divisions among various elements of the terrorist organization (*Okaz*, June 16, 2009). Al-Awfi was a former inmate of the U.S. Guantanamo Bay prison before being released into a Saudi rehabilitation program in November 2007.

Analysts and observers often hesitate to trust Yemeni authorities when they issue their periodic announcements regarding their fight against terrorism. Their often exaggerated or cosmetic claims of their anti-terrorist activities and victories are not as credible as claims made, for instance, by the Saudi authorities, who have a better history of credibility. The uncertainty surrounding the arrest of Alwan should cause any independent observer or analyst to have two hypotheses on the matter, each supported by evidence from openly available sources:

Hypothesis I: Yemen's claim is true and reliable

- The announcement of the arrest of Alwan was followed by the al-Harbi surrender. The Yemeni authorities are now expected to hand over two individuals to Saudi security, in order to implement the security agreement between these two countries. It is difficult to imagine that Yemen would knowingly put itself in an embarrassing situation with Saudi Arabia just to achieve a temporary media victory that is not true in reality.

- After the Yemeni authorities announced the arrest of Alwan, nine foreign citizens were abducted in the province of Sa'ada. They were allegedly kidnapped from an area near Jubara military camp, which hosts returnees from Afghanistan (Aleshteraki.net, June 27, 2009). Despite the fact that the Yemeni authorities tried to accuse north Yemen's Houthi insurgents of the kidnapping, the killing of three of those hostages indicates that al-Qaeda is probably behind the crime, which was presumably an act taken in revenge for the arrest of Alwan. Knowing that al-Qaeda had similarly killed three Americans in Jebla in 2002 in almost the same fashion would support this conclusion (*Asharq al-Awsat*, December 31, 2002). The Houthi insurgents have no history of killing foreigners.

• Although the name Alwan did not appear on jihadi websites prior to his arrest in Yemen, the fact that the jihadis did not come out with an immediate denial in the media lends credibility to Yemen's official account. Al-Qaeda can usually be expected to deny any false news suggesting the defeat or arrest of any of its operatives.

• Although the arrest of Alwan was not announced in an official statement issued by the Yemeni Interior Ministry, as is the usual procedure, the *26 September* newspaper published the story instead. The newspaper is owned by the Ministry of Defense and supervised by two advisers to President Ali Abdullah Saleh, Ali Hassan al-Shater and Abdo Bourji. Reuters News Agency also published the same story. The Reuters correspondent in Yemen, Muhammad Saddam, is the official translator to President Saleh. He would not send a story out without the approval of the president, who directly oversees the terrorism file.

Hypothesis II: The story of Alwan's arrest has an ulterior political motive.

Because of the unreliable record of the Yemeni authorities in the dissemination of information relating to the war on terrorism, the story of Alwan's arrest is questionable in some respects:

• In comparison to the Alwan case, the Saudi Arabian family of al-Harbi has confirmed his surrender to Yemeni authorities. His brother informed *Asharq al-Awsat* newspaper that al-Harbi's family had provided the Saudi Government with information about the suspect (*Asharq al-Awsat*, June 19, 2009). However, Alwan, described by the Yemeni authorities as a Saudi national, does not seem to have any trace of family or relatives in Saudi Arabia. No one from Saudi Arabia has said anything about him. Saudi Arabia normally relies heavily on relatives of terrorist suspects to compile information about them. It is strange that there is no information about Alwan from the Saudi side.

• Alwan's name does not appear on the "85 Most Wanted Terrorists" list promulgated by Saudi Arabia. This puts the Yemeni claims about his prominence and danger level in considerable doubt. The Saudi list contains the names of 83 Saudis and two Yemenis. Yemen's Ministry of the Interior maintains its own list of 154 wanted terrorists, 90 of whom are of Saudi origin and include a large number of the 83 Saudi fugitives named on the Saudi list (yemenembassy.org, March 30, 2009). Alwan's name does not appear in the Yemeni list of suspects either (*Yemen Observer*, June 15, 2009).

• Jihadist websites have ignored the alleged arrest of Alwan, and a few of them even expressed doubt about this news item (al-Faloja, June 2009).

• There are several plausible explanations as to why the story of the arrest of Alwan might be spurious. In Yemen, the NSA and the PSO compete in the field of controlling terrorism. According to a Yemeni writer, the NSA, which took credit for Alwan's arrest, has been criticizing the PSO for not doing enough against terrorism and for possibly being infiltrated by terrorists (Aleshteraki.net, January 12, 2009). This could, therefore, be a manipulative and suspect claim, especially given the present international pressure on Yemen for anti-terrorism activity.

Conclusion

If, in the near future, Saudi Arabian official sources confirm that Yemen has actually transferred two individuals (Alwan and al-Harbi) to Saudi Arabia, this would prove the first hypothesis. Should they transfer only al-Harbi, this would support acceptance of the second hypothesis and would also place Yemeni claims about Houthi responsibility for the abduction of the nine foreign citizens in Sa'ada into doubt as well.

[Original Publication: *Terrorism Monitor* 7 (19) – July 2, 2009]

Al-Qaeda's Purpose in Yemen Described in Works of Jihad Strategists

By Michael W.S. Ryan

It appears that al-Qaeda in the Arabian Peninsula (AQAP) is currently following a new version of a classic al-Qaeda strategy. Developed by al-Qaeda's strategic thinkers, the strategy behind AQAP's latest operations is to draw American military forces into Yemen. If successful, AQAP would strengthen its position in the near term within the traditional tribal structure and potentially benefit its recruitment efforts and broaden its financial support. Such an outcome would also open another front in a strategic location, even as the United States is planning and executing a drawdown in Iraq. In light of the United States' current refusal to take this bait, we should expect AQAP to attempt further provocative operations aimed at America.

In October 2009, Sheikh Anwar al-Awlaki published an article in English on a jihadi website with the title: "Could Yemen be the Next Surprise of the Season?" (tawhed.ws, October 20, 2009). Born in the United States, this is the same ideologue who was linked to Major Nidal Hasan, the Fort Hood shooter, and the young Nigerian who attempted to blow up Northwest Airlines Flight 253 en route to Detroit on December 25, 2009. Very little notice was taken of this article in the Western press initially, perhaps because Al-Awlaki gave no details and had not yet achieved his current notoriety, but he did make some telling points.

Al-Awlaki, a resident of Yemen, did not call for jihad against Yemen's president, Ali Abdullah Saleh, who is both a Zaidi Shiite and the long-serving secular ruler of the Republic, even though the Shiite and secular governments are often targets of al-Qaeda. Instead, his focus was on jihad against America and the Saudi royal family. Yemen has had a mixed relationship with al-Qaeda, ranging from intense security operations aimed at destroying the organization to periods of relative quiescence. Although al-Qaeda in Yemen has attacked government forces, its main focus has been foreign targets [1]. Al-Qaeda members based in Yemen began anti-U.S. operations over ten years ago with the attack on the U.S.S. Cole on October 12, 2000, in which 17 Americans were killed and 38 wounded. More recently, the group was responsible for the attempted bombing of Northwest Airlines Flight 253 on December 25, 2009 [2]. The successful attack on the U.S.S. Cole prompted a determined campaign by the government of Yemen and the United States against al-Qaeda in Yemen, including the killing of local leader Abu Ali al-Harthi by a Predator strike in 2002. It appeared to most observers that by 2004 the government of Yemen, with American help, had rendered al-Qaeda in Yemen relatively powerless. The reemergence of al-Qaeda as the player it is today began in 2006, when 23 jihadists escaped from prison in the Yemen capital of Sana'a. Among the escapees was a former aide to Osama bin Laden in Afghanistan, Nasir al-Wuhayshi, who was later to become the leader of al-Qaeda in Yemen (see *Terrorism Monitor*, March 18, 2008). At least two former inmates of Guantanamo were among the escapees who later became local al-Qaeda leaders (*Asharq al-Awsat*, December 29, 2009).

A Base for al-Qaeda?

Yemen presents al-Qaeda with ideal conditions in which to operate. The government is hard pressed on all sides. It is battling an insurgency by the Shiite minority "Houthi" faction in the north along the border with Saudi Arabia. Houthi incursions into territory claimed by the Kingdom drew a sharp Saudi military response starting in November 2009, amid near-universal Arab claims that Iran is supporting the rebellion to destabilize the Arabian Peninsula (*Asharq al-Awsat*, December 13, 2009). Unrelated to the Houthi rebellion, a simmering al-Qaeda-endorsed secessionist movement in the south presents another challenge. Yemen's economy appears to be locked in a downward spiral with declining oil reserves and a severe shortage of water. The nation is also facing massive unemployment in the context of a dramatically increasing population.

The January 2009 consolidation of the two branches of al-Qaeda in Saudi Arabia and Yemen into al-Qaeda in the Arabian Peninsula (AQAP) was likely a practical move, prompted by the increasing success of Saudi security forces inside the Kingdom and by consequence need to take advantage of a safe haven in Yemen (see *Terrorism Monitor*, September 11, 2009). Saudi officials became concerned about the presence of al-Qaeda in Yemen as increasing numbers of Saudi al-Qaeda members began to migrate south. After AQAP was formed, Saudi officials published a list of the 85 most wanted members of al-Qaeda, most if not all of whom were believed to be operating out of the Yemen safe haven. Meanwhile, Saudi forces continued to have success inside the Kingdom, rolling up al-Qaeda cells, arresting individual supporters and uncovering large caches of weapons. But in Yemen, AQAP had breathed new life into jihad. When AQAP leader Nasir al-Wuhayshi (referred to in AQAP publications as Amir Abu Basir) announced the merger, he made it clear that AQAP would target the government of Yemen as well as Saudi Arabia and America. Al-Qaeda's deputy, Dr. Ayman al-Zawahiri, confirmed that al-Qaeda's central organization considers al-Wuhayshi the amir of AQAP and endorsed the merger (al-Jazeera TV, December 22, 2009).

Yemen has always been a high priority in al-Qaeda's global strategy. The strategist Abu Musab al-Suri tried to convince bin Laden to move al-Qaeda's central organization to Yemen as early as 1989. Although Bin Laden had long-term strategic plans for Yemen, his ancestral homeland, he thought that al-Suri's plan would be too difficult to carry out at that time because it would require the cooperation of a number of diverse Yemeni Islamist groups [3]. Like other jihadis, al-Suri thought that Yemen, because of its conservative tribal social structure, size, mountainous terrain and strategic location, would be an ideal location for jihad (see *Terrorism Focus*, February 7, 2008). Although al-Qaeda's leaders in Yemen have ordered some attacks and condemned the nation's secular government, it is likely that AQAP's intention was to stay below the threshold of activity that would incite the government to renew the kind of attacks that nearly destroyed it previously. Clearly, the Houthi rebellion and the secessionist movement in south Yemen are existential threats in a way that al-Qaeda is not [4]. It was natural for AQAP to assume that the traditionally bad relations between Yemen and Saudi Arabia would allow plotting against the Saudis without triggering a strong response from President Saleh. Jihadis in Yemen have traditionally used al-Suri's writings and tapes (sometimes under the alias Khaled Zayn al-Abidin) about the jihad experience in Syria and Afghanistan as training materials and should be well-schooled in his strategic analysis concerning the use of safe havens and the setting up of resistance fronts.

Deciphering AQAP's Strategy

With the establishment of AQAP, the tempo of operations has increased and become more dramatic, if not more effective, in both Yemen and Saudi Arabia. What is the organization trying to achieve? From al-Awlaki's article and the consistent statements by al-Qaeda over the years, we would have assumed that the ultimate goal of AQAP is the establishment of an Islamic emirate throughout the Arabian Peninsula, beginning with the withdrawal of U.S. forces, followed by the overthrow of the Saudi ruling family. Al-Suri had argued that a hierarchal structure mixing secret operations with overt propaganda operations was the source of the destruction of many jihadist organizations in the modern period. Accordingly, we might have expected the relatively modest AQAP organization to encourage clandestine operations inside Saudi Arabia and restrict its operations in Yemen to a steady stream of polemic and only occasional attacks on Yemeni forces. When AQAP stepped forward to claim the attempted Christmas bombing of Flight 253, al-Wuhayshi was deliberately painting a target on himself and AQAP for the United States. He surely would have expected the government of Yemen to bow to American pressure to take strong measures against AQAP. Yet, Nasir al-Wuhayshi changed the game and dramatically increased the risk to himself and his organization [5].

AQAP's actions only make sense if the group is following the doctrine found in Abu Bakr al-Naji's *Idarat al-Tawahhush* (The Administration of Savagery) [6]. In al-Naji's thinking, the Afghan jihad defeated the Soviet Union, not by driving its forces out of Afghanistan, but by drawing them in until they exhausted their ability to fight and the Soviet economy collapsed. Al-Naji's doctrine, drawn from the Afghan experience, is based on a simple formula: enrage the United States so that it oversteps local security forces and engages directly with local jihadis, which in turn incites other Muslims to join the fight against the "occupying" power, thereby increasing al-Qaeda's strength and prestige. The strategy assumes that local Muslims will have much greater staying power than the United States because they can fight so much more cheaply and have a greater tolerance for casualties. Another strategist who became prominent after al-Suri's arrest, Muhammad Khalil al-Hakaymah, has emphasized the importance of jihadists working closely with the local Muslim populations in whose sea they must swim and upon whom they depend for recruitment, protection, and financing [7]. Therefore, al-Qaeda operatives should avoid killing Muslim civilians in general attacks against buildings or market places and should also avoid creating scandals by using brutal methods such as videotaped beheadings. Hakaymah, like al-Suri, argues that individual attacks unconnected to a central organization are the best tactic when the jihadist group is not in a position to take on the local government.

If AQAP's intention is to start its attempt to create the Islamic Emirate of the Arabian Peninsula in Yemen, the Christmas attack may have been intended to draw U.S forces into Yemen, as al-Naji's doctrine recommends. When a jihadist organization is facing "occupying forces" the strategy calls for setting up a front in a remote area and fighting the logistically strained Western forces with the full support of the local populace, which is expected to be inflamed by the foreign presence. A statement signed on January 14, 2010 by 150 Yemeni clerics that called for jihad if any party invades the country appears to support the notion that AQAP is following al-Naji's prescription and taking advantage of al-Hakaymah's recommendations (*al-Bawaba*, January 14, 2010; *Asharq al-Awsat*, January 14, 2010). One cannot help but think that al-Qaeda's leadership would welcome another American entanglement in addition to Iraq and Afghanistan.

Conclusion

Days prior to the Christmas Day attack, AQAP's leadership stated that they are fighting America, not the Yemeni military (al-Jazeera TV, December 22, 2009). With President Obama having stated that the United States will not send troops to Yemen, it seems that AQAP will be fighting Yemeni security forces exclusively, albeit with American technical help. President Saleh's offer to talk to al-Qaeda "if they lay down their weapons and denounce violence" was basically an offer to talk to AQAP if they stop being al-Qaeda, a statement framed to sound reasonable without in any way constraining Yemen's military forces from attacking AQAP. Unless President Saleh's forces are extraordinarily successful, however, we should expect al-Qaeda to stage more provocative attacks against U.S. citizens and interests outside Yemen, perhaps using American citizens as foot soldiers. Yemen is not the new Afghanistan. Instead, Yemen, Iraq, Afghanistan, and Pakistan are all players in the new phase of al-Qaeda's adaptive strategy aimed at exhausting U.S patience and resources. At this stage, however, AQAP is still relatively small and vulnerable to local forces.

[Original Publication: *Terrorism Monitor* 8 (4) – January 28, 2010]

Notes

1. In August 2009, AQAP forces attacked Yemeni military forces in Marib. See NEFA Foundation for translation of AQAP communication about this attack.
www.nefafoundation.org/miscellaneous/AQIY%20battle%20in%20Mareb.pdf.

2. In addition to the failed attack on flight 253, Abdullah Hassan Asiri failed to kill Saudi Prince Muhammad bin Nayef (August 28, 2009); Saudi Arabian forces also announced killing two would-be suicide bombers on the border with Yemen (October 13, 2009). For other highlights of the past decade see:
www.aawsat.com//details.asp.

3. See Jim Lacey (ed.), *A Terrorist's Call to Global Jihad* (Naval Institute Press, Annapolis, 2008), pp 145-54.

4. In January 2010 the chairman of the board of directors of the Yemen News Agency repeated the accusation that Iran is supporting the Houthis and stated that al-Qaeda cannot pose the same level of threat as the northern rebellion. www.sabanews.net/en/news203619.htm .

5. An audiotape allegedly recorded by Osama bin Laden appeared to claim responsibility for the attack, though

not explicitly. The authenticity of the message has not been confirmed (al-Jazeera, January 25, 2010).

6. In January 2010 the chairman of the board of directors of the Yemen News Agency repeated the accusation that Iran is supporting the Houthis and stated that al-Qaeda cannot pose the same level of threat as the northern rebellion. www.sabanews.net/en/news203619.htm .

7. A translation of this work in full may be found at www.tawhed.net/c.php .

8. See Jim Lacey (ed.), *The Canons of Jihad*, (Naval Institute Press, Annapolis, 2008), pp.147-161.

Yemeni Clerics Announce Mandatory Jihad Against Foreign Intervention

By Murad Batal al-Shishani

In his Friday sermon on January 15, 2010, the well-known Yemeni Islamist and U.S. designated terrorism supporter Sheikh Abdul Majid al-Zindani called for jihad to defend Yemen in the event of a foreign military intervention. Al-Zindani noted that some American media reports said the "Yemeni regime is about to collapse and U.S. forces and Marines should intervene to protect oil sources in Yemen." Al-Zindani considered such media reports (which he did not cite specifically) a declaration of war by the United States. Al-Zindani announced, "As soon as the enemy comes down into our land and comes to colonize us, jihad is obligatory according to our religion... This ruling is from Allah; no one can abolish it; neither king, president, commander, scholar, not anyone" (al-Jazeera TV, January 15, 2010; Ennahar Online, January 15, 2010).

Al-Zindani's remarks came a day before the sheikh and 149 other Yemeni clerics issued a fatwa in the name of the "Association of Scholars of the Yemen" declaring that jihad is "fard ayn" (a compulsory duty) in the event of military intervention in the country, and thus rejecting any military cooperation with Washington, the use of Yemeni territory for foreign military bases, and Yemen's commitment to any security or military agreements that are contrary to Islamic Shari'a (*al-Bawaba*, January 14, 2010; *Asharq al-Awsat*, January 14, 2010). In what appears to be a reference to strikes on foreign nationals by al-Qaeda in the Arabian Peninsula (AQAP), the fatwa also condemns the killing of innocent people, whether Yemenis or foreigners who work or live legally in the country. Furthermore, the fatwa strongly condemns the "bloodshed" in Abyan province, Shabwa province and the city of Arhab (Lahij province) [1]. These last three tribal southern areas of Yemen recently witnessed several missile attacks against al-Qaeda members.

Regardless of the probability of a U.S. military invasion of Yemen, the increasing importance of Yemen is obvious from the security perspective of the United States, particularly after the foiled Christmas Day suicide attack on a Detroit-bound passenger plane, which was "prepared" in Yemen. Yemen has also emerged as a safe haven for Salafi-Jihadi militants. The growing importance of Yemen's national security comes as the U.S. administration of President Barack

Obama expresses reluctance to open another front in the "war on terror," just as the occupation of Iraq is drawing down, and a new focus is being put on military operations in Afghanistan. U.S. President Barack Obama announced through *People Magazine* on January 10, 2010 that he had no intention of sending U.S. troops into Yemen.

However, the reaction to the Detroit incident shows that a shift in U.S. policy remains possible; until then, the United States will give a greater role to the U.S. military base in Djibouti in the fight against al-Qaeda in Yemen and Somalia. In November, 2002 the leader of al-Qaeda in Yemen, Sinan Qa'id al-Harthi (a.k.a. Abu Ali al-Harthi) was killed by a U.S. Predator drone launched from Djibouti (*Asharq al-Awsat*, January 19, 2003).

However, such a role might also be in the interest of al-Qaeda and affiliated Salafi-Jihadi groups. In contrast to the U.S. strategic vision, the Salafi-Jihadis and al-Qaeda hope to lure U.S troops to the region as al-Qaeda's new strategy is based on the creation of multiple safe havens instead of a single safe haven. The policy is designed to attrite the U.S. on multiple fronts, with Yemen lying in the center of these safe havens (see *Terrorism Monitor*, September 10, 2009).

The entry of the clerics in Yemen to the growing crisis, regardless of whether they are linked to al-Qaeda or not, indicates the development of an environment that is sympathetic to the growing presence of al-Qaeda. Among the factors that helped al-Qaeda to find a foothold in Yemen is their integration with the tribal structure in southern Yemen. A review of the names of those affiliated with al-Qaeda in Yemen show that a respectable number of them are from the southern tribes. The Salafi-Jihadis failed in Iraq and Chechnya, for instance, because they lost the support of their local host communities. According to the Yemeni government, al-Qaeda was in the process of appointing a parallel system of al-Qaeda "provincial governors" (much as the Taliban have done in Afghanistan) before recent air strikes on al-Qaeda leaders disrupted the process (*Asharq al-Awsat*, January 14, 2010).

Al-Qaeda's tribal alliances and the ideological convergence with local forces in Yemen are playing to the interests of al-Qaeda. This trend may be reinforced by changing security conditions as well as Yemen's unique political and socio-economic factors. Al-Qaeda considers Yemen important because, among other factors, it can serve as a base to launch attacks on neighboring Gulf States. Across the strategic Bab al-Mandaab strait there is also proximity to other Salafi-Jihadi groups such as al-Shabaab in Somalia. All of these factors show that the presence of al-Qaeda in Yemen has regional and international implications and there is every prospect that the conflict between al-Qaeda and the United States will escalate there.

[Original Publication: *Terrorism Monitor* 8 (4) – January 28, 2010]

Notes

1. See the full Arabic text of the fatwa at sa7t-ye.net/vb/showthread.php

An Assessment of the Anatomy of al-Qaeda in Yemen: Ideological and Social Factors

By Murad Batal al-Shishani

Yemen has become one of the most important strongholds and safe havens for al-Qaeda. The impact of Yemen's Salafi-Jihadist movement is no longer limited to that nation and its national security alone. The threat posed by Yemen's militant Salafists has spread to neighboring countries such as Saudi Arabia and more distantly to the United States, as indicated by the failed Christmas Day suicide bombing of a Northwest Airways passenger plane by Nigerian Umar al-Faruq Abd al-Mutalib, who received his training in Yemen.

Al-Qaeda in Yemen, or al-Qaeda in the Arabian Peninsula (AQAP), as it calls itself at the moment, has gone through different phases. During the era of the Afghan Jihad, Arab fighters recruited a large number of Yemenis, and Osama bin Laden relied on them as personal bodyguards [1]. After the U.S. invasion of Afghanistan in late 2001, they returned to Yemen and Saudi Arabia, focusing their operations on the latter. In February 2006, Yemen's "Great Escape" of over a dozen leading al-Qaeda suspects paved the way for a process of reorganization of a movement in Yemen and coincided with their withdrawal from Saudi Arabia after three years of armed confrontations with the authorities (see *Terrorism Focus*, February 7, 2006). Thus, Yemen became a destination for Saudi jihadis and AQAP was born as a coalition of Saudi and Yemeni jihadis (al-Jazeera.net, January 18, 2010).

Given the pivotal role that Yemen's militant Islamists are playing as a host for al-Qaeda and a magnet for jihadis from abroad, this article seeks to analyze the structure of al-Qaeda in the Arabian Peninsula and identify the social and ideological structures that led to its success. In order to obtain reasonably accurate results, the author has collected the names of about 75 people associated with al-Qaeda in Yemen as published, and analyzed them in order to help understand the structure of the organization.

Organization of AQAP

It appears that AQAP draws on three main groups for its recruits: Yemenis, Saudis, and foreigners [2]. According to the author's analysis, Yemenis form the majority with 56%, followed by Saudis at 37% and foreigners, 7%. This is a key

51

indicator of the level of success that al-Qaeda and Salafi-Jihadists have had in disseminating their ideology among local Yemenis. It also raises the question, in what areas of Yemen in particular have al-Qaeda and the Salafi-Jihadists been most successful.

Upon analyzing the tribal and regional origins of the persons under study, the author found that Yemeni recruits were equally distributed between northern and southern tribes (52% and 48% respectively). The reason for this relatively equal distribution is that al-Qaeda's discourse finds a ready audience among tribal people, whether in the south or the north. Yemeni journalist Nabil al-Sufi argues that al-Qaeda's area of influence in Yemen forms a large triangle that is half the size of the country (al-Hayat, January 31, 2009). The triangle starts from Abyan in the west and extends to al-Jawf in the south, passing through large areas of Shabwa governorate as far as Hadramaut. From the north, it is connected to the capital city of Sana'a by Arhab directorate, overlooking the Maqfar triangle that connects it to another three provinces: Sana'a, Ghamran and Sa'da. The result is the formation of an area known for its tribal affiliations rather than its affiliation to the state and an area where there are few state institutions and where tribal laws dominate.

A focus on tribes in Yemen has been a main reason behind al-Qaeda's success in finding a safe haven there. Abu Musab al-Suri, the first to see Yemen's potential as a safe haven for the jihadist movement, has said that the main reason for considering Yemen a stronghold for jihadis is the tribal nature of its people and the solidarity between tribes [3]. It was for similar reasons that Osama bin Laden addressed the southern tribes of Saudi Arabia in 2004, specifically in Asir province (which borders Yemen), naming the tribes and encouraging them to fight in Iraq. "Oh heroes of Asir and champions of Hashed, Madhaj, and Bakeel, do not stop your supplies to assist your brothers in the land of Mesopotamia [i.e. Iraq]. The war there is still raging and its fire spreading" [4].

Abdulelah Hider Shaea, a prominent Yemeni journalist, confirms that al-Qaeda has succeeded in building an alliance with the tribal system in Yemen because the country has not been "tamed" or "civilized" like other countries. Tribes are still in control and thus it was easy to build alliances with them [5]. Shaea said that al-Qaeda wanted to recruit young people who were not afraid of death and found these young people in Yemen's tribal and Bedouin societies, where acts of revenge and battles between tribes are still dominant, given the absence of state institutions (al-Jazeera.net, January 21, 2010).

Conditions of Militancy in the South

Southern Yemenis, who form the majority of the population, were the first to join the Salafi-Jihadi movement. Political conditions in the south have made tribes closer to al-Qaeda. Saeed al-Jahmi, author of an Arabic language text on al-Qaeda in Yemen, has said that the number of al-Qaeda members in the southern part of Yemen is higher than that in the north and gives the following reasons for this phenomenon: the political conditions in the south; the repressiveness of the former Marxist regime; and the political use of violence ingrained in the south during that period. Moreover, the Salafis of the south are different from those of the north, busying themselves with generalities while northerners focused on details. A key element in the development of southern militancy was migration to Saudi Arabia, where many joined Islamic Shari'a schools and first became introduced to the Salafist ideology. Many Yemeni emigrants wanted to return to their home country and seek revenge on those who had deprived them from living in their homeland. In addition, the charismatic personality of Bin Laden (perceived as a hero and savior by some) and the failure of the Muslim Brotherhood to attract southern Salafists to their movement made it easy for al-Qaeda to recruit fighters from the south [6].

Political conditions in the south and predominant feelings of unequal treatment by the central government made people there vulnerable to al-Qaeda's rhetoric and ideology. This becomes clear when one reads the letter of Nasir al-Wuhayshi, the leader of al-Qaeda in Yemen, entitled "To Our People in the South" (May 13, 2009):

The events, [suppression of protests by Yemeni security forces] in Lahaj, al-Dale, Abyan, Hadramaut and other areas, and the injustice and suppression of people who have no weapons to defend themselves, have gone beyond all acceptable limits. It is our duty to support these people, assist them and lend them a helping hand. Oh free men, resistors of injustice and oppression in Yemen and in the Arab Peninsula, what you are preaching is a right that God and your religion have urged you to preach. It is because you by your nature do not accept injustice and humiliation. With your faith, you were able to resist the British occupation [of the Aden Protectorate, 1839-1967] and to force the [British] troops to leave your country. Then you have practiced your right to peaceful protests. Now even this right, given by the

53

oppressor, is taken away from you. When you protested, you were badly oppressed although your cause was just. If you demand justice, it does not mean that you want separation [7].

With regard to Saudi operatives in AQAP, most came from the south of Saudi Arabia (up to 50%), while 39% came from the central area (mainly from al-Qassim) and 11% from other areas (*al-Ghad*, January 6, 2005). Al-Qaeda members coming from al-Qassim are tribal and conservative in nature. This geographical distribution reflects the huge impact of al-Qaeda's defeat in Saudi Arabia after confrontations with Saudi troops and the movement's departure for Yemen.

Al-Qaeda's focus on recruitment from the south of Saudi Arabia led to an increase in the number of Saudi al-Qaeda members who have tribal connections to Yemeni tribes. The emphasis on tribal unity can becomes clear in a 2004 letter by militant Saudi Salafist ideologue Fares Shuwail al-Zahrani (a.k.a. Abu Jandal al-Azadi), also entitled "To the People of the South":

I hereby say to the people of the south, the south of the Arabian Peninsula, avoiding all colonial division of our countries, from the Yamani side to the Arabian Sea, to our proud tribes, who God has favored with Islam and made them occupy the world, I say to them that I am proud of being one of them … I tell them that our country is in the middle of the world, we have the Qiblah, Mecca and Medina. We have the richest seas, the most important straits and the greatest reserves of oil. Do you accept that the crusaders and their agents control you? Do you accept that they steal your money and your resources? Would you allow them to kill your sons and daughters? Oh people of the Arabian Peninsula, oh people of the Arabian Peninsula, you are the strategic depth of your fellow jihadists [8].

Among the al-Qaeda members recruited from southern Saudi Arabia were seven of the fifteen Saudi 9/11 bombers. Bin Laden highlighted this fact in a recorded speech, saying, "Asir's tribes formed the lion's share [of the 9/11 perpetrators], [including] those from Ghamed, Zahran and Bani Shahr [all Asir tribes] [9].

Conclusion

Based on the above, it is evident that al-Qaeda is attempting to build tribal alliances in the area extending from the south of Saudi Arabia to the south of Yemen. These alliances are made possible by the conservative nature of the Salafi-Jihadi movement's ideology. If we examine the structure of al-Qaeda, it is clear that the Salafi-Jihadis are succeeding in mobilizing youth in both Saudi Arabia and Yemen, even when their families have good relations with the authorities. It seems that al-Qaeda's ideology is becoming more influential and is benefiting from injustices in the south of Yemen.

Local alliances have helped al-Qaeda find a safe haven at the strategic level. This has given the movement the capability of carrying out attacks, not only inside Yemen but also outside the country. Examples of this new reach include the attempt to assassinate Saudi Deputy Minister of the Interior Prince Muhammad bin Nayef and the attempt to bomb the Northwest Airlines plane heading from Amsterdam to Detroit. It is clear that traditional tribal relations, injustice, and local grievances are the best allies of al-Qaeda in the Arabian Peninsula.

[Original Publication: *Terrorism Monitor* 8 (9) – March 4, 2010]

Notes

1. Abdel Bari Atwan, The Secret History of al-Qaeda, al-Saqi Books, 2006, p.59.
2. In a February 18, 2010 phone interview with the author, Yemeni journalist Abdul-Ilah al-Sha'e, the only journalist to interview Abu Basir al-Wuhayshi, al-Qaeda's leader in Yemen, said that on his visit to an al-Qaeda stronghold for the interview, he had seen foreign operatives with al-Qaeda, but did not speak with any of them.
3. Abu Musab al-Suri, "The Responsibility of the People of Yemen Regarding the Sanctuary of Muslims," www.tawhed.ws/r.
4. His letter entitled "Oh People of Iraq", May 7, 2004. The full text can be read on Abu Mohammad al-Maqdisi's website: www.tawhed.ws/r.
5. Phone interview with Abdul-Ilah al-Sha'e, February 18, 2010.
6. Saeed al-Jahmi, Tanthim al-Qa'ida: al-nasha'at, al-khalfyat al-adyolojya, al-imtidat (al-Yaman nomouthdjan (Al-Qaeda: Its Emergence and its Ideological Background (Yemen as an example)), Madbouli Bookshop, Cairo, 2008, p. 303, pp 306-318.
7. The audio can be downloaded from: www.as-ansar.com/vb/showthread.php.
8. Fares Shuwail al-Zahrani letter entitled, "To Our People in the South," May 2004. The audio can be downloaded from: www.ukht-benladn.net/mhadrat_show-446.html
9. Osama bin Laden videotape, September 9, 2002, The full text can be accessed at www.alqimmah.net/showthread.php

Mass Arrests of al-Qaeda Suspects in Saudi Arabia Illustrate Security Threat from Yemen

By Murad Batal al-Shishani

The Interior Ministry of Saudi Arabia released a statement announcing the arrest of 113 persons "constituting a network and two cells" tied to al-Qaeda on March 24, 2010. The network was comprised of 101 individuals, including 47 Saudi nationals, 51 Yemenis, a Somali, a Bangladeshi and an Eritrean (*Arab News*, March 25, 2010). The suspects are alleged to have planned attacks on oil installations and security centers in al-Sharqiyah (Eastern) province of Saudi Arabia (*al-Watan*, March 25, 2010).

At a news conference on the same day, the Saudi Interior Ministry's security spokesperson, Major General Mansur al-Turki, said that each of the two cells was composed of six individuals (two suicide bombers and four assistants), all of whom were Saudi nationals and one Yemeni national. He said that both cells worked independently but were affiliated with al-Qaeda in Yemen, and were tied to Abu Hahjir (a.k.a. Sa'id al-Shihri). Al-Turki said that the arrested individuals (including a woman) were aged between 18 and 25 years-old (*al-Watan*, March 25, 2010).

Al-Turki pointed out that the deaths of Yusuf al-Shihri and Ra'id al-Harbi (both disguised in women's clothes) in clashes at the al-Hamra checkpoint in Jazan on October 13, 2009 "opened a window for the security agencies to determine that the al-Hamra checkpoint fire fight was a prelude to a broader plan, not a separate incident." From there the Saudi security agencies started to investigate more cells, which led to the latest arrests. (*Asharq al-Awsat*, March 25, 2010; *al-Watan*, March 25, 2010).

Al-Turki gave details on the methods that al-Qaeda in Yemen use to smuggle individuals and weapons into Saudi Arabia. He said that there was evidence of cooperation between al-Qaeda and the Houthist rebellion in north Yemen, adding that al-Qaeda exploited the war to smuggle operatives, weapons, and ammunition into Saudi Arabia. He suggested that al-Qaeda was exploiting the general confusion that prevailed along the southern border of Saudi Arabia, particularly the large number of simple civilians who enter Saudi Arabia illegally in search of jobs. Trained al-Qaeda operatives were smuggled under the guise of Yemeni civilians seeking livelihoods across the border (*al-Watan*, March 25,

2010). The next day, al-Turki commented on the presence of non-Saudis among the arrested individuals, telling the Saudi press that al-Qaeda is facing difficulties in recruiting large numbers of Saudis.

The details of the arrest as publicized by Saudi Arabia indicate three important developments in the behavior of al-Qaeda in Saudi Arabia since it moved to Yemen and merged with Salafi-Jihadis there, creating al-Qaeda in the Arabian Peninsula (AQAP):

1. Easy targeting of Saudi Arabia is considered to be one of the benefits of al-Qaeda's creation of a safe haven in Yemen. This is not the first time that al-Qaeda has attempted to infiltrate Saudi borders; one of these attempts reached the Saudi Deputy Interior Minister, Prince Muhammad bin Nayef, in an assassination attempt by a suicide bomber in August 2009. AQAP's ability to recruit all of these members and distribute them in different cells indicates that AQAP represents a legitimate threat to Saudi national security; especially as al-Qaeda continues to target Saudi oil installations to guarantee a greater international impact.

2. In addition to AQAP's aim of recruiting non-Saudis inside Saudi Arabia, the Salafi-Jihadis' main target for recruitment remains Saudis, as 47 of the arrested individuals are Saudi natives. Moreover, the age range of 18-25 indicates that they represent a new generation of Saudi al-Qaeda members as the majority appear to be younger than those al-Qaeda suspects named by the Saudi government since 2003. This suggests that al-Qaeda has succeeded in developing new methods to attract youngsters despite Saudi efforts to counter al-Qaeda on the ideological level.

3. Finally, the arrests show the increasing role of AQAP deputy leader Sa'id al-Shihri, who seems to be in charge of operations inside Saudi Arabia. This suggests that al-Shihri's profile will increase as the operative in charge of Saudi Arabia, one of the most important areas for al-Qaeda. In his latest tape, for instance, al-Shihri said that the foiled 2009 Christmas day suicide attack by 23 year-old Nigerian Omar Farouk Abdulmutallab on Detroit-bound Northwest Airlines flight 253 was coordinated directly with Osama bin Laden (alfaloj/vb/showthread.php, February 8, 2010).

[Original Publication: *Terrorism Monitor* 8 (14) – April 9, 2010]

Wooing Bin Laden: Cooperation Between Somalia's al-Shabaab Movement and Yemen's al-Qaeda Movement

By Andrew McGregor

In early April 2010, there were reports that 12 to 15 al-Qaeda operatives and leaders had left Yemen for Somalia, though no names were cited. The men are said to have embarked from al-Mukallah, a Yemeni port in the Hadramaut region commonly used for smuggling or shipping weapons to Somalia (alsahwanet.net, April 5, 2010; Somaliland Press, April 8, 2010). Though numerous Yemeni officials have insisted the Coast Guard is highly active off the coast of Yemen, the UN Monitoring Group on Somalia reports little Coast Guard activity in the area, which despite being controlled by the President's Republican Guard continues to be a center of drug smuggling as well. Other reports suggest the al-Qaeda group reached Somalia via airplane, disguised as humanitarian workers. Somali Treasury Minister Abdirahman Omar Osman claims some of the al-Qaeda operatives came by ship from Yemen, while others crossed overland from Eritrea (AHN, April 7, 2010). According to Abdirahman, the al-Qaeda operatives are not Yemenis, but came all the way from Afghanistan and Iraq to escape the military offensives in those countries and because they "believe they can do what they like" in Somalia (BBC, April 7, 2010). The Treasury Minister also suggested that this was only an advance party, designed to determine if al-Qaeda's "biggest military bases" could be moved to Somalia. (Reuters, April 7, 2010). Despite this announcement, none of the "al-Qaeda leaders" were named, nor were their positions in the organization announced. The entire story was called into question on April 14, 2010 when an al-Qaeda source in Yemen denied all such reports, calling them baseless and promising to issue a statement on the allegations soon (al-Wasat, April 14, 2010).

The current concern over cooperation between militants in Yemen and Somalia began in early January 2010, when al-Shabaab's Sheikh Mukhtar Robow Abu Mansur announced that the movement had decided to send fighters to Yemen to aid their "Muslim brothers" in their battle against Yemen's regime. The decision was characteristic of al-Shabaab's short attention span – the movement always seems to find something else to do other than complete its conquest of Mogadishu.

Somalia's Hizb al-Islam movement, once a solid ally of al-Shabaab, has also courted controversy in recent days by extending an invitation to Osama bin Laden to come to Somalia. Hizb al-Islam says it is also prepared to welcome "every Muslim fighter" to Somalia to fight the enemies of Allah. These now presumably include al-Shabaab, with which Hizb al-Islam is now engaged in bitter fighting in a three-way battle with Mogadishu's Transitional Federal Government (TFG) (Mareeg, April 3, 2010; AFP, April 3, 2010). According to senior Hizb al-Islam official Moallim Hashi Muhammad Farah; "The West may call him a criminal, but we call him our brother and he is not a criminal. Questioning the relationship between us and al Qaeda is like questioning the relationship between two brothers, and that is not realistic" (Reuters, April 7, 2010).

Despite these reports of al-Qaeda operatives heading for Somalia, there are other reports coming from inside that nation that say the number of foreign fighters active in Somalia is actually decreasing due to fear of being cornered there by the much anticipated TFG offensive, leading many of these fighters to return home (Jowhar, February 6, 2010).

Evidence of Militant Movement between Yemen and Somalia?

Somalia's Information Minister, Dahir Mahmud Gelle, claims the new goal of al-Shabaab is to "foment jihad in Yemen," going so far as to join the Shiite Houthist rebellion in north Yemen (Asharq al-Awsat, February 4, 2010). Though the latter is an unlikely development, persistent rumors place Somali volunteers in the front lines of the rebellion.

Al-Shabaab spokesman Sheikh Ali Mahmud Raage regards al-Qaeda as nothing more than Muslims who have suffered massacres for practicing Shari'a law and religion in their own country. Al-Shabaab and al-Qaeda share only the "Muslim faith and freedom fighting," nothing else (BBC, January 17, 2010). Beyond noting that al-Shabaab's strength is derived internally rather than from foreign fighters, the Sheikh refuses to discuss the exchange of fighters between Somalia and Yemen in the media.

Al-Qaeda fighters were reported by U.S. authorities to be leaving Pakistan for Somalia and Yemen a year ago, but, at least so far as Somalia goes, it seems that many of these were actually misidentified Tablighi Jamaat missionaries, many of whom paid for this confusion with their lives shortly after reaching Somalia. In recent months, al-Qaeda in the Arabian Peninsula (AQAP) has announced an exchange of fighter with Somalia (*al-Hayat*, February 9, 2010). This was confirmed by al-Shabaab's spokesman, who said Yemeni fighters would play a major role in al-Shabaab's military campaign (AllPuntland, January 19, 2010). One al-Qaeda leader, Sheikh Abu-Sufyan Al-Sa'di, announced how pleased the movement was with Shabaab's decision to send fighters to Yemen, saying the two movements would soon seize the southern entrance to the Red Sea (Radio Gaalkacyo, February 9, 2010).

Taking the Bab al-Mandaab Strait: Dream or Possibility?

A videotape released in early February 2010 by AQAP deputy leader Sa'id al-Shihri declared that al-Qaeda was determined to seize both sides of the vital Bab al-Mandaab Strait at the southern end of the Red Sea in cooperation with their allies in al-Shabaab. The narrow Bab al-Mandaab is one of the most important seaways in the world – most of the Western world's oil supplies pass through the strait. Closing the strait to the 3,000 tankers a year that use it would effectively close the Suez Canal to most traffic, dealing a deadly blow to Egypt which relies on the canal's revenues. The only alternative for these vessels would be to sail around Africa's Cape of Good Hope, adding another 6,000 miles to their journeys.

According to al-Shihri, controlling this strait and returning it to the "bosom of Islam" would represent a great victory for al-Qaeda and would give the organization "international influence" (*al-Hayat*, April 2, 2010; Shabelle Media Network, February 9, 2010).

There are reports of other plans to carry out acts of maritime terrorism. The African Union peacekeeping mission in Somalia (AMISOM) and the armed Somali Sufi movement Ahlu Sunna wa'l-Jama'a have both said in recent days that they have intelligence regarding an impending Shabaab attack on the ports of Mogadishu, Bossaso as well as various Yemeni ports using vessels packed with explosives (Reuters, April 2, 2010).

Messages have recently begun to appear on jihadi internet forums from Somali extremists, urging Yemenis to look at the Somali example, where threats to invade by land and sea have only emboldened and strengthened the radical Islamists; one such message told the Yemenis "the fate of the battle is to be determined in your land and sea and it is in your own hands. After that, the turn of Jerusalem will come, and then it will be time to restore the caliphate." The message further claims the tribes of Yemen and Somalia will rendezvous at the

Bab al-Mandaab Strait, where they will eventually be joined by the people of Sudan, Nigeria, South Africa and Uganda.

Jihadi websites have been studying the means of disrupting shipping in the Bab al-Mandaab Strait. Among the ideas are:

- Using small fishing boats to deploy barrels full of explosives in the shipping lanes. Inner tubes could be wrapped around the barrels to prevent them from sinking.
- Deploying a large number of empty barrels or barrels filled with sand to exhaust the efforts of minesweeping teams.
- Mounting ambushes on minesweeping ships.

In a true example of asymmetric warfare, the jihadis say military supplies to Coalition forces in Iraq and Afghanistan could be disrupted and estimate $1 billion in damages could be caused for the expenditure of $1,000.

The TFG's State Minister of Defense, Sheikh Yusuf Muhammad Si'ad Indha Adde, threw fuel on the fire by maintaining Osama bin Laden is looking to "make his biggest base in Somalia," and is determined to threaten global security by cutting off the Red Sea and the Gulf of Aden. Indha Adde also claims Yemeni rebels are shipping arms to al-Shabaab through the southern Somali port of Kismayo, which is currently in al-Shabaab hands (al-Qimmah.com, February 1, 2010).

Impact on the Somali Refugees in Yemen

Interestingly, this year has seen a dramatic drop in the number of refugees reaching Yemen from the Horn of Africa; from 17,000 in the first three months of 2009 to roughly 9,400 in the first quarter of 2010. However, this is not due to a dramatic improvement in conditions in Somalia, but rather to even greater insecurity and poverty within that country, preventing many would-be refugees from making their way to Bossaso for the passage to Yemen (VOA, April 9, 2010). Puntland also appears to be taking long-awaited measures to curtail the human-smuggling industry, long an important source of revenue (together with piracy) in semi-autonomous Puntland (IRIN, March 13, 2010). As a result, the cost of buying passage on a smuggling boat has quadrupled recently. Many of those making the trip now are natives of Ethiopia rather than Somalia (IRIN,

April 6, 2010). Hundreds die in the passage each year, many of whom are thrown from the boats in deep water by the Puntland smugglers.

Yemen's deputy foreign minister Ali Muthan says there are over 700,000 African immigrants in Yemen, of which only 200,000 have refugee status (IRIN, January 18, 2010). Somali migrants are granted automatic refugee status, though many fail to register with the government.

The Somalis in Yemen have been subjected to greater scrutiny since al-Shabaab's declaration that it was sending fighters to join al-Qaeda in Yemen. Patrols have been stepped up in Somali neighborhoods and refugee camps, registration has been made mandatory, travel outside the camps has been banned and Somalis found in a motor vehicle are subject to arrest and interrogation by security forces (Shabelle Media Network, January 23, 2010; Saba, January 28, 2010). Two Somali men were even reported to have been decapitated and left in the streets of a Somali area in Sana'a as a warning (Dayniile, January 10, 2010). With typical disregard for the wellbeing of Somalis, al-Shabaab has made the often miserable lives of Somali refugees worse. In Yemen, they have gone from economic burden to security threat (*Yemen Times*, January 4, 2010).

With pressure growing on the Somali community in Yemen, community leaders have issued a letter addressed to "the people of Yemen," condemning all threats of terrorist activity in Yemen by al-Shabaab while asserting al-Qaeda was only interested in creating hostility between the Somali refugees and their "Yemeni brothers" (*Yemen Observer*, February 13, 2010). With nearly a million refugees within the borders of an already impoverished nation and growing complaints of the economic, social and cultural impact of so many refugees, Yemen may use the new security threat from Somalia as an excuse to close its borders to further migration (*Asharq al-Awsat*, March 11, 2010).

The governor of Yemen's Marib province, Naji al-Zayid, claims it is not only Yemen's refugee population that is being targeted by al-Qaeda recruiters, but also its many African students, including young Somalis (Voice of Mudug, February 14, 2010).

Since it controls little more than a few neighborhoods of Mogadishu, Somalia's transitional government can do little to prevent the arrival of foreign fighters from Yemen or elsewhere. Yemen, however, still has a working government despite speculation regarding its eventual collapse. Sana'a claims to have redoubled its efforts at maritime security as well as establishing an anti-piracy center and opening a diplomatic office in the unrecognized breakaway state of

Somaliland as part of an effort to secure the Red Sea. Competition between Israel and Yemen for influence in Somaliland may lead to one of these nations becoming the first to recognize the Hargeisa government.

Conclusion

Oddly enough, the greatest threat posed by enhanced cooperation between Somalia's al-Shabaab and al-Qaeda in the Arabian Peninsula is not at the Bab al-Mandaab Strait, or any other part of the Horn of Africa. Rather, it is in the Western nations such as the United States, Canada, Great Britain and Sweden whose diaspora Somali communities provide recruits and funding for al-Shabaab. With a few rare exceptions, the Somali radicals have focused their activities in the Horn of Africa so far, but greater integration with al-Qaeda will inevitably lead to a new emphasis on targeting the West.

Is there any truth to the story of a dozen or more leading al-Qaeda operatives arriving in Somalia from Yemen in recent days? Somalia's Transitional Federal Government is hampered by chronic divisiveness, but the one thing all government officials can agree on is the need for drastically increased levels of funding. The al-Qaeda threat is consistently advanced as a means of opening the gates to a flow of cash from the United States and its Western allies, though these funds, like the accompanying arms supplies, typically vanish soon after their arrival in Mogadishu.

It must be noted that al-Qaeda and al-Shabaab are utterly incapable of seizing and holding the Bab al-Mandaab Strait. Any attempt to do so would inevitably result in their utter destruction and the permanent occupation of the region around it by Western militaries and the resultant damage to the sovereignty of the largely Arab and Muslim nations on both sides of the strait. However, these movements are capable of causing a vast amount of mischief in the area, delaying cargos, forcing hikes in maritime insurance rates, instigating hikes in fuel prices and forcing costly deployments of naval forces to sweep the area for mines and prevent the deployment of attack boats or bomb-laden suicide ships.

There is also the China question. Closing or even interfering with the Bab al-Mandaab Strait would cause havoc to China's petroleum supplies from Sudan. Chinese tankers must load their fuel at Port Sudan in the Red Sea and then proceed south through the Strait. China already has a naval presence in the Gulf of Aden and it is entirely possible these ships may take an active role to prevent any interference with China's energy supply lines (see *Terrorism Monitor*, April 5, 2009).

Of course, mining seas effectively requires a great deal more than dumping a few barrel bombs into the water. The tactic was recently tried by Gaza insurgents off the coast of Israel – total damage amounted to the temporary closure of a few beaches.

Al-Shabaab's assertions it is sending fighters to aid al-Qaeda in Somalia should be viewed in the context of the movement's repeated efforts to ingratiate itself with al-Qaeda's leadership. Despite declarations of allegiance to bin Laden and their ideological identification with al-Qaeda, the non-Arab Somali movement has yet to be incorporated into al-Qaeda in the way Algeria's Arab Islamists became al-Qaeda in the Islamic Maghreb.

[Speech given at the Jamestown Foundation conference, *Yemen On The Brink: Implications for U.S. Security Interests in the Horn of Africa*, given on April 15, 2010 at the Carnegie Endowement for International Peace, Washington, DC]

Breaking Yemen Apart: Al-Qaeda Exploits Social Divisions to Further its Agenda

By Sarah Phillips

Since its announced inception in January 2009, the Yemeni al-Qaeda franchise, (al-Qaeda in the Arabian Peninsula – AQAP) has become much more ambitious with the international terrorist operations it has attempted to execute. What began with the group's stated desire to overthrow the Yemeni regime quickly became farther reaching, first into Saudi Arabia and then, on Christmas Day, into the United States.

The group's online magazine, *Sada al-Malahim*, articulated this shift in August 2009, apparently perceiving its battle against the Yemeni regime largely won: "We concentrate on Saudi Arabia because the government of [Yemeni President] Ali Abdullah Saleh is on the verge of collapse." That month an AQAP operative attempted to assassinate Saudi Arabia's Deputy Interior Minister, Prince Mohammed bin Nayf. While the attempt was unsuccessful it demonstrated the group's willingness to undertake brazen attacks outside of Yemen and advertised itself as a new vanguard group for al-Qaeda internationally. Since the attempted bombing of a U.S. passenger jet on Christmas Day, a number of significant planned operations have also been linked to Yemen, including a thwarted attack on Saudi oil facilities (al-Arabiya, March 24, 2010) and seemingly, an elaborate plan involving a British Airways employee, who was passing inside airline security information to AQAP leaders in Yemen [1]. As the Yemeni state becomes more dysfunctional, AQAP is attempting to wedge the cracks wider and position itself as a legitimate political actor against a regime that is widely seen as corrupt. As it simultaneously becomes more internationally aggressive it is welcoming foreign recruits with Western passports to join its fight against the West [2].

While Yemen's problems extend far beyond those involving al-Qaeda, AQAP's traction is symptomatic of the wider fragmentation within the country's political and economic system. The level of decay apparent in the economy is providing a window for AQAP in the short/mid-term, although it faces a number of likely obstacles in the longer term [3]. However, the short/mid-term provides AQAP with a combustible mix of economic decline, widespread perceptions of injustice, wayward foreign recruits to militant teachings of Islam and, perhaps most concerning, a steady rise in communally framed violence in parts of the south.

To understand the interconnectedness of these issues, a brief explanation of Yemen's political economy is in order. Like many oil-based economies, the Yemeni political system is based on patronage relations, and functions according to the regime's ability to maintain a wide network of elites who are reliant upon the largesse from center. The less money the regime has to distribute through its networks, the less influence in has with stakeholders around the country. In a country with few functional formal institutions, it is this informal "influence" that keeps the center connected to the periphery, and thus keeps the country running. The regime now has less money to distribute through its networks: around three-quarters of the government's operating budget comes from oil revenues but its oil reserves are rapidly depleting. Oil revenue dropped by around 40 percent last year, which further crippled the government's already anaemic budget. The influence of the regime is, therefore, also waning.

Yemen has always been a poor country, and its people are certainly resilient, but something significant has shifted in recent years. The gravitational center of this shift is the highly visible disparity of income between those included in the regime's networks and those excluded from them. Perceptions of injustice are now rife – something that AQAP has proven adept at articulating in its propaganda [4]. That deep sense of injustice is helping to create to an environment in which violence may make more sense against a perceived threat than it did just a few years ago. However, what is most striking in Yemen today is that legitimate grievances, including those from southerners against the northern-based regime, appear to be metastasising into communally framed animosities, to the extent that vigilantism is on the rise [5].

The unfolding of these events has been disturbingly rapid. Just two years ago it was possible for a foreigner to travel relatively freely throughout most of the former south; now Yemenis report fearing vigilante gangs, particularly in Shabwa, Dhala'e, Lahj, and Abyan. In July 2009, for example, four members of a family were kidnapped by their neighbour in the southern governorate of Lahj, who accused them of being spies for the northern regime. The father, one of his sons and his brother-in-law were executed while the other son escaped (*Yemen Observer*, July 18, 2009).

Two things in particular stood out about this crime and the others like it that Yemenis now speak of. The first was that the father had emigrated to the south from the north 25 years ago (that is, before unification) and his two sons were born in the south. This points to a seeming shift in the way the north-south division is being characterised in parts of the south, from one of political and economic inequality perpetrated by the regime, to one of ethnicity, or at least perceived ethnicity. The murdered men were considered northern by virtue of their family heritage being in the north, not because they settled in the south after unification, when the perceived occupation is being traced back to. By this logic, the family was not part of the political occupation of the south but rather part of an ethnic occupation.

If these murders had occurred in isolation, it would not necessarily be indicative of a broader trend, but crimes of this nature have since been on the rise. Shortly after the murders, a northerner was found dead hanging from a tree in the south, and a northern contractor was kidnapped and tortured in Hadramaut, and only freed when he promised to leave the south. In the southern governorate of al-Dhala'e, where anti-regime sentiments are particularly high, stores belonging to northerners are being quite regularly burnt down, and other threats are being made against northerners who refuse to leave the area and return to the north. This type of violence carries the very clear potential to provide a spark for much wider unrest.

An editorial in the *Yemen Post* last year illustrated the degree to which these sorts of attacks have increased:

> [The country's discouraging situation] does not mean that southern mobility followers have the right to attack a northerner just because he is one. It does not mean that any car passing by a southern governorate with a car plate showing that he is a northerner should be attacked and have rocks [s]mashed through its windows. This is what southern mobility followers have been doing over the last month as they killed a number of people just because they did not agree with their way of thinking or because he was a northerner [6].

One northern Yemeni reported travelling in a share taxi throughout the south in March 2009, during which time he was told that because he was from the north he was putting the entire car at risk. The driver informed him that people are establishing makeshift checkpoints, searching cars for northerners and that some have even been killed on this basis. He described driving through towns where locals told him they have been operating under a self-imposed curfew for the past two months because crime has become so pervasive in the hours of darkness [7]. While this may be a further indication that identity politics are taking hold in a new way, it is possible that anti-northerner animosity is also sometimes being used as a cover for simple banditry. However, this caveat does not belie the fact that this is remarkably new and almost certainly related to the same political decay that AQAP is attempting to remake in its own image.

These animosities are not a re-emergence of old cross-border tensions that unification had tried to paper over. The pre-unification border between north and south Yemen was a product of Ottoman and British colonial intervention, not communal feelings of "otherness" between Yemenis on either side of the border. The sporadic conflict between the former northern and southern states prior to unification in 1990 was based on divisions that were largely between the competing elites in each state, not communal identities relating to either state. When unification was announced in 1989, both northern and southern Yemenis welcomed the decision, and both regimes had – correctly – perceived unification as a way of enhancing their popular legitimacy. One obvious illustration of this is the fact that the opening sentence of the South Yemeni 1970 constitution was: "Believing in the unity of the Yemen, and the unity of the destiny of the Yemeni people in the territory…" [8]. The feelings of cultural and historical unity were strong on both sides of the border, as was the belief that the main obstacle to Yemen's ascendance in the Arab world was the fact that its people – the Yemenis – remained artificially divided.

The threads keeping the Yemeni state together are under increasing stress. While AQAP is not a natural alternative contender to power, it willingness to prey on the social trauma caused by injustice and exclusion gives it certain advantages in the prevailing climate. The potency of AQAP rests on its ability to offer only slightly more to communities in crisis than what the government is offering. If the regime is not willing to negotiate a more inclusive political settlement with its citizens, there is little likelihood that the country's situation will improve in the foreseeable future. It is in the regime's own self-interest to respond to the threat that it faces by becoming less extractive and more inclusive, and it is on this point that external pressure might be usefully applied.

[Original Publication: *Terrorism Monitor* 8 (19) – May 13, 2010]

Notes

1. Sam Greenhill and Paul Sims, "BA worker 'planned to use strike to become suicide bomber and passed on secrets to terror masterminds in Yemen,'" *Daily Mail*, March 12, 2010.

YEMEN: AL-QAEDA'S NEW PLAYGROUND

2. "Americans suspected of terror-related activities," Associated Press, March 17, 2010. See also Abdulsattar Hatitah, "Yemen: A Talk with Al-Qaeda Expert Abdul-Ilah Haydar" *Asharq al-Awsat*, March 9, 2010. In this interview, Haydar notes in passing that at one AQAP meeting "There are some titles and people without names, some were Saudi and some probably not Arab [judging] by their features, and with whom we did not have any conversation." This is both concerning and consistent with other evidence to suggest that there are a significant number of foreigners mixing with AQAP.

3. This argument, that the more AQAP asserts itself politically, the more likely it is to come into conflict with local communities, is expanded upon in Sarah Phillips "What Comes Next in Yemen: Al-Qaeda, the Tribes, and State-Building," *Carnegie Endowment for International Peace*, Carnegie Paper Number 107, March 2010.

4. For example, an article in the August 2009 issue of *Sada al-Malahim* argued that: "The inhabitants of [the oil richer areas, Marib, Shabwa and Hadramaut] are paying for their own oppression" with the oil wealth misappropriated by their government. This was an important shift in the way that oil is usually discussed in al-Qaeda propaganda: the argument was not about the West greedily obtaining oil at any cost, but rather about local communities not receiving what was rightfully theirs because the government is corrupt and unjust.

5. It should be noted that the Yemeni government also established its own vigilante militias in the south, purportedly in defence of unity. Mohammed al-Qadhi, "Civil war anniversary splits Yemen" *The National*, July 6, 2009.

6. It is important to note, however, that the attackers are not necessarily attached to the southern movement as the author implies. See Hakim Almasmari, "Difference Between Southern Mobility and al-Qaeda," *Yemen Post*, July 26, 2009.

7. Correspondence with the author, March 2010.

8. Cited in Michael Hudson, *Arab Politics: The Search for Legitimacy* (New Haven, CT: Yale University Press, 1977), p. 357.

Chapter Two

Yemen's War on Terrorism

Yemen's Innovative Approach to the War on Terror

By Eric Watkins

Yemeni President Ali Abdullah Saleh appears to have weathered the worst of his terrorist problem. Indeed, with no al-Qaeda related incidents in two years, Saleh's previously suspect security credentials are beginning to look brighter. A high-profile visit from then German Chancellor Gerhard Schroeder scheduled for March 2005, following a February 2005 trip by the Chairman of the U.S. National Democratic Institute Kenneth Walk to launch the NDI's regional bureau in Yemen, only serves to enhance this image. Not least, Saleh's government is also being praised for developing a new approach to the war on terrorism based on dialogue, even as it seeks to distance itself from men long suspected of supporting the al-Qaeda network.

There have been some surprises, though. In August 2004, during the trial of five men accused of plotting the October 2000 attack on the U.S.S. Cole when their lawyer presented a document in court that alleged a government role in facilitating the attack. The document took the form of an official letter by former Interior Minister Hussein Arab instructing security authorities to give "safe passage to Sheikh Mohammed Omar al-Harazi with three bodyguards without being searched or intercepted. All security forces are instructed to cooperate with him and facilitate his missions." In the letter, Arab said the order was valid from April 2000 until the end of 2000. Harazi is one of the names used by Abd al-Rahim al-Nashiri, the sixth defendant and the alleged mastermind of the suicide attack that killed 17 U.S. sailors aboard the ship.

It was not immediately clear how the defense obtained a copy of the letter, but significantly enough it was considered authentic by the court and accepted as evidence in the trial. Its meaning was not lost on observers. "This document confirms that there is a breach in the Yemeni security system. This system has been infiltrated for a long time by terrorist elements, because of old relations," political analyst Mohammed al-Sabri told the Associated Press. Another analyst, Jamal Amer, said al-Nashiri's possession of such a letter "proves that there is a link between security authorities and these groups" [1]. Such observations also appeared to confirm suspicions of U.S. investigators of the Cole bombing, who wanted to interrogate upper echelons of the Yemeni regime but who were blocked from doing so by Hussein Arab, among others. The observations also shed light on the ability of al-Qaeda operatives to obtain Yemeni identification documents and travel papers – both of which are issued by the interior ministry.

Even as Saleh's government remained silent over the letter which implicated the former minister in terrorism, an Internet newspaper run by the president's ruling General People's Congress (GPC) launched a broadside against another former high official. On December 30, 2004, the GPC's al-Motamar newspaper [www.almotamar.net] claimed that that the military wing of the al-Iman University received instructions to prepare for acts of anarchy, looting, and to close roads to civilians as part of a plan to create chaos and sedition in Yemen. Al-Motamar.net quoted what it called "informed sources" who also described the university as a "nest for terrorism." The story was a thinly disguised attack on Sheikh Abdul Majid al-Zindani, President of al-Iman University and a member of the Shura Council of the opposition Islah Party, who has long been accused by the U.S. of helping to bankroll al-Qaeda. In fact, the *al-Motamar* story seemed to echo the very words of former U.S. Ambassador to Yemen Edmund Hull who in March 2005 told a local newspaper that "[W]e are worried about the activities of al-Iman University; we aim to stop the foreign funds to al-Zindani so as to stop his fund for the university and the activities that promote terrorism and finance terrorism" [2].

Al-Iman University filed a lawsuit against *al-Motamar's* editor-in-chief Abdullah al-Hadrami in January 2005, but the report has been enough to demonstrate that al-Zindani no longer enjoys official favor. He seems to understand that as well, having – for the second time in less than a year – sought the government's help in denying other charges laid against him by the U.S. government. In January 2005, just weeks after the *al-Motamar* story, al-Zindani demanded that the Yemeni government sue the U.S. at the International Court of Justice for its accusations against him of supporting and financing terrorism. Those allegations were made public on February 28, 2004 when the U.S. Treasury Department announced that Zindani had been added to the U.S. government's list of people suspected of supporting terrorist activities. The U.S. Treasury

Department described al-Zindani as a "loyalist" to al-Qaeda leader Osama bin Laden and said he "has a long history of working with bin Laden, notably serving as one of his spiritual leaders." It also said that al-Zindani actively recruited for al-Qaeda's terrorist training camps and played a role in the purchase of weapons for al-Qaeda and other terrorists. Soon after, the UN Security Council added Zindani's name to its list of terrorist financiers. At the time, al-Zindani unsuccessfully petitioned the Yemeni government to ask the UN Security Council for another debate of the resolution which was taken in the absence of Yemen's representative – a significant absence in and of itself.

Al-Zindani's pleas for help from the Yemeni government are clearly designed to evince sympathy among his own Islamist followers and to stir their ire against Saleh. But the Yemeni president seems to have pre-empted such moves by taking a relatively benign approach against potential rank and file recruits to al-Qaeda. To be sure, the Yemeni president has not been hesitant to order military action against hardened extremists when necessary – as he did in the November 2002 assassination of Sinan Qa'id al-Harthi, believed by U.S. and Yemeni authorities to be a close friend of Osama bin Laden and al-Qaeda's key operative in Yemen. In fact, at the time, there were concerns that the al-Harthi assassination may have made Yemen's government more of a target for al-Qaeda than it already was, due to Saleh's growing cooperation with the U.S. In addition to his willingness to liquidate al-Qaeda supporters, Saleh has also shown a knack for using gentler weapons on them, too, and with felicitous effects.

Perhaps the most interesting of these weapons is a Yemeni qadi, or religious judge, named Hamoud al-Hattar, who was named by Saleh as "chairman of the committee for religious dialogue with al-Qaeda supporters in Yemen" in August 2002. In an interview with the Arabic *al-Quds al-Arabi* newspaper in December 2004, Hattar said Saleh summoned a group of senior Yemeni ulema – including Hattar – for a private meeting [3]. In this meeting, which was attended by senior state officials, there was a discussion of the idea of dialogue with the young people who returned from Afghanistan and others who have ideological convictions that are contrary to the notions held by Muslim ulema in general. According to Hattar, Saleh raised the problem saying: "We have a group of young people who hold dangerous beliefs. Those people have not committed any crime, but if we leave them on their own, they could cause great harm to themselves and to the country. We need to talk to them."

Hattar said the group launched the dialogue on September 5, 2002 and has conducted four rounds since then. "We believe that we have eliminated 90 percent of the ideology that had formed the basis for terrorist operations in Yemen," Hattar told *al-Quds al-Arabi*. As for evaluating the work of the committee, he said, "[W]e cannot assess ourselves, but we will give others a chance to speak about the work of this committee and what it has achieved." In his view, "many political analysts and others who follow Yemeni affairs and the issues of security and terrorism worldwide say that the committee succeeded in taking more steps toward the achievement of security and stability. Since late December 2002 and until now, there has been no significant terrorist incident in Yemen."

Hattar's methods have doubtless caused a stir, leading him to a five-day visit to France at the invitation of the French government. Hattar told the official Saba news agency that he would conduct an interview with French radio concerning Yemen's experience in dialogue with militants, and that he would also hold talks with French officials in the foreign, interior, and justice ministries, as well as at the Arab Institute and the Council of French Muslims [4]. While winning friends abroad always helps, the general point of Saleh's undertaking with Hattar is to comply with the demands of the Bush administration's war on terrorism without being seen by his own people as one of Washington's henchmen. Whether Saleh actually intends to go after and eventually uproot alleged supporters of the al-Qaeda network such as Hussein Arab or Abdul Majid al-Zindani remains to be seen. But Saleh knows that any such job will be much easier to undertake if the ground around such men is softened by people like the loquacious Hamoud al-Hattar, chairman of the Committee for Dialogue with al-Qaeda supporters in Yemen.

[Original Publication: *Terrorism Monitor* 3 (4) – May 5, 2005]

Notes

1. Ahmed Al-Haj, "USS Cole Follow Up: Yemeni Government Abetted Terrorists," Associated Press, August 25, 2004.

2. For this paragraph and the next, see: "Yemen: Islamic cleric denies al-Iman University runs military wing," in *Asharq al-Awsat*, January 3, 2005; "Yemeni university sues internet paper over terror claims," on *Yemen Observer* website, January 12, 2005; and "Yemeni cleric asks government to sue U.S. over terrorism allegations," on *Yemen Times* newspaper website, January 13, 2005.

3. Mahmud Ma'ruf, "Yemeni Judge on Dialogue With Al-Qaeda Supporters, Change in 'Convictions'," *Al-Quds al-Arabi*, December 18, 2004.

4. Yemen News Agency Saba website, February 15, 2005.

The Yemeni Arms Trade: Still a Concern for Terrorism and Regional Security

By Shaun Overton

The November 28, 2002 attack on an Israeli airliner in Mombassa, Kenya, focused attention on Yemen and it arms markets. A United Nations report tasked with assessing arms trafficking to Somalia found that the shoulder fired missiles used in that attack likely originated from Yemen. Furthermore, follow-up reports cite Yemen's weapons availability as a significant risk factor for al-Qaeda's procurement of arms.

Yemen's efforts at internal control started after 9/11 with the new international focus on terrorism. The Yemeni government embarked upon a widely known weapons buyback program, hoping to disarm the tribes and thus neutralize the threat they posed to government control, in a non-confrontational manner. Sources connected to the markets believe the tribes have largely participated, relieving themselves of artillery, missiles, tanks and other forms of heavy weaponry. Surprisingly, the widespread rumor of American financing of the buyback program seems to exercise little impact on the tribes' willingness to participate.

Weapons purchases in the markets have fallen drastically since 1999, a period coinciding with a marked decrease in intertribal violence. Tribal mini-wars created a market for weapons of all sizes and varieties, leading to a flourishing trade in arms. The decrease in activity led to a drop in supply accompanied by significant price hikes. Currently, the market's major customers are tribesmen hoping to adorn themselves with rifles or pistols, as is customary in Yemeni tribal tradition. Anything heavier, and ammunition in general, is in low demand as no large customer groups have any great need for such items.

This decrease in demand has accompanied other limited Yemeni government efforts to affect control over weapons in Yemen. The government implemented a ban on carrying weapons inside major cities. The results did not reach their intended marks with tribal cities like Marib and al-Hazm, though more urbanized areas such as Sana'a, Aden and Taiz successfully implemented the ban. Yemeni internal efforts have likely interfered with the free trade of weaponry with the closing of the weapons market at Souq al-Talh and Marib. Souq al-Talh used to be the largest arms market in the country. It served local tribal needs and acted as a distribution center, supplying markets not easily supplied by border or maritime smuggling to places like Jihana, a major market about 250 km southeast of the capital [1]. Souq al-Talh closed in spring 2004 as a result of the al-Houthi rebellion due to a heavy government crackdown and its continued presence within the market. The Marib market closed approximately six months prior to the al-Houthi rebellion, though the circumstances surrounding its closing and what provoked it remain ambiguous.

A November 2003 trip to Souq al-Talh revealed how the market concealed its full selection. When purchases of heavy weapons were involved, the market served merely as a meeting point for buyer and seller. Sellers maintained small stores in the market stocked with pistols, rifles and ammunition. Other items, such as RPGs, missiles and heavier weapons were available off-site if one found the right dealer and if buyer and seller established enough trust. Interviews with arms dealers proved impossible due to security concerns, but people connected to the market insisted that nearly any conceivable conventional weapon was obtainable through the right contacts.

The al-Houthi rebellion serves as an excellent guideline to the status of Yemen's weapons markets in the spring of 2004. Al-Houthi managed to arm his supporters by simply visiting weapons markets across the country according to a Yemen-based journalist who covered the Houthi rebellion extensively and wishes to remain anonymous due to current employment with a Western embassy. Flush with cash from decades' worth of khums (a Shi'a religious tax) al-Houthi and his followers encountered little difficulty in financing the operation. They apparently were able to purchase all the materials for their uprising from within the country. What remains unclear, however, is the type of weaponry employed in the rebellion and whether al-Houthi managed to acquire heavy arms or not.

Significant levels of arms trading appear to continue in these areas despite the market closures. Note, for example, the March 19 2005, killing of al-Houthi followers as they attempted to acquire weapons in Souq al-Talh despite the closure of the weapons section. Numerous sources insist that the market is indeed closed. A likely scenario is that the market, while closed, still serves as a covert rendezvous point for buyers and sellers. Alternatively, as Sana'a University professor Abdullah al-Faqih points out, closing the markets only drives such activity underground, potentially doing away with the need for open markets altogether. The government presence also is unlikely to have significantly interrupted existing dealer-client relationships.

Marib also appears under limited control. The government only managed to officially implement the ban on carrying weapons inside the city in January 2004, years behind most other cities [2]. That effort has not gone smoothly either. *Asharq al-Awsat* newspaper reported on February 2, 2005 a clash between security forces and tribesmen attempting to bring their personal weapons into the city. The conflict escalated further when the tribesmen retaliated, attacking government buildings and checkpoints. Continued tensions between the Abeeda tribe, whose members were exclusively involved in the incident, and the security apparatus are near certain as both parties took casualties in the violence. The Abeeda tribe is the same tribe accused of sheltering Sinan Qa'id al-Harthi (a.k.a. Abu Ali al-Harthi), the al-Qaeda leader assassinated by the CIA in November 2002 [3]. Others in the city complain of unequal application of the law, saying that some days weapons are permitted past checkpoints while on others the law is enforced.

Yemen's extensive boundaries provide a further challenge to limiting the flow of weapons into and out of the country. The nation's incipient coast guard still lacks anything close to enough resources to effectively patrol nearly 2,000 km of coastline. American support has enhanced their capabilities, building the coast guard's numbers of ships and men at a modest pace. At the present time, however, the coast guard remains unable to implement a significant presence.

The country's land boundaries prove equally challenging. The Saudi governor of Jizan, Prince Mohammed bin Nasser bin Abdul-Aziz, complained publicly in August 2003 that Saudi authorities captured Yemeni arms smugglers on an hourly basis. The two nations only recently demarcated an official location for the border. Perhaps the greatest problem is the geography of the border itself. The border runs 1,458 km with Saudi Arabia through the Empty Quarter, an area nearly devoid of inhabitants and permanent settlements. Patrolling such an area is a near impossible task for the government and its limited resources.

Many people believe that Yemeni military officers bear responsibility for the distribution of weapons in the country. Arms can flow legally into Yemen for the legitimate purpose of supplying the army. Military officials, most of whom are paid under $100 per month, stand to gain a great deal by illegally selling supplies of weapons under their care. Moreover, they have little to fear from government recordkeeping and are unlikely to face weapons inventory inquiries. A conversation unrelated to smuggling with an officer in the military police highlights the government's dilemma of balancing officials' pay with their responsibility. He noted that on his official salary he makes YR 9,000 per month, a little more than $45. When bribes are factored in, he estimates an income of YR 60,000-70,000, about $320-370. Such corruption is rampant throughout the government.

The Yemeni government itself suffers from inadequate commitment to the weapons issue. The Yemeni Parliament cannot resolve its differences over a proposed law to thoroughly regulate arms distribution and ownership in the country. The speaker, Sheikh Abdullah bin Hussein al-Ahmar, remains unenthusiastic about the proposal. Most of the tribal elements feel likewise. They are reluctant to cede on an issue where enhanced government control is an almost certain outcome. Instead, they point to the current 1992 law as satisfactory, despite major shortcomings like the government's inability to seize weaponry even after an offender commits a weapons violation.

The Yemeni government's progress on weapons availability is weak. The buyback program has taken significant quantities of heavy weapons out of private hands, though those groups were unlikely to use those weapons against the government in the first place. Otherwise, they would not willingly disarm. Knowledgeable individuals who visited the Jihana market late last year noted that the heaviest weaponry on offer in the stalls were RPGs and their launchers. They were apparently of near unusable quality given their extreme age. Such signs are encouraging though they are partially negated by the now even more discreet trade of heavy weapons due to the market closures and continued hostility between the government and the tribes. Reopening the markets to monitor weapons traffic seems an unfeasible option. The government has made little progress in improving its relations with the tribes since the country's unification in 1990. There seems to be little reason to believe the government will gain control over the weapons situation and the factors affecting it anytime within the next few years. Consequently Yemen will likely remain a potential supply source for weapons to interested parties for some time to come, including al-Qaeda.

[Original Publication: *Terrorism Monitor* 3 (9) – May 6, 2005]

Notes

1. www.yementimes.com/99/iss35/report.htm
2. "Hamla amniyya li-mana'a haml as-silah fi madinat Marib," www.almotamar.net/11027.htm, January 8, 2004.
3. al-Jarbani, Hussein, al-Yemen: "Maqtal sita ashkhas baynahum jundiyan fi ishtibak bi Ma'rib," *Asharq al-Awsat*, February 2, 2005.

Yemen's Committee for Dialogue: Can Jihadists Return to Society?

By Michael Taarnby

Well before 9/11, Yemen was faced with a terrorist threat on a scale matched by few other countries. It was not a case of unraveling the occasional sleeper cell but rather a question of how to handle thousands of militants, many of whom returned to Yemen from Afghanistan and other battlefields with impressive combat experience and deep ideological motivation.

This complex and dangerous situation required delicate handling and perhaps the most interesting aspect of Yemen's war on terrorism is the Committee for Dialogue. The Committee was established in August 2002, when Yemeni President Ali Abdullah Saleh summoned five senior clerics who subsequently formed the nucleus of this pioneering enterprise. Since its inception, the Committee has expanded to 24 members, which also includes four ministers.

The work of the Committee for Dialogue has confused, aggravated and astounded a number of international observers who follow Yemen's unique approach to counterterrorism. What at first glance might appear as a haphazard strategy is in fact much more complicated and made to fit the local circumstances. Some have accused Yemen of being soft on terrorism, conveniently ignoring the substantial number of terrorists being convicted and executed. It appears that Yemen, while keeping a keen eye on international opinion and developments, has created a counterterrorism strategy which deals harshly with immediate threats, yet focuses on long-term and lasting solutions.

Justice for All

The following is a brief summary and distillation of an interview conducted in Sana'a on 21 June 2005, with the president of the Committee for Dialogue, Judge Hamoud al-Hattar, who is also the president of the court of appeal for Sana'a and al-Jawf governorates.

Since the war on terrorism began in earnest, several hundred young radical Islamists were arrested and imprisoned without trial. Knowing fully well that these suspects were innocent according to the Yemeni penal code, they were nevertheless considered potentially dangerous to society because of their militant views and known associates. Realizing that the suspects eventually had to be either put on trial or released, a decision was made to approach them to see if they could be convinced of the futility of the Jihadist lifestyle. The Committee for Dialogue was to be the instrument for conducting what amounted to a dialogue with known al-Qaeda sympathizers.

Expecting little and hoping for the best, the members of the Committee for Dialogue outlined an approach to dialogue with the detainees that would turn out to be as effective as it was simple. The process of dialogue between the clerics and the radical Islamists is founded on a single-page manual. This interesting document differs from any Western interrogation manual both in size, scope and working principle. The foundation of the dialogue is equality and respect; literally a conversation between individuals of equal standing. The basic fact that one party in the dialogue was behind bars appears not to have had much influence on the process. The manual is simple in the extreme in that it stresses the need for mutual respect and recognition, courteous behavior and a duty to speak the truth, common definition of goals and methods, recognition of differences and agreement to revert to common ground when the dialogue stalls. As such the manual more resembles a form of social contract than an interrogation checklist, which it is certainly not.

In this context, it would be misleading to speak of an interrogation. The dialogue is decoupled from whatever questioning and interaction that takes place between the detainees and the intelligence and security services. The basic pre-requisite is voluntary participation; coercion does not serve any purpose in this setting. For this reason the content of the manual is presented to the detainees and the topics and format is discussed until mutual agreement has been reached.

At the first meeting between the detainees and the clerics there is the unavoidable suspicion that must be dealt with immediately. Not surprisingly, the detainees have been quite skeptical about the motives of the clerics and have often bluntly enquired into their "true" motives. The clerics would then proceed to explain that the purpose of the visit was to initiate a dialogue to exchange views on important matters of mutual interest, although seen from different angles. Knowing fully well the detainees' obsession with religion, it was explicitly stated that the foundation of the dialogue would be the Quran and the Sunna and nothing else.

The way to attract their interest was through the proposal of an all or nothing deal. The clerics who approached the detainees insisted that the dialogue would center on the interpretation of the Holy Scriptures. If the detainees could persuade the clerics of the legitimacy of their Jihad they would join them. If not, the detainees would have to give up the idea of armed struggle. Somewhat surprisingly to the clerics, the detainees were eager to accept the deal. However, their arrogance and zeal was seldom matched by their knowledge of the scriptures, and in the end they were not able to present a convincing concept of Jihad based on the authoritative sources. Over time it was proven that the legitimacy of Jihad as outlined by Osama bin Laden and al-Qaeda does not stand up to close scrutiny.

This approach has proven useful because it deliberately ignores the unavoidable positioning that occurs when current events are brought up. U.S. foreign policy in the Middle East, the Palestinian problem and the situation in Iraq are not central topics, and as such tend to be deliberately avoided. Instead the focus is exclusively on Islam and what it means to be Muslim. For instance, the detainees are challenged to find the passages in the Holy Scriptures that allow indiscriminate killings of non-Muslims. Lengthy discussion of these passages, their context and interpretation, more often than not lead to the conclusion that the foundation of the Jihadist ideology is very fragile indeed. By focusing on the religious angle exclusively, the dialogue maintains momentum and avoids intractable entrenchment.

The detainees are a heterogeneous group with members from the Aden-Abyan Islamic Army, the al-Houthi rebellion, Takfir Wal-Hijra, al-Qaeda and a number of Afghan veterans. These members are self-taught and not very responsive to sincere religious dialogue. This rogue's gallery represents a variety of challenges. When asked about the significance of Afghan veterans among the detainees, al-Hattar was quick to emphasize that an Afghan experience did not necessarily turn Muslims into mindless killers. While it is certainly true that the hardcore of al-Qaeda in Yemen are more often than not recruited through a lengthy stay in Afghanistan, quite a few gave up the Jihad or got involved in legitimate domestic political activity. Those detainees who had been exposed to al-Qaeda's ideology for some time were among the hardest cases. Their belief in the mission, their sense of superiority and the endless reference to the Holy Scriptures made them uniquely difficult partners in an open dialogue.

In terms of their social background, there is no clear profile of the al-Qaeda sympathizer. They come from all segments of society, including the very top and the very bottom, and are united only in their adherence to al-Qaeda's ideology and their dedication to the cause.

Future Prospects

Being turned around is not enough if the suspect to be released relapses into his old habits and circle of friends. An unspecified period of surveillance follows immediate release, though this is probably less complicated than a similar arrangement in a Western European country. Great care is being taken to carefully reinsert the former militant Islamists into society in a viable manner. If possible they are returned to their jobs or alternatively a new job is secured for them. Those who dropped out of school or university are encouraged to continue their studies and are provided with loans if needed. Unconfirmed stories circulate in Yemen about former detainees who are now working for the security services. While this may be true in a few cases, it was never a planned affair.

The work of the Committee for Dialogue is nearing its third year and the results are worth noticing. The Yemenis are generally quite happy about the work of the Committee and share the impression that its efforts have contributed to improve the security situation and internal stability. The criticism that has occurred over the years has less to do with the idea behind the initiative than local political agendas. Critics have found the work of the Committee an expedient and indirect way of criticizing the government, though rarely addressing the actual content. Members of the Committee for Dialogue have been labeled as government stooges, an accusation al-Hattar does not accept. In his view, the members represent themselves, but are willing to work with the government to try to solve a national security problem.

As of June 2005, 364 suspects have been released, an astonishing number by any standard. The answer to the sensitive question of how many of those released have returned to their previous militant lifestyle was evasive. Yemen understands that international critics are keen to point out the futility of the project. Assuming that a handful, an unverifiable number obtained by asking others familiar with the work of the Committee for Dialogue, is true, this raises another important question in itself: What percentage should be considered an acceptable threshold for success?

Perhaps there are other measures of success within this relatively new field of counterterrorism. Judge Hamoud al-Hattar has received a number of death threats, a point he did not bother to mention himself, perhaps considering it too trivial. He currently lives under armed protection, an indication that someone is following his work and has drawn the conclusion that the soft-spoken cleric is a danger that should be eliminated. Another way of assessing the work of the

Committee for Dialogue is through the words of al-Hattar himself. Before the Committee started there were two options for the Jihadists – to kill or be killed themselves. Now there is a third choice, a return to society.

[Original Publication: *Terrorism Monitor* 3 (14) – July 15, 2005]

Al-Qaeda Suspects on Trial in Yemen

By Andrew McGregor

Yemen is preparing to try a number of prisoners who are accused of being associated with al-Qaeda terrorist activities in Yemen and abroad. The most notable prosecution involves Muhammad Hamdi al-Ahdal (a.k.a. Abu Asim al-Makki) and his associate Ghalib al-Zaidi, who have been held since December 2003. Al-Ahdal is described as a veteran of fighting in Chechnya and Afghanistan (where he lost a leg) before returning to Yemen to conduct terrorist operations. He is a former deputy to Sinan Qa'id al-Harthi, an al-Qaeda operative killed by an American drone aircraft in 2002.

U.S. lawyers from the Center for Constitutional Rights visited Yemen last week to meet with families of the men being held at the Guantanamo Bay prison. A lawsuit is being prepared on behalf of 60 Yemeni citizens still held in the Cuba-based prison. On January 23, 2006, it was announced that four men released from Guantanamo a year ago will be tried on charges of being al-Qaeda members. It had been widely expected that the men would be released for lack of evidence. A fifth suspect released from Guantanamo is being tried in a separate action on charges of drug trafficking. Karama Sa'id Khamsan was arrested near the Afghanistan/Pakistan border by Pakistani police and was turned over to U.S. forces in 2001, although it is now alleged that he was there to take delivery of two tons of hashish bound for Yemen (*Gulf Times*, January 24, 2006).

In addition, 19 people suspected of planning the assassination of U.S. officials and planning other terrorist acts in Aden have been delivered for prosecution. The 19 are accused of having returned from jihad in Iraq with orders from then al-Qaeda leader in Iraq Abu Musab al-Zarqawi to begin operations in Yemen.

There are conflicting reports about the whereabouts of Yemeni businessman and member of the ruling General People's Congress Abdul Salaam al-Hilah. Last week, Amnesty International reported that al-Hilah was now in Guantanamo Bay, but the Yemeni Foreign Ministry claimed he was still in a prison in Afghanistan. Al-Hilah told Amnesty that he was kidnapped in Egypt in September 2002 before being transported to prisons in Azerbaijan and Afghanistan (*Yemen Observer*, January 21, 2006).

Also at Guantanamo Bay prison, another Yemeni was put on trial by U.S. military authorities this month, one of the first two prisoners to face a military commission. In a 10-minute speech before the commission, Ali Hamza Ahmad

83

Sulayman al-Bahlul denounced American support for Israel, declined the services of his court-appointed U.S. military lawyer (who faced four prosecutors) and declared a boycott of the entire proceedings. Al-Bahlul was a media specialist for Osama bin Laden who created a video lionizing the al-Qaeda attack on the U.S.S. Cole in Yemen in 2000. Additional charges of conspiring to carry out terrorist activities means al-Bahlul could face a life sentence. The trial had been adjourned until May 15, 2006.

The government of President Ali Abdullah Saleh has been one of the United States' staunchest allies in the war on terrorism. Yet, while the Yemeni government cracks down on Sunni terrorism, it faces renewed fighting from Zaidi Shiite rebels in the mountainous north of the country. The insurgents, who ambushed an army column on January 19, 2006 are believed to be ex-followers of preacher Hussein al-Houthi, who was killed along with many supporters in battles with security forces in 2004. The renewed attacks are sure to disappoint the government, which has made concerted efforts at reconciliation with the restive North.

[Original Publication: *Terrorism Focus* 3 (4) – February 1, 2006]

Al-Qaeda's Great Escape in Yemen

By Andrew McGregor

Yemen's U.S.-sponsored fight against al-Qaeda suffered a severe blow in early February 2006, with the escape of 23 convicts from a high security prison in the capital of Sana'a. Among the escapees were 13 al-Qaeda suspects imprisoned for their roles in the 2000 bombing of the U.S.S. Cole and the 2002 attack on the French oil tanker Limburg. On February 5, 2006, Interpol issued a global alert that described the fugitives as a "danger to all countries." The prison break came only one day before the trial date of Muhammad Hamdi al-Ahdal and 14 other al-Qaeda suspects. Al-Ahdal is accused of directing the U.S.S. Cole bombers, but was to be tried on charges of financing terrorism. That trial has now been postponed indefinitely.

The escape took place February 3, 2006, from the Sana'a national headquarters of the Political Security Organization (PSO), Yemen's leading intelligence agency. The possibility of inside help for the mass escape from Yemen's most tightly guarded prison has raised the question of whether the state security services harbor agents sympathetic to al-Qaeda. The prison's previous commander and deputy were dismissed just two weeks ago after two Zaidi militants escaped. Government sources initially claimed that the al-Qaeda fugitives escaped through a 70-meter tunnel that emerged in a nearby mosque (http://www.26sep.net, February 4, 2006). Later reports suggested that the tunnel was 140 meters long and was dug from the mosque into the prison.

Unlike Yemen's three other major security agencies, the PSO leadership is recruited solely from military officers and reports directly to President Ali Abdullah Saleh. Like the army, the PSO is believed to include many Salafists and Ba'athist sympathizers, a legacy of Yemen's broad support for the 1980s anti-Soviet jihad in Afghanistan and a long alliance with Saddam Hussein's Iraq (*Gulf States Newsletter*, December 9, 2005). The U.S. war in Iraq is widely opposed in the officer corps, many of whom were trained in Iraq. The PSO has been accused within Yemen of mass extra-judicial arrests made in an effort to flush out al-Qaeda members. In July 2002, the home of PSO Vice Chairman Ali Mansur Rashid was attacked by armed men seeking the release of "173 Mujahidin" (*al-Ahram Weekly*, August 15-21, 2002).

The escapees included two notable figures. Jamal al-Badawi was charged as one of the main plotters in the strike on the U.S.S. Cole. President Saleh commuted the sentence of death that followed al-Badawi's conviction to a prison term of 15 years. In politically volatile Yemen, prosecutions are often dependent upon the political consequences of a conviction, and occasional commutations and amnesties are part of maintaining Saleh's presidency. Al-Badawi was one of 10 al-Qaeda members who escaped from an Aden prison in April 2003. Like the prison in Sana'a, this facility was also run by the PSO.

The other fugitive of note is Fawaz al-Rabihi, another leading al-Qaeda figure in Yemen. Al-Rabihi came to the attention of the FBI in early 2002, when the agency issued a warning that al-Rabihi had left Afghanistan with the intent of striking U.S. interests in Yemen or the U.S. homeland. Al-Rabihi struck in October 2002, attacking the Limburg with a primitive bomb-boat under the alleged direction of al-Ahdal. The explosion killed one sailor, and the consequent three-fold increase in maritime insurance for the area severely damaged Yemen's economy. In an outburst after receiving the death sentence from a Sana'a court, the Saudi-born al-Rabihi claimed he had given his pledge to Osama bin Laden to kill Americans. The escapees may be heading to Salafist strongholds in Shabwah, Marib or al-Jawf provinces.

[Original Publication: *Terrorism Focus* 3 (5) – February 7, 2006]

Yemen's Passive Role in the War on Terrorism

By Gregory D. Johnsen

For the past five years, Yemen has been what is best described as a passive partner in the U.S.-led war on terrorism. It has taken a number of steps to limit the activities of al-Qaeda and other like-minded groups within the country, but most of these have been at the behest of the U.S., and it is often schizophrenic in its pursuit of Islamic militants. In April 2004, Prime Minister Abdul Qadir Bajammal claimed that Yemen had eradicated 90 percent of the al-Qaeda organization in the country. Yet rumors that factions within the country's political and security establishment assisted in the recent jailbreak of 23 militants, including prominent figures in the attacks on the U.S.S. Cole and the Limburg, have once again raised questions about Yemen's reliability as an ally in the war on terrorism (*Terrorism Focus*, February 7, 2006).

In the immediate aftermath of the September 11, 2001 terrorist attacks, Yemen was often mentioned in the same breath as Afghanistan as a possible hideout for al-Qaeda. Many Yemenis, including prominent government officials, felt their country was next on a "hit list" after the U.S. finished in Afghanistan. That fear has been expressed more recently by President Ali Abdullah Saleh, during a speech in Aden in December 2005, when he claimed that he dissuaded the U.S. from occupying the country following the attack on the U.S.S. Cole in October 2000 (al-Arabiya, December 1, 2005).

The country's fears stemmed from a long and close history with Islamic militants. Following the withdrawal of Soviet troops from Afghanistan in 1989, many of these fighters – known as Afghan Arabs – made their way back to their countries of origin, full of religious zeal and the thrill of victory, and eager to replicate their successes at home. The governments of the Arab world, however, were not as excited with the prospect of a local jihad within their borders. Massive crackdowns by many of these governments forced a number of the Afghan Arabs to flee their countries yet again. Many of them seized on an apocryphal hadith of the Prophet Muhammad: "When disorder threatens, seek refuge in Yemen." Even Osama bin Laden has alluded to the ideas expressed in the hadith and the situation in Yemen during the mid-1990s when he told Abd al-Bari Atwan of *al-Quds al-Arabi* in an interview in November 1996 that he would like to live in Yemen because it was one of the few places in the Arab world where one could still breathe the air of freedom.

The Yemeni government largely welcomed these fighters, and in 1994 it managed to turn them into an effective paramilitary force that helped the government put down a secession attempt by the socialist south. The Afghan Arabs were led by Sheikh Abdul Majid al-Zindani, who has since been listed as a "specially designated global terrorist" by both the U.S. and the UN, and Ali Muhsin al-Ahmar, a close relative of the president and one of the most powerful military leaders in the country. Both men had extensive contacts among the fighters. Al-Zindani made frequent trips to Afghanistan in the 1980s and early 1990s, and, according to the U.S. Treasury Department, has been a "spiritual leader" of bin Laden. Al-Ahmar is married to the sister of Tariq al-Fadhli, one of the most prominent Yemeni veterans of the war in Afghanistan, and the former head of the Aden-Abyan Islamic Army. Yet, much like U.S. support for the Afghan Arabs in the 1980s, Yemen's use of these fighters has since come back to haunt the government.

In addition to the attack on the U.S.S. Cole, which killed 17 sailors, the French oil tanker Limburg was also attacked in 2002, resulting in the death of a Bulgarian sailor who drowned after jumping overboard. Not everyone, however, attributes the attack on the Limburg directly to al-Qaeda operatives in Yemen. Nasser al-Bahri, bin Laden's former chief bodyguard, who is also known as Abu Jandal, claimed in an interview with *al-Quds al-Arabi* in 2004 that the bombing was a rash reaction to the killing of Yahya Saleh Al-Mujalli, a local al-Qaeda operative, by government forces in Sana'a in late September 2002.

Earlier that year, Yemen had invited U.S. Special Forces into the country as advisers and trainers, and following the attack on the Limburg, it cooperated with the unmanned Predator drone strike on Sinan Qa'id al-Harthi, the suspected head of al-Qaeda in Yemen, and five of his companions in November 2002. The Yemeni government paid a high price domestically for allowing the U.S. to strike inside Yemen's borders, following a leak from the Pentagon that broke the agreement of secrecy between the two countries. President Saleh felt personally betrayed by the leak, and when Yemen captured al-Harthi's replacement, Mohammad Hamdi al-Ahdal, one year later in November 2003, it refused to allow U.S. officials to interrogate him directly.

The recent escape of 23 prisoners occurred only a day before al-Ahdal was due to stand trial. In the aftermath of the prison break, there has been a great deal of confusion as to whether al-Ahdal escaped or not. Hussein al-Jarbani of *Asharq al-Awsat*, reported on February 5, 2006, that al-Ahdal was among the escapees. On

February 4, 2006, the *Yemen Times* also published what it called the "official list" of the escapees, noting that the list contained only 22 names, "excluding [Mohammad] Hamdi al-Ahdal." Other agencies, however, have stated that the judiciary has merely delayed his trial by a week, and that he is still in custody. On February 13, 2006, the Yemeni government finally announced that al-Ahdal was still in custody, as it officially began his trial under extremely tight security.

Al-Ahdal was originally captured in 2003, reportedly on a tip from a former militant who had recently been granted his freedom under a government program, Committee for Dialogue, headed by judge Hamoud al-Hattar. The program, which was initiated at the request of President Saleh in September 2002, is designed to convince suspected militants that carrying out violent actions in the name of Islam is not sanctioned by the Quran or the Sunna. It has since released 364 suspected militants in six separate pardons, following their pledges to abstain from violence. Bin Laden's former bodyguard, al-Bahri, is one such graduate. The Committee for Dialogue, which was initially started as part of a multi-pronged approach to remove Yemen from a "hit list" in Washington, appears to have been caught up in its perceived success through a combination of Western media reports and fewer terrorist attacks in Yemen from late 2002 to early 2005. This early euphoria led to the release of more and more detainees in greater frequency, and eventually to Bajammal's claim that Yemen was 90 percent al-Qaeda free.

Yet by the summer of 2005, as the war in Iraq continued to drag on, the Committee for Dialogue ran into problems. On June 1, 2005, al-Hattar told the *Khaleej Times*: "Resistance in Iraq is legitimate, but we cannot differentiate between terrorism and resistance in Iraq's situation because things are not clear in this case." Within a few months, however, his views had shifted slightly and he would only say: "Iraq is not a subject of the dialogue" (AP, October 11, 2005). This shift in thinking, or at least public descriptions of the dialogue sessions, seems to have been brought about by an incident in July 2005 when two former detainees, which al-Hattar had recommended for release, carried out a suicide bombing on U.S. forces in Baghdad. Al-Hattar initially denied this claim, which was originally reported by "anonymous Yemeni security sources" in the armed forces weekly newspaper *26 September* (October 13, 2005). Yet Jamal al-Amir, the editor of the weekly independent newspaper *al-Wasat*, has argued that the story is true, and that at least eight men from al-Hattar's program have found their way to Iraq to fight U.S. forces there.

These revelations have essentially spelled the end of al-Hattar's program. In December 2005, while al-Hattar was in Washington participating in a State Department sponsored conference on religious dialogue, Khalid al-Hammadi of *al-Quds al-Arabi* reported that sources within Yemen's security forces were convinced that al-Hattar's program had failed, and that it should be stopped (*al-Quds al-Arabi*, December 10, 2005). The sources pointed to the fact that al-Hattar had not been able to persuade the released militants to renounce violence, as a number of the former detainees were still in Iraq fighting. Yemen, of course, has worked extremely hard to keep its young men from traveling to Iraq, turning away suspicious passengers at the airport. Yet the borders are simply too porous to keep everyone in the country and out of Iraq.

The threat of violence is no longer one-way. In January 2006, Yemen announced that it had arrested 19 men, who had recently returned from Iraq and were planning to carry out terrorist attacks in the country. The men were reportedly acting on the orders of Abu Musab al-Zarqawi and his al-Qaeda in Iraq organization. One of the targets was a hotel in Aden frequented by Westerners; the men also had instructions to kill U.S. citizens. The *Yemen Observer*, which has recently been closed by order of the prime minister as a result of a story on the "cartoon riots," reported that one of the men, Ali Abdullah Asyan, called himself "Abu Ali al-Harthi, Jr." in honor of the slain al-Qaeda commander (*Yemen Observer*, January 28, 2006).

The return route of fighters from Iraq to Yemen with the intention of striking Western targets in the country suggests that Yemen's period of relative calm could be nearing an end. It is too soon to tell if this is a new generation of fighters, as the "junior" in Asyan's assumed name would suggest, but what is clear is that Yemen has not destroyed 90 percent of al-Qaeda in the country. Furthermore, following the recent prison break, it is not even clear if the Yemeni government is 90 percent al-Qaeda free. For Yemen to truly reach Bajammal's figure, it will have to cease being passive and become a more active ally.

[Original Publication: *Terrorism Monitor* 4 (4) – February 23, 2006]

Prosecuting Terrorism: Yemen's War on Islamist Militancy

By Andrew McGregor

Any observer of Yemen's political scene cannot help but notice that Yemen appears to be awash with al-Qaeda suspects. Mass trials follow mass arrests as hundreds of suspects flow through Yemen's legal system. Some are selected for execution and others for lengthy prison sentences, but many avail themselves of early release or periodic amnesties. The system seems designed to weed out those who present a direct threat to Yemen or its regime, while relieving U.S. pressure in the war on terrorism by offering a constant demonstration of activity. In the wings of this performance is the constant threat of an insurgency led by Yemen's powerful Islamist movement.

The Legal Frontline

A continuing irritant in Yemen-U.S. relations is the status of Sheikh Abdul Majid al-Zindani, the country's most prominent Islamist and leader of the al-Iman University in Sana'a. In February 2004, the U.S. Treasury Department identified al-Zindani as a "specially designated global terrorist" (*Terrorism Monitor*, April 6, 2006). The U.S. would like to see the sheikh extradited for his al-Qaeda connections and possible involvement in the U.S.S. Cole bombing, but al-Zindani enjoys the personal protection of Yemen's president, Ali Abdullah Saleh, who describes him as "a moderate." The president called such extradition attempts "unconstitutional" and noted that "we are not the police of any other country" (*Yemen Observer*, March 1, 2006).

The sheikh met in early April 2006 with Khaled Meshaal, the Syrian-based leader of Hamas. At a fundraising event for the new Palestinian government (which has lost nearly all foreign aid from the West), al-Zindani referred to Hamas as "the jihad-fighting, steadfast, resolute government of Palestine" (UPI, April 14, 2006). Al-Zindani is a leading member of the Islah Party, an Islamist opposition party that often works closely with the government. The leader of the Islah Party is Sheikh Abdullah al-Ahmar, chief of the powerful Hashed tribe. Saleh and many other government figures are members of the Hashed. Al-Ahmar is close to the Saudis, and it is partly through his mediation that many long-standing territorial and security disputes have been resolved in recent years.

Al-Zindani is one of many Yemeni "Afghans," the term used for veterans of the anti-Soviet jihad in Afghanistan. Rather than alienate the so-called Afghans, Saleh's regime has used them to eliminate opponents of the government, most notably in the assassination campaign against members of the Yemen Socialist Party in the period 1990-94. Others are reported to have been deployed against Zaidi Shiite militants in northern Yemen.

Meanwhile, Saudi-born Muhammad Hamdi al-Ahdal is facing the death penalty in another U.S.-related prosecution. A veteran of conflicts in Afghanistan and Chechnya, al-Ahdal is charged with being a leading member of Yemen's al-Qaeda network, raising funds and organizing bomb attacks on U.S. interests in the country. He has admitted to collecting over one million Saudi riyals to buy the allegiance of Yemeni tribesmen in the Marib region. Nineteen security men were killed in a three-year pursuit of al-Ahdal that ended in 2003. Al-Ahdal used his chance to speak in court to charge Saudi and U.S. authorities with pressing Sanaa for a conviction. Al-Ahdal's onetime superior in al-Qaeda, Sinan Qa'id al-Harthi, was killed in Marib in 2002 by a U.S. unmanned Predator aircraft.

Nineteen men currently on trial in Sana'a are accused of planning attacks against U.S. interests as revenge for the killing of al-Harthi. The suspects, including five Saudis, are accused of operating under the instructions of Abu Musab al-Zarqawi, leader of the al-Qaeda faction in Iraq (*Yemen Times*, April 16, 2006). Two of the accused have admitted to possessing arms and explosives for use in training fighters for Iraq and Afghanistan, but proclaimed that their war was with the United States, not Yemen (*Yemen Observer*, March 4, 2006).

In an interesting case that attracted little attention, a group of former Iraqi army officers were acquitted on appeal in March 2006 on charges of plotting to attack the U.S. and UK embassies in Sana'a. Other former Iraqi officers are reported to have found employment in Yemen's military. The two armies cooperated extensively in the Saddam Hussein era, and a large part of Yemen's military received training in Iraq. The Iraqis have spent three years in prison, but appealed to be allowed to stay in Yemen over fears for their safety in Iraq.

Furthermore, on April 19, 2006, a group of 13 Islamists led by Ali Sufyan al-Amari were handed prison terms of up to seven years for plotting attacks against political and security officials in Yemen. Prosecutors announced in late April 2006 that 60 more suspected members of al-Qaeda are being brought to trial (26September.com, April 25, 2006).

Though the mass prosecutions suggest Yemen is mounting a successful campaign against Islamist militants, hundreds of convicted extremists have found a quick route to freedom through cooperation with Yemen's Committee for Dialogue, which engages the prisoners in a Quran-based rehabilitation program. Other convicted Islamists are released in periodic amnesties, while suspects with political connections are often never brought to trial. Over 800 Zaidi Shiite rebels were freed in March 2006 in order to resolve the 2004-2005 conflict that erupted in the mountains of northern Yemen. While the "revolving door" system of Yemeni justice frustrates U.S. security agencies, dispute resolution, mediation and reconciliation are all traditional art forms in Yemen's fractious social framework. They are what prevent the state from disintegrating, and Saleh's proficiency in these skills keeps the regime afloat.

Hunting Fugitives

Yemeni security forces continue the hunt for the 23 Islamists who escaped prison in Sana'a in February 2006. The facility was run by Yemen's leading intelligence service, the Political Security Organization (PSO). Particularly distressing to the U.S. was that many of the fugitives had been involved in terrorist attacks against U.S. interests, while some were making their second escape from PSO prisons. Eight of the escapees have surrendered or been captured, but the two most prominent fugitives, Jamal al-Badawi and Jaber Elbaneh, remain at large. Al-Badawi was sentenced to death in 2004 for planning the attack on the U.S.S. Cole, while Elbaneh was one of the so-called "Lackawanna Six," a terrorist cell based in upper New York state. Of the six, five are serving sentences in U.S. prisons, but Elbaneh escaped to Yemen where Yemeni police eventually detained him.

Security forces are reportedly using tribal and religious leaders in negotiations with the other fugitives for their surrender (*Yemen Observer*, April 3, 2006). Several PSO prison governors were put before a military tribunal on April 27, 2006 on charges of "inadequate conduct" in relation to the escape. The PSO is widely believed to include Islamists in its ranks, and there were serious questions raised at the time of the escape regarding PSO assistance to the escapees.

The escape has created barriers to the release of over 100 Yemeni detainees in Guantanamo Bay. The Yemen government maintains that 95 percent of the prisoners have no involvement in terrorism. According to a government study, most of the captive Yemenis worked in Afghanistan as teachers of the Quran or the Arabic language (26September.com, March 21, 2006). Nevertheless, some prisoners already released from Guantanamo Bay have been charged in Yemen with membership in al-Qaeda. One Yemeni prisoner who is unlikely to be released anytime soon is Sheikh Muhammad Ali Hassan al-Moayad, who is serving 75 years in a Colorado prison for financing terrorism. The sheikh was a member of the Shura Council of the Islah Party and imam of the main mosque in Sana'a before he was arrested in Germany in 2003 and extradited to the U.S. Al-Moayad complains of mistreatment in the U.S. and his family is appealing to President Saleh to intervene.

Yemen and the War in Iraq

U.S. intelligence has identified Yemen as a leading source of foreign fighters in the war in Iraq. The leader of the Aden-Abyan Islamic Army (one of Yemen's largest Islamist militant groups), Khalid Abd al-Nabi, has complained that members of his group were arrested by PSO officers and then taken before U.S. operatives for interrogation regarding plans to fight coalition forces in Iraq (*Yemen Times*, April 4, 2006). The Islamic Army was formed in 1994 from "Afghans" who had helped Saleh's regime defeat southern Yemen's socialists. They are accused of maintaining ties with al-Qaeda while sending fighters to join al-Zarqawi's network in Iraq.

In 2002, the government mounted a largely ineffective assault with heavy artillery and helicopter gunships on the group's training camp in the mountains near Hatat in Abyan district. Abd al-Nabi surrendered to the government, but was only briefly detained before being released without charges. Convicted Islamist militants released through the Committee for Dialogue program agree to avoid further militancy within Yemen, but there is no mention made of Iraq.

Conclusion

A report released in April 2006 by Yemen's Ministry of Planning and International Cooperation revealed that 41 percent of Yemenis are below the poverty line and lack access to basic health and educational services (*Yemen Times*, April 25, 2006). Rising food prices, a 17 percent unemployment rate and a general lack of opportunity for Yemen's youth provide a pool of dissatisfied recruits for Islamist organizations.

The number of Yemenis currently fighting in Iraq is probably not large, but the presence of the conflict provides an external outlet for Yemen's most militant Islamists, much like Afghanistan once did. With the Islamist opposition forming the largest political force in Yemen outside of the current government, the United States will continue to find it difficult to leverage the Saleh regime. Any U.S. intervention at this point would present serious consequences for the stability of the region. For now, Yemen will remain a troubling ally in the war on terrorism.

[Original Publication: *Terrorism Monitor* 4 (9) – May 4, 2006]

Yemen Convicts PSO Members Involved in the Great Escape

By Andrew McGregor

In Yemen's "war on terrorism," the legal merry-go-round continues. On July 12, 2006 a dozen officers from Yemen's Political Security Organization (PSO) received sentences between eight months and three years and indefinite suspensions from work for collusion in the sensational escape of 23 al-Qaeda suspects from a Sana'a PSO prison in February (*Terrorism Focus*, February 7, 2006). The defendants, however, remain entitled to retirement benefits (26September.com, July 14, 2006). The suspects were tried in a military court, although Yemen's National Organization for Defending Rights and Freedoms protested that the court had no jurisdiction since security employees were part of the civil service (*News Yemen*, July 17, 2006).

Nine of the 23 escapees have been captured, but none of the 13 who were convicted of involvement in the bombing of the U.S.S. Cole (including their leader, Jamal al-Badawi) are currently detained. With the exception of Ahmad al-Raimi, all those recaptured have since been released for lack of evidence. The same cause has been cited in the release of 315 al-Qaeda suspects in recent months (26September.com, May 31, 2006). The PSO, like many institutions in Yemen, is thoroughly infiltrated by Islamists, some of whom are sympathetic to the aims of al-Qaeda. The Islamists are also well represented in the parliament by the Islah Party, which, despite its opposition status, is closely tied with the ruling General People's Congress. With al-Badawi and his colleagues still on the loose, the PSO convictions will do little to mollify the U.S. administration, which views the escape as a major setback in U.S.-Yemen cooperation in the war on terrorism.

Perhaps indicative of the current mood in Yemen was the unlikely acquittal earlier this month of 19 men charged with the possession of weapons and explosives intended for attacks on U.S. interests in Yemen (*Terrorism Focus*, July 11, 2006). Sana'a Primary Court judge Muhammad al-Badani ruled that the defendants (14 Yemenis and five Saudis) had only been charged because of their participation or intention to participate in jihad in Iraq under the direction of the late Abu Musab al-Zarqawi, and that the prosecution had failed to prove that the arms were not meant for that purpose. In a move sure to be applauded by Yemen's Islamists, the judge relied on Shari'a law in ruling that "when the enemy collects its forces to occupy a part of the defender's homeland and seeks to occupy the whole land, so jihad is a duty for all Muslims to break off the occupation" (*News Yemen*, July 9, 2006; *Terrorism Focus*, July 11, 2006). The defendants remain in prison as the decision is being appealed in the Court of Criminal Appeals by state prosecutors, who have suggested that the acquittals "undermined trust in justice" (*Arab News*, July 13, 2006). With a presidential election coming up in September, there is considerable speculation within Yemen that President Ali Abdullah Saleh is courting Yemen's considerable and influential Islamist constituency. His main challenger will be Faisal Othman bin Shamlan, a vocal opponent of al-Qaeda running on an anti-corruption platform (*Yemen Times*, July 8, 2006).

U.S. operations in Iraq are a daily sore-point for much of Yemen's population, making President Saleh's cooperation with the United States politically dangerous. Yemen's army had especially close ties to the Iraqi military under Saddam Hussein, many of whose ex-members now form the core of the Iraqi resistance. U.S. support for Israel's current attacks on Lebanon and the Gaza Strip has brought thousands into the streets in protest and calls from some members of parliament for the expulsion of U.S. Ambassador Thomas Krajesky. Other MPs have called for a portion of the country's oil revenues to be dedicated to Palestinian and Lebanese resistance to Israel (*Yemen Observer*, July 18, 2006). Simmering anti-U.S. sentiment may soon endanger the already tenuous security links between the United States and Yemen.

[Original Publication: *Terrorism Focus* 3 (29) – July 25, 2006]

Al-Qaeda Oil Attack Thwarted in Yemen

By Christopher Heffelfinger

On September 15, 2006, Yemen's Interior Ministry announced that during a shootout it had blown up four cars laden with explosives, killing the four suicide bombers in the process before they could reach their intended targets. The foiled attack came within days of al-Qaeda second-in-command Ayman al-Zawahiri's calls for mujahideen to attack oil installations in Gulf countries. The attacks, which targeted facilities in Marib and Hadramaut, were apparently meant to be carried out simultaneously by two sets of cars in the early morning hours of September 15, 2006. Security guards at the facilities opened fire on the vehicles – which contained 10 gas canisters rigged with TNT – as they sped toward the facilities, killing the attackers as the explosives detonated. One security guard was killed; no serious damage was done to the facilities (*Asharq al-Awsat*, September 15, 2006; *Yemen Observer*, September 15, 2006).

The notoriously trigger-happy nature of the Yemeni security forces appears to have been advantageous in thwarting this attack; such shootouts, however, have often killed innocents in the past. Despite the dramatic nature of the foiled attacks as described by the Interior Ministry, the incident provides little hope of quelling support for al-Qaeda and the mujahideen in Yemen.

One day following the attacks, Yemeni security services arrested four alleged al-Qaeda members suspected of planning attacks in the capital, Sana'a. "A cell linked to the al-Qaeda network was arrested Saturday morning in the capital city of Sana'a," Yemeni Interior Minister Rashad al-Alimi said in a statement. "The cell had links to terrorist attacks on oil installations Friday in Hadramaut and Marib governorates" (*Gulf News*, September 16, 2006). Security services also confiscated 12 bags of highly explosive material, disguises – including women's clothing – fake IDs and forged license plates.

While the foiled attacks were the first against an oil-related target in Yemen since the 2002 al-Qaeda attack on the French oil tanker Limburg off the Yemeni coast, there are still significant concerns about al-Qaeda's strength in the country – the homeland of Osama bin Laden's father. Fears of another attack have been growing in the country since 23 al-Qaeda members escaped via a tunnel from a Yemeni jail in February 2006 with help from prison guards; fourteen of the prisoners remain at large.

The foiled attacks and the arrests the following day – as well as the arrest of a bodyguard of Saleh's main opponent accused of al-Qaeda involvement – were immediately placed into the context of Yemeni President Ali Abdullah Saleh's fight against terrorism as he was campaigning for re-election. Saleh, who has been in power since 1978, won with more than 77% of the vote in the September 2006 elections. His cooperation with the United States since the September 11, 2001 terrorist attacks has been largely unpopular among Yemenis, but his government framed these attacks as against the Yemeni people and their national interests, and he went to lengths to publicize the events of September 15-16, 2006 as a victory for the economy and also for the safety of Yemenis.

Most analysts have explicitly linked the foiled attacks to al-Zawahiri's message, released on September 11, 2006, warning against the theft of Muslim oil and of new attacks in the Persian Gulf. "You should worry about your presence in two areas—the first is the Gulf, from where you will be expelled, God willing, after your defeat in Iraq, and your economic ruin will be achieved," he said in the statement issued on the often-used al-Sahab website.

Considering that the attackers timed the operations to coincide with the end of the security guards' shift, it seems unlikely that they would have selected and monitored the targets, gained knowledge of the shifts at both facilities, then prepared for and carried out the attacks within only four days of al-Zawahiri's message. Moreover, the Yemeni government announced a tightening of security around oil facilities on September 3, 2006, in response to information about potential attacks or sabotage. The attacks were in all likelihood carried out by al-Qaeda members or supporters, but probably not prompted by al-Zawahiri's message.

By "Persian Gulf," the al-Qaeda leader was referring to the much greater oil-producing countries of the UAE and Kuwait (Yemen has less than 20% the production capacity of Kuwait and is one of the poorest countries in the region). Nonetheless, the timing of the attacks must be seen as advantageous to al-Qaeda and its ability to incite attacks around the region with messages delivered on the Internet.

In fact, this has not been the first call from al-Zawahiri to attack oil installations in the region. In December 2005, he also called for the targeting of oil facilities in the Gulf in order to damage the U.S. economy. Bin Laden and others have been calling for attacks against these targets for much longer, decrying the loss of Muslim wealth to Western interests.

In February 2006, al-Qaeda members in Saudi Arabia attempt to attack the world's largest oil production facility at Abqaiq, but that attack was also unsuccessful. Despite the repeated calls to target these facilities, it appears that al-Qaeda has so far been unable to inflict serious damage on oil production in the Gulf region. In accessing this failure, al-Qaeda may well decide that more, well-planned, well-resourced operations are necessary if they are to really inflict damage against the oil infrastructure in the region.

[Original Publication: *Terrorism Focus* 3 (37) – September 26, 2006]

Suspects Arrested in Yemen for Supporting Somali Islamists

By Andrew McGregor

Confusion continues to surround the case of eight foreign nationals and 15 Yemenis arrested in Yemen in October 2006 in relation to an alleged al-Qaeda plot to smuggle small-arms to Islamists in Somalia. The accused include three Australians, a Dane, a Briton, a Somali and an unidentified European. An eighth suspect, a German, was released on November 5, 2006. Although the detainees were arrested three weeks ago, charges have yet to be filed.

According to Yemeni security forces, the suspects were identified as al-Qaeda members (Saba News, November 1, 2006). Early reports claiming that all eight foreign suspects, including the Australians, were studying at Sheikh Abdul Majid al-Zindani's al-Iman University appear to be false. Sheikh al-Zindani is a controversial figure, a radical Islamist closely tied to the Yemen government, but wanted by the United States for terrorism offenses (*Terrorism Monitor*, April 6, 2006). Al-Zindani denies any connection to the arrested suspects (*News Yemen*, October 31, 2006). The suspects were also said to be close to a Somali al-Qaeda operative known as al-Ansar and to Imam Anwar al-Awlaki (Abu Atiq), a lecturer at al-Iman University and a suspected al-Qaeda member who was arrested several weeks earlier.

The most prominent of the detainees are Muhammad and Abdullah Ayub, the Australian-born sons of Abdul Rahim Ayub, former co-leader with his twin brother Abdul Rahman of the Mantiqi 4 cell of Jamaah Islamiya, an Indonesian terrorist group tied to al-Qaeda. Abdul Rahim fled Australia for Jakarta days after the 2002 bombing in Bali. Their mother is Rabiah Hutchison, an Australian who converted to Islam in 1984 when she married Abdul Rahim Ayub. Hutchison was a frequent visitor to Afghanistan, Iraq and Iran before her passport was revoked at the urging of the Australian Security and Intelligence Organization (ASIO). She divorced Abdul Rahim Ayub in the mid-1990s and is reported to have been briefly married to Abu al-Walid al-Masri, a leading al-Qaeda member in Afghanistan. Hutchison claims to have sent her two sons to study Islam in Yemen three years ago. Their sister Ramah is married to Khalid Cheikho, who is currently charged with conspiracy in a planned terrorist operation in Sydney.

The third Australian is Polish-born Marat Sumolsky (Abdul Malik), a 35-year old convert to Islam who took his wife and child to Yemen two years ago. Yemeni authorities suggest that Sumolsky may be released soon (*Yemen Observer*,

November 4, 2006). All of the Australian suspects appear to have been subjects of interest for the ASIO, though Australian Foreign Minister Alexander Downer denies any government involvement in the arrests (*Yemen Times*, November 1, 2006). The Australian consul was not given access to the prisoners until November 4, 2006. Australian officials have been assured that the prisoners will not be transferred to Guantanamo Bay. The Danish suspect is Kenneth Sorensen (Abu Zakaria), a 24-year old convert to Islam who moved to Yemen with his wife and child.

The Australians moved to an apartment building in the Yemeni capital of Sana'a close to al-Zindani's university. The Danish and British suspects also lived there and were already under U.S. and British surveillance as possible terrorists. The group became targets of an investigation that was unexpectedly disrupted by raids conducted by Yemeni security forces on October 17, 2006. According to one account, the sudden arrests infuriated American and British intelligence services (*The Australian*, November 4, 2006). Australian police firmly denied media accounts that the Australian detainees were tied to a plot to bomb a railway station in Sydney. The suspects in this case include another Australian convert to Islam, 26-year old Jill Courtney (*The Age*, November 2, 2006).

The arrests come at a time when the foreign minister of Somalia's faltering transitional government, Ismael Mohamoud Hurreh, claims that al-Qaeda operatives from Yemen, Saudi Arabia, Pakistan, Eritrea and Chechnya are pouring into Somalia to fight on behalf of the Islamic Courts Union (*The Independent*, November 3, 2006).

[Original Publication: *Terrorism Focus* 3 (43) – November 8, 2006]

Yemen Faces Second Generation of Islamist Militants

By Gregory D. Johnsen

The July 2, 2007 suicide attack in Marib, which killed eight Spanish tourists and two Yemeni drivers, painfully illustrated the degree to which al-Qaeda in Yemen has reorganized itself into an effective force (*Terrorism Focus*, July 10, 2007). The Yemeni government was caught largely unaware by the attack, as it believed the al-Qaeda threat had been neutralized. Yet, while the government managed to deter one generation of militants, it neglected to maintain the initiative through the second generation. This second generation of fighters, many of whom have spent time in Iraq, coalesced around the leadership of some of the 23 men who escaped from a political security prison in Sana'a in February 2006 (*Terrorism Focus*, February 7, 2006). The government attempted to negotiate for the surrender of many of these escapees, 10 of whom have turned themselves in, but much of its resources over the past few years have been devoted to ending the al-Houthi revolt in the north, which it determined was a more immediate threat (*Terrorism Focus*, July 31, 2007).

Yemen did, however, react quickly in the aftermath of the suicide attack. It arrested a handful of suspects in the days following the attack, and on July 4, 2007, it killed Ahmad Baysawani Duwaydar, an Egyptian it claimed masterminded the strike (*Terrorism Focus*, July 10, 2007). Yet, after a more thorough investigation, the government modified its claims, and released the details of the 11-man cell it said was behind the attack (*26 September*, August 2, 2007). Duwaydar's role in the report was reduced to providing material support to the other members of the cell. Among the suspects were three of the 23 escapees, including the head of al-Qaeda in Yemen, Nasir al-Wuhayshi. Yemen also identified the suicide bomber as Abdu Muhammad Said Ruhayqah, a 21-year-old who was living in the Sana'a neighborhood of Musayk, which has become known over the past few years as a haven for Islamic militants.

Yemen responded to the most recent threat from al-Qaeda by renewing tribal alliances it had established in 2001 and 2002 to counter the militants. On August 5, 2007, three days after Yemen revealed the make-up of the cell, President Ali Abdullah Saleh traveled to Marib and al-Jawf to meet with tribal leaders and ask for their assistance in combating al-Qaeda (*Asharq al-Awsat*, August 6, 2007). This was reminiscent of a similar trip Saleh made in late 2001, after more than a dozen soldiers were captured during a failed attempt to arrest two suspects in

Marib. The early morning raid Yemen launched on an al-Qaeda hideout three days later demonstrates the success of the negotiations.

The raid, which took place in the border region between Marib and al-Jawf governorates, resulted in the deaths of all four al-Qaeda suspects. Three of the suspects – Ali Ali Nasir Doha, Naji Ali Salih Jaradan and Abd al-Aziz Said Jaradan – were wanted in the March assassination of Ali Mahmud Qasaylah, the chief criminal investigator in Marib, as well as for their role in the July 2, 2007 attack (*Terrorism Focus*, May 22, 2007). The fourth suspect was Amar Hasan Salih Haryadan, an 18-year-old from the Mahashimah tribe in al-Jawf. According to Yemen's Interior Ministry, Haraydan had been recruited to be another suicide bomber in an upcoming attack that al-Qaeda in Yemen was planning (al-Motamar.net, August 9, 2007).

Attacks on army checkpoints, government buildings and an electrical sub-station the following day in Marib appear to be retaliatory strikes by the suspects' relatives and not a response from al-Qaeda. The attacks did little damage, but they do illustrate some of the problems the Yemeni government must navigate as it attempts to dismember al-Qaeda. This is not simply a two-sided battle between the government and al-Qaeda in Yemen, but rather one of multiple and shifting alliances among a variety of different actors. The murky world of tribal loyalties and militant Islamism in the region has led Arafat Madabish, a Yemeni journalist, to label it "Maribistan" in an unflattering comparison to Pakistan's Waziristan (al-Tagheer.com, August 9, 2007).

If Yemen is to succeed in dismantling this second generation of al-Qaeda-like militants, it must have significant tribal assistance. President Saleh's August 5, 2007 meeting was an important step, but a consistent and ongoing effort is necessary if Yemen does not want to face a third generation of militants.

[Original Publication: *Terrorism Focus* 4 (27) – August 14, 2007]

Chapter Three

The Radical Faces of Yemen

Profile of Sheikh Abdul Majid al-Zindani

By Gregory D. Johnsen

February 2006 was not a good month for Sheikh Abdul Majid al-Zindani, a man the U.S. has labeled a "specially designated global terrorist." First, a Yemeni government weekly, *26 September*, published a report claiming that then President George W. Bush had sent a letter to President Ali Abdullah Saleh demanding that Yemen arrest al-Zindani and freeze his assets (*26 September*, February 23, 2006; *Terrorism Focus*, March 7, 2006). Then, over the course of the next two weeks, al-Zindani was involved in two vehicle accidents, which were later determined to have been assassination attempts against the aging sheikh (al-Jazeera, March 4, 2006).

Like most incidents involving al-Zindani, the details of the stories were in constant flux, and in the end few really knew exactly what happened. Despite the fact that the newspaper's website eventually published the purported text of the letter from Bush to Saleh on March 4, 2006, it was eventually discovered that no such letter existed. The story of the assassination attempts had a similar feel of fluidity.

Al-Zindani's son, Abdullah, told *Asharq al-Awsat* on March 5, 2006 that it was not true that his father had been the target of an assassination attempt. Just a week later, however, his father corrected this version of the story in an interview with Khaled al-Hammadi of *al-Quds al-Arabi*. He said that the first accident, in which a tire on his car had "exploded," was worrisome, but he became convinced that he had been targeted a week later when an entire wheel fell off the car. "It is well known that assassination operations designed for cars are carried out in this manner," he said (*al-Quds al-Arabi*, March 12, 2006).

Al-Zindani refused to implicate the U.S. in the affair, saying, in a rare moment of discretion, that "we do not know who the person responsible is, nor do we know who is behind him" (*al-Quds al-Arabi*, March 12, 2006). Nevertheless, despite all of al-Zindani's tact, the issue has strained U.S.-Yemeni relations, and has initiated a meeting between President Saleh and then U.S. Ambassador Thomas Krajeski. A video of this meeting was later aired on Yemeni Television, with a voice-over by President Saleh: "Sheikh al-Zindani is a rational, balanced and moderate man and we know him well, and the Yemeni government guarantees [his actions], and I guarantee his character" (*al-Quds al-Arabi*, March 12, 2006).

The battle between Yemen and the U.S. over the fate of al-Zindani began on February 24, 2004, when the U.S. Department of Treasury named al-Zindani a "specially designated global terrorist" for his financial support of al-Qaeda (the UN added him to its list of "individuals belonging to or associated with al-Qaeda," in accordance with Security Council Resolution 1267, three days later).

Al-Zindani is inevitably taken at face-value, as a fire-breathing radical intent on the destruction of the U.S. This image of him as a wild-eyed militant is further aided by his striking appearance, which is set-off by a bright red, henna-dyed beard, as well as by his oratorical presence, which often borders on bombastic despite his occasional difficulties with Arabic grammar.

All of this, however, tends to disguise the fact that al-Zindani defies labels. His thought is a much more nuanced response to the modern world than the simple tags of Wahhabi or Salafi indicate. In the political arena he is a frightening man, who has advocated violence and destruction for those who disagree with him. On the other hand, intellectually he has tackled some of the most difficult issues facing religion in today's world, namely the tension that exists between religion and science. Additionally, he also specializes in the study of tawhid, or the oneness of God. One of his books on the subject is used as a textbook in Yemeni public schools.

In a country with an unacknowledged HIV/AIDS crisis, he is one of the few public figures working to combat it, opening a treatment center in Sana'a. His methods are rather unorthodox – he believes he can heal patients through Quranic intercession – but he refuses to ignore the problem, unlike many that argue that Muslims do not contract the disease (*al-Quds al-Arabi*, March 12, 2006).

In 2003, he issued a controversial fatwa that was designed to make marriage easier for Muslims living in the West. He was attacked for legitimizing sin, but he maintained his position, saying it was a way for Muslims to interact successfully in modern societies (*Asharq al-Awsat*, September 12, 2003).

He heads al-Iman University in Sana'a, where John Walker Lindh studied before heading to Afghanistan to join the Taliban, although al-Zindani has denied that Lindh ever attended the school in numerous interviews (al-Arabiya, August 4, 2004). He is also the head of the consultative council for Islah, the country's largest opposition party, and in the opaque world of Yemeni politics he remains very close to President Saleh, who has often delivered the commencement address at al-Iman University.

His following in Yemen is mostly derived from cassette tapes of his sermons that are sold in stores throughout the country. Large signs in stores around the new campus of Sana'a University promise that cassettes of his Friday sermons are available by 7:00 PM on the day they are delivered. He is also a writer, despite the criticisms of some Western-educated Yemenis that he "doesn't really know Arabic grammar," and has authored at least 14 books on subjects from the rights of women to his latest on fasting (author's interview, Sana'a, 2004). He often contributes the front-page editorial to the monthly newspaper of al-Iman University, Saut al-Iman, or the Voice of Faith.

Two years ago, very little was known about al-Zindani in Western circles, and much of what was known was wrong. This is not necessarily surprising; even Western academics specializing in contemporary Yemeni history seemed unsure of his origins. While this is no longer the case, thanks largely to the internet and the large number of interviews that al-Zindani has given in recent years, the U.S. seems to have done little to update its files. Even the birth date that the U.S. government has for him, "circa 1950," is wildly off the mark (U.S. Treasury Department, February 24, 2004).

Al-Zindani was actually born closer to 1940 – most likely in 1938 – on Mount Ba'dan, near a village of the same name, which overlooks the southern city of Ibb, a date that becomes clear from reading through al-Zindani's numerous interviews and writings. He spent his primary years in school in Ibb, before moving to Aden, which was under British rule at the time, to continue his studies. In his late teens, he moved to Cairo to attend Ain Shams University.

It was in Cairo, where al-Zindani went to study pharmacology that he first became interested in the relationship between science and the Quran, which is often termed al-*i'jaz al-'almi*, or the scientific wonders of the Quran. In an interview with the Yemeni magazine *al-Shaqa'iq* in February/March 2004, al-Zindani said that in 1958, a group of Egyptian communists published what he called "a gray pamphlet" attacking the Quran and claiming that it contradicted modern science. "This started me on my path," he told the magazine, "of answering those challenging communists." The fact that al-Zindani studied in Cairo during the late 1950s and early 1960s has also been confirmed by his fellow Yemeni students who were in Cairo at the time (author's interview, Sana'a, 2004).

This would eventually become al-Zindani's life, although he spent time fighting with Yemen's "third-way force," Hezbollah, during the civil war in the 1960s. (There is no relationship between the Yemeni Hezbollah and the Lebanese grouping of the same name). He spent most of the 1970s shuttling back and forth between Saudi Arabia and Yemen, as he slowly imported a more conservative version of Islam into Yemen through the education system.

Finally in the 1980s, following a splintering of the Yemeni Muslim Brotherhood, he convinced Sheikh Abd al-Aziz bin Baz, the Grand Mufti of Saudi Arabia, to support him in establishing the Institute for the Scientific Inimitability of the Quran and Sunnah, which was based at King Abd al-Aziz University in Jeddah (*al-Shaqa'iq*, February/March, 2004). It was here where he first met Osama bin Laden, and where he found a base to recruit and transport thousands of young Yemeni and Saudi Arabian men to Afghanistan to fight against the Soviet Union.

The U.S. Department of Treasury calls him one of "bin Laden's spiritual mentors," and while al-Zindani did guide and teach the younger man during the 1980s, he started downplaying the relationship even before 9/11. He told *Asharq al-Awsat* that bin Laden did not finance any part of al-Iman University (*Asharq al-Awsat*, June 3, 2001). He went even further after the attacks on New York and Washington, although he was careful to remain ambiguous. In 2004, he avoided a question by Hassan M'awdh of al-Arabiyya regarding his relationship with bin Laden, saying only that during the 1980s everyone, even the U.S., had been against the Soviet occupation of Afghanistan (al-Arabiya, August 4, 2004).

Still, the fact remains that he was able to utilize his contacts with the Afghan Arabs to help the Yemeni government put down a secession attempt by the Socialist south in 1994. He returned to Yemen following unification, lured back to his country of birth with promises of positions of power. In 1993, he was named to the five-man appointed presidential council, where he remained until 1997.

More recently in 2000, he was involved in a case labeling the late writer Muhammad Abd al-Wali an infidel for a line in his book, Sana'a: The Open City, that allegedly blasphemies God. The fact that al-Wali had been killed in a plane crash in 1973 seemed to matter little to al-Zindani. He has also led the charge, collecting donations, to pursue the prosecution of Muhammad al-Asadi, the editor of the English-language *Yemen Observer*, for re-publishing the now infamous "Muhammad cartoons," despite the fact that the newspaper published them with a line through the cartoons. The case is still pending.

His fatwas have also been linked to the killing of a Socialist Party politician, Jarallah Omar, on December 28, 2002, as well as the murder of three Baptist missionaries two days later. There have also been rumors that he gave the fatwa that led to the bombing of the U.S.S. Cole in 2000, which killed 17 U.S. sailors. He has refused to appear in court to answer questions regarding any of these accusations.

Al-Zindani's future remains unclear, but for the moment he remains what he has always been: an intriguing and complex figure in both the political and intellectual arenas, loathed by the U.S. and championed by Yemen.

[Original Publication: *Terrorism Monitor* 4 (7) – April 6, 2006]

Yemeni Sheikh al-Zindani's New Role as a Healer

By Andrew McGregor

Despite being designated by the United States and the United Nations as a "global terrorist," Yemen's Sheikh Abdul Majid al-Zindani continues to be protected by the Yemeni government. Most recently, Sultan al-Barakani, chairman of the ruling General People's Congress Caucus, said that the U.S. government had failed to send the Yemeni government information incriminating al-Zindani in terrorism, stating that, "we don't have any evidence that Sheikh al-Zindani was involved with al-Qaeda" (*Yemen Times*, April 2, 2007).

Sheikh al-Zindani is one of the most perplexing characters to emerge from the war on terrorism (*Terrorism Monitor*, April 6, 2006). Politically powerful and revered by some as one of the Islamic world's leading educators, al-Zindani's alleged ties to al-Qaeda have brought him to the attention of international counter-terrorism authorities. Despite his official U.S. and UN designations as a "global terrorist," the red-bearded scholar remains free and highly active in the political, religious, educational and medical fields, the latter representing a new and somewhat questionable addition to al-Zindani's career. Al-Zindani is a leading member of the opposition al-Islah Party, although in Yemen's complex political structure al-Zindani and the nominally oppositionist al-Islah frequently work closely with Yemen's ruler, President Ali Abdullah Saleh. The sheikh's real political enemies are found in the ranks of Yemen's secular Socialist Party. Al-Zindani recently declared that both the socialists and the unity constitution are "infidel" (*al-Thawri*, March 8, 2007).

Al-Zindani is also a leading exponent of the scientific basis for Islam, as outlined in various passages of the Quran that the sheikh interprets as descriptions of everything from black holes to photosynthesis. In December 2006, al-Zindani, a former pharmacist, claimed to have developed a cure for HIV/AIDS. Unlike other HIV/AIDS medicines, the sheikh's discovery allegedly has no side effects while eliminating the disease in men, women and even fetuses. Al-Zindani asserts that he will reveal the herbal formula for "Eajaz-3" once a copyright has been obtained. Although the sheikh claims the inspiration of his creation "came from God," no proof of the cure's effectiveness has yet been presented (*Yemen Observer*, December 19, 2006). In the last few months, five Libyan children receiving treatment for HIV at al-Zindani's al-Iman University have been deported in response to allegations of Libyan assistance to Shiite rebels in Yemen's Sa'ada province (*Yemen Observer*, March 6, 2007; *Terrorism Focus*, February 20, 2007).

According to a statement from the U.S. Treasury Department, al-Zindani's involvement with al-Qaeda includes recruiting, purchasing weapons and acting as a spiritual leader for the movement, as well as acting as a contact for Kurdish Iraq's Ansar al-Islam [1]. The Yemen government has ignored appeals from Washington for the arrest of the sheikh and the seizure of his assets (*Arab News*, February 24, 2006). Al-Zindani was recently identified in a U.S. federal court as the coordinator of the October 2000 suicide attack in Aden harbor on the U.S.S. Cole. A two and a half year-old lawsuit filed in Virginia by the families of the 17 servicemen killed in the bombing has recently finished by finding the country of Sudan responsible for the attack, opening the way for compensation payments from the $68 million in Sudanese assets frozen by the U.S. government. The suit also alleged that al-Zindani selected the two suicide bombers that carried out the strike, although the sheikh was never charged by Yemeni authorities with complicity in the attack (*The Virginian-Pilot*, March 12, 2007). Yemen's minister of foreign affairs, Dr. Abu Bakr al-Qirbi, welcomed the decision, ignoring the alleged role of al-Zindani, while declaring the verdict proof that Yemen was in no way involved in the attack on the U.S. destroyer.

There is no indication that al-Zindani will lose the protection of Yemen's government in the foreseeable future. While the controversial sheikh continues to hold radical Islamist views, al-Zindani has lately made a slight retreat from the Islamist global arena, focusing on domestic politics while assuming a lower international profile, no doubt with the encouragement of President Saleh (who continues to represent himself as an ally in the war on terrorism). Sheikh al-Zindani appears to be trying to create a more respectable international image for himself through his unlikely claim to have developed a cure for HIV. This effort may quickly backfire if it turns out that the sheikh has fraudulently treated HIV sufferers who may have sought more useful and proven medical treatments elsewhere.

[Original Publication: *Terrorism Focus* 4 (8) – April 6, 2007]

Notes
1. See http://www.treasury.gov/press/releases/js1190.htm

Tracking Yemen's 23 Escaped Jihadi Operatives – Part 1

By Gregory D. Johnsen

In mid-September 2007, Yemeni President Ali Abdullah Saleh issued a stern warning to the Wa'ilah tribe in northern Yemen: turn over the six al-Qaeda suspects you are sheltering or face serious repercussions (*al-Wasat*, September 12, 2007). The six men that Saleh believes have found refuge with the tribe near the Saudi border are the remnants of a group of 23 prisoners that escaped from a Yemeni political security prison on February 3, 2006. The escapees included a number of prominent al-Qaeda militants, among whom were individuals convicted of carrying out attacks on the U.S.S. Cole in 2000 and on the French oil tanker Limburg in 2002.

Six of these suspects have since been killed in clashes with Yemeni or U.S. forces, 11 have either turned themselves back in to authorities or have been recaptured and six of the suspects remain at large. Many of these individuals have continued to fight for al-Qaeda since their escape, and one of them, Nasir al-Wuhayshi, has since been named the new head of al-Qaeda in Yemen.

Despite differences of age and background, the 23 men who were being held in the cell were linked together through shared experiences. Nearly half of the escapees, 11, were born in Saudi Arabia to Yemeni parents. Several of the men were arrested in late 2002 after a series of bombings in Sana'a and Marib. Seven of these men were part of a 15-man cell that was later charged with planning to attack five foreign embassies as well as to assassinate the then U.S. Ambassador Edmund Hull. Three of the men were convicted of being part of an 11-man cell that was charged with plotting to carry out attacks in Yemen and abroad. Among the escapees, there are also two sets of brothers, Hizam and Arif Mujali and Mansur and Zakariya al-Bayhani, who are themselves brothers of Ghalib and Tawfiq al-Bayhani, who are currently in U.S. custody in Guantanamo Bay. Two other escapees, Qasim al-Raymi and Fawaz al-Rabay'i, also have brothers in Guantanamo.

This two-part series presents a biographical sketch of each escapee, along with his current status.

The Dead

Umar Sayd Hasan Jarallah (1979-2006)

Jarallah was from the Red Sea port city of Hudaydah. Jarallah was also known as Abdullah al-Gharib and Ibn Hafiz. He was sentenced to 10 years in prison in February 2005 for his role in the attack on the Limburg. Along with al-Umda, Huwaydi and Zayd, Jarallah was hidden for one month following their escape by Muhammad Hajir (*22nd May*, April 29, 2007). He killed himself along with Ahmad Muhamad al-Abiyad in a failed suicide attack on an oil facility in Marib on September 15, 2006. One guard was killed in the attack on the Safir facility (*Asharq al-Awsat*, September 21, 2006).

Shafiq Ahmad Umar Zayd (?-2006)

Zayd was born in Saudi Arabia to Yemeni parents and is known by the kunya Abu Abdullah. He was extradited to Yemen from Saudi Arabia along with two other individuals in 2003. He was part of an 11-man cell, which was charged with forging passports, weapons and explosives possession, planning to travel to Iraq and forming an armed gang to carry out attacks in Yemen. Along with Mansur al-Bayhani and Abdullah al-Wada'i, he was convicted only of forging passports. Ibrahim al-Muqri, who was part of the same trial, was cleared of all charges (*Yemen Times*, March 24-27, 2005). All of the men, however, remained in prison until they managed to escape in February 2006. As was mentioned above, Zayd was sheltered by Muhammad Hajir for one month following his escape. He killed himself along with Hashim Khalid al-Iraqi in a failed suicide attack on an oil port in Hadramaut on September 15, 2006.

Fawaz Yahya Hasan al-Rabay'i (1979-2006)

Al-Rabay'i was born in Saudi Arabia, the third of four brothers and four sisters (*News Yemen*, October 9, 2006). He is also known by the kunya Furqan al-Tajayki (*al-Ghad*, October 2006). He attended al-Falah school in Saudi Arabia, where he learned to recite the Quran. Along with nearly one million Yemenis, the family was expelled from Saudi Arabia in 1990 as a result of Yemen's support for Saddam Hussein following his invasion of Kuwait. His mother is known as Umm Hasan, after her oldest son. Hasan is a bus driver with six children. According to his family, Hasan is no longer close to them, as he was arrested on two separate occasions in order to put pressure on his younger brothers. Hasan complained that his brothers were trouble makers, and that when he was in jail his children went hungry.

The second brother, Abu Bakr, is currently awaiting sentencing in Yemen for his role in a series of al-Qaeda plots. The youngest brother, Salman, is being held by the United States in Guantanamo Bay (*News Yemen*, October 9, 2006). According to his father, he was sent to Afghanistan by his family to search for Fawaz, and was subsequently arrested and turned over to the United States. His father denies that either Abu Bakr or Salman have any links to al-Qaeda (*News Yemen*, October 9, 2006).

During the late 1990s, al-Rabay'i took a job in the personnel department in the presidential office in Yemen. In early 2000, he traveled to Afghanistan with two other men, including a former agent in Yemen's Political Security Organization (*News Yemen*, October 9, 2006). Like many young men who head off to fight in Afghanistan or Iraq, al-Rabay'i did not tell his family where he was going. Later, he called his father, Yahya, to tell him that he was in Afghanistan. The family claims that they knew nothing of his activities in Afghanistan, although he did mention to his father that his salary contradicted Islamic law and that his goal was to die as a martyr (*News Yemen*, October 9, 2006). According to one source, al-Rabay'i trained with Abu Musab al-Zarqawi in an al-Qaeda training camp in Afghanistan (*al-Ghad*, October 2006). He is also known to have spent time with at least two of the 9/11 hijackers, Muhammad Atta and Zayd Jarah (*al-Ghad*, October 2006).

Al-Rabay'i spent one year in Afghanistan before returning to Yemen in 2001, as the head of a 12-man cell (*News Yemen*, October 9, 2006). In 2002, the United States asked Yemen to arrest him on the suspicion of belonging to al-Qaeda. He escaped security forces two separate times that year before finally being captured in 2003. In August, he managed to escape a raid on his house in Sana'a dressed only in his pajamas (*Asharq al-Awsat*, October 2, 2006). The raid did result in the death of one member of his cell, Samir al-Hada. He also escaped from a security checkpoint, when the car he and Hizam Mujali were traveling in was stopped in the southern governorate of Abyan. Instead of allowing their car to be searched, the two shot one of the two soldiers, Hamid Khasruf, manning the checkpoint and fled (*Yemen Times*, April 7-13, 2004). The pair was later arrested in March 2003 in Marib (BBC, April 5, 2003). During the time that al-Rabay'i was on the run, he was sheltered by different tribes in Marib and Abyan.

On August 30, 2004, al-Rabay'i was sentenced to 10 years in prison for attacking a Hunt Oil helicopter in November 2002, which was reportedly done with the authorization of Sinan Qa'id al-Harthi (a.k.a. Abu Ali al-Harthi) (*Yemen Times*, May 31-June 2, 2004). He was also fined 18.3 million Yemeni riyals, roughly $99,450, for his role in a 2002 attack on the Civil Aviation Authority building in Sana'a (*News Yemen*, October 1, 2006). Six months later, in February 2005, al-Rabay'i was again on trial for his role in the attack on the French oil tanker, Limburg, and for killing a soldier. The court sentenced him to death on these charges. During his trial, al-Rabay'i frequently alleged that he was being tortured by Yemeni security officers (*Yemen Times*, December 27-January 2, 2004-2005). He did, however, find time during his trial to arrange to be married to a daughter of Yahya Salih Mujali, the brother of Hizam and Arif (*News Yemen*, October 9, 2006).

Following his escape from the security prison in February 2006, he was charged with planning the dual suicide attacks in Marib and Hadramaut on September 15, 2006. This operation was partially funded by four million Saudi riyals that al-Rabay'i received from Bandar al-Akwa through Said al-Akbar. Both al-Akwa and al-Akbar are currently awaiting sentencing for their roles in the attack (*22nd May*, April 29, 2007). During this time, he also paid a visit to his father, Yahya, who was in the hospital. According to reports that surfaced after his death, al-Rabay'i did not wear a disguise when he made the visit (*News Yemen*, October 9, 2006). Al-Rabay'i was killed on October 1, 2006 along with Muhammad al-Daylami during an early morning shoot-out with Yemeni security forces in the Bani Hashish region just north of Sana'a. In a story about the escapees, the Yemeni newspaper *al-Ghad* mentioned that some sources claim that al-Rabay'i was murdered in "cold blood" after he surrendered himself to soldiers (*al-Ghad*, June 25, 2007). Security forces also arrested three individuals it claimed had assisted the pair (*Asharq al-Awsat*, October 2, 2006).

Muhammad Ahmad Abdullah al-Daylami (c.1978-2006)

Al-Daylami was charged with participating in the November 2002 attack on a Hunt Oil helicopter, planning to attack five foreign embassies and a 2003 plot to assassinate Edmund Hull, then the U.S. Ambassador in Yemen. He was sentenced to five years in prison in February 2005. In October 2006, he was killed along with Fawaz al-Rabay'i in a shootout with Yemeni security forces in the region of Bani Hashish.

Yasir Nasir Ali al-Hamayqani (c.1978-2007)

Al-Hamayqani was also known by the kunya Abu Khalid. He was charged with traveling to Iraq. Al-Hamayqani was killed in clashes with Yemeni security forces in the Sabah district of the southern governorate of Abyan on January 15, 2007 (*Asharq al-Awsat*, January 17, 2007). According to a security official, al-Hamayqani was in possession of a machine gun and two hand grenades when he was surrounded by security forces. He managed to wound two officers before he was killed (*Asharq al-Awsat*, January 17, 2007).

Mansur Nasir Awadh al-Bayhani (1974-2007)

Al-Bayhani was born in 1974 in the city of Tabuk in Saudi Arabia to a Yemeni migrant worker from al-Rida'a in the governorate of al-Baydha. He took his kunya, Abu Assam al-Tabuki, from his boyhood home. Mansur's brother, Zakariya, was also among the escapees. Additionally, both his older brother Tawfiq (1972) and his younger brother Ghalib (1980) are currently in U.S. custody in Guantanamo Bay. Al-Bayhani made his way to Afghanistan via Pakistan in the 1990s, where he joined the Taliban. Later that decade, he was part of Samir Salih Abdullah al-Suwaylim's Arab brigade that fought in Chechnya against Russian forces. During their time in Chechnya, al-Suwaylim, who was better known as al-Khattab, was poisoned by Russian security forces, while al-Bayhani was wounded in the right eye. Following the death of Suwaylim, he traveled back to Afghanistan to fight U.S. forces, before returning to Saudi Arabia where he was arrested and extradited along with five companions, including his brother Zakariya, to Yemen.

Al-Bayhani was eventually brought to trial, along with 10 others, on charges of forging passports, weapons and explosives possession, planning to travel to Iraq and forming an armed gang to carry out attacks in Yemen. He was acquitted in March 2005 of all charges save for forging Saudi, Iraqi and Yemeni passports (*Yemen Times*, March 24-27, 2005). Shafiq Umar and Abdullah al-Wada'i were also convicted of forging passports. Ibrahim al-Muqri, who was part of the same trial, was acquitted of all charges. All of the men, however, remained in prison until they managed to escape in February 2006. Al-Bayhani later turned himself in to Yemeni authorities, and was later released following a security guarantee. Mansur eventually made his way to Somalia, where he was killed in a U.S. naval strike by the USS Chafee on June 2, 2007.

[Original Publication: *Terrorism Monitor* 5 (18) – September 27, 2007]

Tracking Yemen's 23 Escaped Jihadi Operatives – Part 2

By Gregory D. Johnsen

In mid-September 2007, Yemeni President Ali Abdullah Saleh issued a stern warning to the Wa'ilah tribe in northern Yemen: turn over the six al-Qaeda suspects you are sheltering or face serious repercussions (*al-Wasat*, September 12, 2007). The six men that Saleh believes have found refuge with the tribe near the Saudi border are the remnants of a group of 23 prisoners that escaped from a Yemeni political security prison on February 3, 2006. The prisoners escaped by tunneling out of their cell and into a neighboring mosque, which has since been detailed in a lengthy narrative written by one of the escapees and published by the Yemeni paper *al-Ghad*. The escapees included a number of prominent al-Qaeda militants, among whom were individuals convicted of carrying out attacks on the U.S.S. Cole in 2000 and on the French oil tanker Limburg in 2002.

Six of these suspects have since been killed in clashes with Yemeni or U.S. forces, 11 have either turned themselves back in to authorities or have been recaptured and six of the suspects remain at large. Many of these individuals have continued to fight for al-Qaeda since their escape, and one of them, Nasir al-Wuhayshi, has since been named the new head of al-Qaeda in Yemen.

Despite differences of age and background, the 23 men who were being held in the cell were linked together through shared experiences. Nearly half of the escapees, 11, were born in Saudi Arabia to Yemeni parents. Several of the men were arrested in late 2002 after a series of bombings in Sana'a and Marib. Seven of these men were part of a 15-man cell that was later charged with planning to attack five foreign embassies as well as to assassinate the then U.S. Ambassador Edmund Hull. Three of the men were convicted of being part of an 11-man cell that was charged with plotting to carry out attacks in Yemen and abroad. Among the escapees, there are also two sets of brothers, Hizam and Arif Mujali and Mansur and Zakariya al-Bayhani, who are themselves brothers of Ghalib and Tawfiq al-Bayhani, who are currently in U.S. custody in Guantanamo Bay. Two other escapees, Qasim al-Raymi and Fawaz al-Rabay'i, also have brothers in Guantanamo Bay prison.

The first part of this series offered a biographical sketch of each escapee who is now deceased (*Terrorism Monitor*, September 27, 2007). This second part of the two-part series presents a biographical sketch of each escapee who is still at large or has surrendered.

118

At Large

Qasim Yahya Mahdi al-Raymi (b. 1977)

Al-Raymi is from Sana'a, and was also known by the kunya Abu Hurayrah al-San'ani. His younger brother, Faris, who fought in Afghanistan and Iraq, was killed in mysterious circumstances in Sana'a in June 2007 after leaving his house in the company of Zakariya al-Yafa'i, another escapee. Another brother, Ali, is listed as being in U.S. custody at Guantanamo Bay. Al-Raymi was arrested in connection with a series of explosions in the al-Qadasayah district of Sana'a in 2002. He was charged with being part of the cell that was planning to attack five embassies in Sana'a. During his trial in 2004, al-Raymi threatened to cut off the leg of Said al-Akil, the public prosecutor. Al-Akil's house was subsequently attacked with a hand grenade later that week. Al-Raymi was sentenced to five years in prison on August 30, 2004, which was later upheld by a superior court in February 2005.

Following his escape, al-Raymi was sheltered for a while by Yahya Muhammad al-Shara'i, who has since been apprehended and is currently awaiting sentencing (*22nd May*, April 29, 2007). On June 21, 2007, al-Raymi posted an audio statement to an Islamist website announcing that fellow escapee Nasir al-Wuhayshi was the new head of al-Qaeda in Yemen. On August 2, 2007, Yemeni authorities announced that al-Raymi was part of the 10-man cell that was responsible for the July 2, 2007 suicide bombing in Marib, which killed eight Spanish tourists and two Yemeni drivers (*Terrorism Focus*, August 14, 2007). That same week, on August 5, 2007, al-Raymi posted another audio message to an Islamist forum, once again warning his colleagues in al-Qaeda against negotiating with the government (*Asharq al-Awsat*, August 6, 2007). Three days later, al-Raymi was rumored to be killed in an early morning raid on his hideout in the al-Suhaym region in the governorate of Marib. That report proved to be premature, as al-Raymi had left the hideout the night before the attack. Instead, later reports revealed that Ali bin Ali Jaradan, Abd al-Aziz Jaradan and Ali Nasir Duha were killed in the raid (al-Arabiya, August 8, 2007). All three were linked to the July 2, 2007 suicide attack in Marib. The trio was also wanted for their involvement in the assassination of Ali Mahmud Qasaylah, the chief criminal investigator in Marib, in March 2007 (*Terrorism Focus*, May 22, 2007).

Ibrahim Muhammad Abd al-Jabar Huwaydi (b. 1982)

Huwaydi is from the Red Sea port city of Hudaydah. He was arrested in the wake of the 2002 bombings in the neighborhood of al-Qadasayah in Sana'a. He was charged with planning to attack foreign embassies as well as plotting to assassinate Edmund Hull, then the U.S. Ambassador in Yemen. He was sentenced to five years in prison in February 2005. During his trial, Huwaydi claimed that he attempted suicide on two different occasions as a result of torture (*Yemen Times*, December 27, 2004-January 2, 2005). Along with Muhammad al-Umda, Umar Jarallah and Shafiq Zayd, Huwaydi was hidden for a month by Muhammad Hajir, who has since been captured and is currently awaiting sentencing (*22nd May*, April 29, 2007). Hajir claimed in his confession that he was worried that the men would kill him if he did not hide them. Huwaydi has yet to be recaptured.

Muhammad Sa'd Ali Hasan al-Umda (b. 1981)

Al-Umda is from the Yemeni city of Taiz and is known by the kunya Abu Ghrayb al-Taizi. He was charged with being involved in the 2002 attack on the Limburg, and in February 2005 was sentenced to 10 years in prison. Al-Umda, as was mentioned above, was sheltered for one month by Muhammad Hajir (*22 May*, April 29, 2007). Al-Umda is still at large.

Jamal Muhammad Ahmad Ali al-Badawi (b. 1966)

Al-Badawi is originally from the southern port city of Aden, and is also known by the kunya Abu Abd al-Rahman. He is charged with being involved in both the attack on the U.S.S. Cole and the one on the Limburg. Prior to his escape in February 2006, al-Badawi also escaped, along with nine others, from a political security prison in Aden on April 11, 2003. He was sentenced to death by Najib Muhammad al-Qadari in 2004, although this was later reduced to a sentence of 15 years by Said Naji al-Qata in February 2005 (*News Yemen*, May 12, 2007). He is wanted by the United States and is still at large.

Nasir Abd al-Karim Abdullah al-Wuhayshi (b. 1976)

Al-Wuhayshi, who is also known by the kunya Abu Basir, is from the southern governorate of al-Baydha. During the late 1990s he worked as a secretary to Osama bin Laden in Afghanistan (*al-Ghad*, June 25, 2007). Following the U.S. attack on the Taliban and al-Qaeda in Afghanistan in late 2001, he escaped across the border to Iran where he was arrested. Iran later extradited al-Wuhayshi and eight others back to Yemen in November 2003 (*Yemen Times*, November 2003). The Yemeni government never officially brought charges against him, although he remained in prison until he escaped in February 2006. In June 2007, he was named the new head of al-Qaeda in Yemen in an audiotape that was posted to an Islamist website. He is still at large. On August 2, 2007, Yemen announced that he was part of the 10-man Marib cell, which was responsible for the attack that killed eight Spanish tourists and two Yemeni drivers (*26 September*, August 2, 2007).

Hamza Salim Amar al-Qayti (b. 1969)

Al-Qayti was born in Saudi Arabia to a family from Mukalla in the eastern Yemeni governorate of Hadramaut. He is also known by the kunya Abu Samir. He was extradited to Yemen from Saudi Arabia in 2003. Al-Qayti was never officially charged with any crime, although he remained in prison until he escaped in February 2006. In March 2007, al-Wasat reported that al-Qayti was injured during a car chase after the Land Cruiser he was riding in with seven others in the southern governorate of Abyan refused a request to be searched at a military checkpoint (*al-Wasat*, March 21, 2007). Officials later found weapons and anti-aircraft missiles in the vehicle. On August 2, 2007, Yemen announced that he was part of the 10-man Marib cell (*26 September*, August 2, 2007)

Surrendered

Fawzi Muhammad Abd al-Qawi al-Wajayhi (b. 1982)

Al-Wajayhi was born in Saudi Arabia to Yemeni parents. His family is from the same neighborhood in Taiz as is Muhammad al-Umda's family. Both men took kunyas that reflect this link, Abu Musab al-Taizi and Abu Ghrayb al-Taizi, respectively. Al-Wajayhi spent time in Afghanistan during the 1990s as a bodyguard to Osama bin Laden (*Washington Post*, July 4, 2007). When he returned to Saudi Arabia in the aftermath of the U.S. attacks on the Taliban and al-Qaeda in Afghanistan, he was arrested and extradited to Yemen along with two other men. He was charged with involvement in the Limburg attack, and was part of the 15-man cell that was sentenced on August 30, 2004. Al-Wajayhi was given 10 years for his role in the attack. Following his escape, he turned himself back in to Yemeni authorities as part of a security arrangement, which allowed him to remain under loose house arrest in exchange for his not taking part in any illegal activities. In Yemen, this process is usually sealed by a security guarantee, which often involves both the money and reputation of the mediator.

Abdullah Yahya Salih al-Wada'i (b. 1978)

Al-Wada'i was born in Saudi Arabia to Yemeni parents from Sana'a. He is also known by the kunya Marwan al-Hashidi. Al-Wada'i was arrested in Saudi Arabia upon his return from Afghanistan, and later extradited to Yemen along with five others, including Mansur al-Bayhani and Ibrahim al-Muqri. He was part of the 11-man cell that was brought up on charges in February 2005 of belonging to an armed gang intent on carrying out criminal attacks in Yemen and abroad, as well as of fighting in Afghanistan and Iraq and possessing forged travel documents. Al-Wada'i was eventually cleared by the court of all charges save forging passports, but was never released from prison. Following his escape, he turned himself back into authorities and is currently free on a security guarantee.

Khalid Muhammad Abdullah al-Batati (b. 1982)

Al-Batati was born in Saudi Arabia and is also known by the kunya Abu Sulayman. His family is from Sana'a. He was extradited to Yemen from Saudi Arabia. In early 2005, he was accused of being part of an eight-man cell formed by Anwar Jaylani, an Iraqi, that was planning to attack the British and Italian embassies as well as the French Cultural Center in Sana'a. The group was also accused of planning to assassinate a number of prominent Yemeni officials, including then Prime Minister Abd al-Qadir Bajammal and Minister of Interior Rashid al-Alimi. Al-Batati was sentenced to three years and two months in prison in August 2005. Following his escape, he turned himself back into security forces in late April 2006 (*26 September*, April 23, 2006).

Abd al-Rahman Ahmad Hasan Basurah (b. 1981)

Like his companion al-Batati, al-Basurah was also born in Saudi Arabia to a Sanaani family. Basurah, who is also known by the kunya, Abu Ghrayb, was also extradited to Yemen from Saudi Arabia and was also charged with being part of the cell formed by Anwar Jaylani in 2005. Basurah's role was apparently collecting information on the French Cultural Center, which was one of the targets in the plot (*Yemen Times*, March 31-April 3, 2005). He also confessed to making a sketch of the British Embassy (*Yemen Times*, June 9-12, 2005). During the trial, Basurah admitted that one of the military uniforms seized by security forces was his, but that he had bought it in order to impersonate Saddam Hussein in a student play (*Yemen Times*, June 2-5, 2005). Later during the trial, Basurah claimed he had been duped by al-Jaylani, and that the leader had exploited his feelings and absconded with his money (*Yemen Times*, June 9-12, 2005). He was sentenced to three years and four months in prison. He later turned himself in alongside Jamal al-Badawi on May 15, 2007. He is currently free on a security guarantee.

Abdullah Ahmad Salih al-Raymi (b. 1977)

Al-Raymi is originally from the city of Taiz. He spent time fighting in Afghanistan, before returning to Qatar where he was arrested. Qatar later extradited him to Yemen in May 2005. Yemeni authorities charged him with forging documents for travel to Afghanistan. He was sentenced to four years in prison. Following his escape from prison, al-Raymi was re-captured in a joint raid by Yemeni security forces and a local counter-terrorism unit in the governorate of Marib on May 5, 2006 (*News Yemen*, May 11, 2006). He was later released.

Zakariya Nasir Awadh al-Bayhani (b. circa 1977)

Like his brother Mansur, Zakariya was born in the northern Saudi city of Tabuk to Yemeni parents. Both his older and younger brothers, Tawfiq and Ghalib, are currently in U.S. custody in Guantanamo Bay prison. Following his return to Saudi Arabia from Afghanistan, he was arrested and subsequently extradited to Yemen. In Yemen, he remained in prison although no charges were ever brought against him. Along with his brother Mansur, he turned himself in to

Yemeni authorities in late 2006. Both were later released in accordance with a security guarantee.

Zakariya Ubadi Qasim al-Yafa'i (b. 1973)

Al-Yafa'i was born in Saudi Arabia, and his family is from the village of Yafa in the southern Yemeni government of Lahj. Saudi Arabia extradited him to Yemen along with two other men in 2003. He was never charged with any crime, although he was kept in prison until he escaped in February 2006. He was re-captured by security forces in a raid on a house in the Shumayla neighborhood of Sana'a on April 17, 2006 (al-Wasat, April 19, 2006). According to reports, he did not resist arrest. Al-Yafa'i was later released on a security guarantee. Following his release from prison, he was involved in the death of Faris al-Raymi, the younger brother of Qasim al-Raymi, who is still at large. According to a report in the Yemeni newspaper al-Ghad, Zakariya agreed to take Faris to see his brother in early June 2007. The two left al-Raymi's house in Sana'a at 7:30 in the morning. Four hours later, Faris' father, Nasir, received a call from a surgical team at the German hospital in Sana'a saying they had removed seven bullets from Faris' head, chest and hands. Faris remained alive for another week, but never regained consciousness. The reason for his killing remains a mystery.

Jabir Ahmad Salih al-Banna (b. 1966)

Al-Banna, who holds dual U.S.-Yemeni citizenship, is also known as Abu Ahmad. His family is from the village of Yahir in the governorate of Dhall'a. Al-Banna was linked to the Lackawana Six, and is still wanted by the United States, which has offered a $5 million reward for information leading to his capture. According to the United States, al-Banna was an admirer of Kamal Darwish, a veteran fighter who was killed along with Abu Ali al-Harthi in missile attack by a CIA-operated drone in November 2002. Al-Banna traveled to Afghanistan on May 14, 2001 to participate in an al-Qaeda training camp along with Mukhtar al-Bakri, Sahim Alwan, and Yahya Goba. Before crossing the border from Pakistan into Afghanistan, al-Banna took up residence for a short time at a guesthouse in Kandahar, which was visited by Osama bin Laden. Later, along with his friends, he received military training at an al-Qaeda camp in Afghanistan. Unlike the others, al-Banna never returned to the United States. One of his former companions, Sahim Alwan, described him as very eager to fight the Northern Alliance and as someone who was actively seeking to become a martyr (PBS, July

24, 2003). He eventually made his way to Yemen, and surrendered himself in Taiz in late 2003, following a lengthy mediation effort headed by a "high-ranking member" of the ruling GPC party (*al-Ghad*, June 25, 2007). Among the guarantees that al-Banna was given was a promise that he would not be extradited to the United States. Al-Banna received a similar pledge from the Yemeni government in May 2007 when he once again turned himself into Yemeni forces along with Abd al-Rahman al-Basurah. He is currently under loose house arrest.

Hizam Salih Ali Mujali (b. 1980)

Hizam is the older brother of Arif Mujali. He is from the governorate of Sana'a. Yemeni forces arrested him along with Fawaz al-Rabay'i in late 2003. The two resisted arrested, and fired at the security forces, killing one soldier, Hamid Khasruf. Hizam, like his younger brother, Arif, was part of the 15-man cell that went on trial in 2004. Hizam was charged with attacking a Hunt Oil helicopter and for participating in the attack on the Limburg. On August 30, 2004, he was sentenced to death for killing Khasruf. This sentence was upheld by a higher court in February 2005. Both Hizam and Arif turned themselves into the government in August 2006 (*al-Wasat*, August 30, 2006). Their surrender was orchestrated by Sheikh Hadi Dalqim, a tribal leader from Marib, who served as a mediator between the government and the brothers. It is unclear whether Mujali's sentence was commuted as a result of the negotiations.

Arif Salih Ali Mujali (b. 1984)

Arif is the younger brother of Hizam Mujali, and is also known by the kunya Abu al-Layth al-San'ani. As his kunya indicates, he is from Sana'a. Another brother, Yahya, is also active in jihadi circles, and had agreed to marry his daughter to Fawaz al-Rabay'i. He was part of the 15-man cell and was charged with involvement in the November 2002 attack on the Hunt Oil helicopter, planning to attack five embassies, and for planning to assassinate then U.S. Ambassador Edmund Hull. He suffered from an injured leg, which he claimed was the result of torture, during his 2004 trial (*Yemen Times*, August 19-22, 2004). In the weeks following his escape from prison in February 2006, security forces managed to corner Arif and three companions in a building in the Musayk neighborhood of Sana'a, which has become known over the past few years as a haven for Islamic militants. The four men were able to escape, and eventually made their way to Marib. Sheikh Dalqim eventually persuaded both Arif and Hizam to surrender themselves to the government in August 2006 (*al-Wasat*, August 30, 2006). Arif is free as part of this arrangement.

Ibrahim Muhammad Abdu al-Muqri (b. 1972)

Like many of his fellow escapees, al-Muqri was born in Saudi Arabia to Yemeni parents from Hudaydah. He has two known kunyas, Abu Muhammad and Abu Musab. Al-Muqri was arrested in Saudi Arabia upon his return from Afghanistan and later extradited to Yemen. He was then kept in a political security prison until he was brought up on charges in February 2005, along with 10 other defendants. The men were charged with forming an armed gang intent on carrying out criminal acts both in Yemen and abroad. The 11 defendants were also charged with training in al-Qaeda camps in Afghanistan between 1998 and 2002, as well as possessing forged travel documents. Also indicted in the case were: Mansur al-Bayhani, Abdullah al-Wada'i and Shafiq Umar. Al-Muqri was cleared of all charges in March 2005, but was not released, and instead remained in prison until he escaped in February 2006. He surrendered himself to authorities a few months after his escape. As part of the deal, he was released but kept under surveillance. Al-Muqri, however, evaded Yemeni security forces and made his way to Somalia. Later, as he was crossing the border into Kenya, he was arrested along with two companions. He is currently in prison in Kenya.

[Original Publication: *Terrorism Monitor* 5 (19) – October 24, 2007]

Al-Qaeda in Yemen Reorganizes under Nasir al-Wuhayshi

By Gregory D. Johnsen

The man most responsible for the growing strength of al-Qaeda in Yemen is a 32-year-old former secretary of Osama bin Laden named Nasir al-Wuhayshi. He took over the leadership of the group when it had all but been eliminated, and has slowly, over the past two years, resurrected al-Qaeda in Yemen.

The publication of the second issue of *Sada al-Malahim* (The Echo of Battles) on March 13, 2008 illustrates the degree to which al-Qaeda has reconstituted and reorganized itself in Yemen. The most recent issue of the online journal was released exactly two months after the first issue was posted on various websites and devoted blogs. But already there have been significant changes to the journal. No longer is it published by al-Qaeda in Yemen, but rather by "the al-Qaeda Organization of Jihad in the South of the Arabian Peninsula." There is also a certainty of tone and authority to the second issue that was lacking in the first. For example, the journal denied that a January 2008 interview between a local Yemeni paper and an individual claiming to be al-Qaeda in Yemen's Information Officer was legitimate. "We say that we are the al-Qaeda organization of Jihad in the South of the Arabian Peninsula, and that the callers are ignorant of the situation and have no relationship with the organization." All of this speaks to an increasingly centralized leadership within the group's ranks in Yemen.

In November 2002, the organization lost its leader, Sinan Qa'id al-Harthi (a.k.a. Abu Ali al-Harthi), in a CIA attack. A year later, al-Qaeda in Yemen seemed defunct after the capture of al-Harthi's replacement, Muhammad Hamdi al-Ahdal. Coincidentally, it was at this time, when al-Qaeda in Yemen reached bottom in November 2003, that al-Wuhayshi was returned to Yemen as part of an extradition agreement with Iran (*al-Ghad*, June 25, 2007). Concentrated efforts by the U.S. and Yemeni governments, various alternative programs, and the lure of the war in Iraq all contributed to more than two years of relative calm in Yemen. But all that changed in February 2006, when al-Wuhayshi and 22 other prisoners escaped from a political security prison in Sana'a (Reuters, February 15, 2006). The escape marked the beginning of the second phase in the war against al-Qaeda in Yemen.

Along with his most trusted lieutenant, Qasim al-Raymi – also known by the kunya (honorific or war-name) of Abu Hurayrah al-San'ani – al-Wuhayshi has completely rebuilt the organization, which is much more ordered now than it was under al-Harthi in 2002. The initial process of rebuilding was slow and it is unclear whether al-Wuhayshi was commanding the group's operations before he was officially announced as al-Qaeda in Yemen's leader in June 2007 (*al-Wasat*, June 27, 2007); but since then he has consolidated control of the group, and now appears to be firmly in command.

Al-Wuhayshi authored a lengthy narrative detailing the prison break, which, in the absence of any official descriptions, has served as the most widely accepted version of the escape (republished by *al-Ghad*, June 25, 2007 and July 7, 2007). Al-Wuhayshi, who is known by the kunya Abu Basir, also eulogized Abu Layth al-Libi, the al-Qaeda commander who was killed in late January 2008 in Pakistan, in the most recent issue of *Sada al-Malahim*. Part of this eulogy may help to explain why al-Wuhayshi was selected as the group's leader in 2007. Early in his statement he lists a series of al-Qaeda figures who have been killed including men such as Abu Hafs, Abu Abaydah, and Abu Ali al-Harthi; implicit in this is not only his duty to speak about al-Libi as the group's commander, but also his connection to these early al-Qaeda figures through his time at bin Laden's side in Afghanistan.

It is unclear exactly when during the 1990s al-Wuhayshi left his home in the southern governorate of al-Baydah to travel to Afghanistan, where he eventually became one of bin Laden's secretaries. But al-Wuhayshi has certainly played up his personal links to bin Laden, which appear to have impressed the relatively young men who now constitute al-Qaeda in Yemen's second generation. This personal connection to the early figures of al-Qaeda in the late 1990s seems to have acted as implicit endorsement of his qualifications as a leader. It could be said that his authority has been certified by his association with the first generation of al-Qaeda.

Following the U.S. attack on the Taliban and al-Qaeda in Afghanistan in late 2001, al-Wuhayshi escaped across the border to Iran where he was arrested. He was later extradited back to Yemen along with eight other Yemenis in November 2003. Yemen never officially brought charges against him, but he remained in prison until his escape in February 2006. The years in Iranian and Yemeni prisons seem to have hardened him. He has complained of torture in Yemeni prisons, and threatened to repay those who torture his comrades with death (*al-Ghad*, June 25, 2007; *News Yemen*, July 2, 2007). Al-Wuhayshi has also accused older members of al-Qaeda of making deals with the Yemeni government. This no-holds-barred approach is a relatively new one in Yemen, where negotiation and compromise are much more common methods. The underlying philosophy that al-Wuhayshi has instituted among his followers in Yemen is articulated in the most recent issue of *Sada al-Malahim*: "Jihad is a religious duty that God has made incumbent." This type of reasoning leaves no room for negotiation, and this is exactly the stance that al-Qaeda in Yemen under al-Wuhayshi has adopted. Under his leadership, al-Qaeda in Yemen has become more strident, better organized and more ambitious than it has ever been before.

[Original Publication: *Terrorism Focus* 5 (11) – March 18, 2008]

Leader of Yemen's Mujahideen Claims al-Qaeda has a Nuclear Weapon

By Abdul Hameed Bakier

In a recent interview posted to jihadi websites, al-Qaeda's leader in Yemen claims the organization possesses nuclear weapons and vows to attack U.S. and Western interests to compel them to withdraw their forces from the region (hanein.info, January 27, 2009).

According to the interview, the leader of al-Qaeda in Yemen, 33-year-old Nasir al-Wuhayshi (a.k.a. Abu Basir), was Osama bin Laden's secretary until he was arrested by Iran and extradited to Yemen in February 2002. Al-Wuhayshi has been a fugitive since he escaped from a Yemeni prison in 2006 (see *Terrorism Focus*, February 7, 2006; March 18, 2008). In 2008, the second man in al-Qaeda, Dr. Ayman al-Zawahiri, commended al-Wuhayshi and named him the Amir of Mujahideen in Yemen. Since then, there has been a growing unity between al-Qaeda's Saudi and Yemeni affiliates and the mainstream al-Qaeda group in the Pakistan/Afghanistan border region. Led by an Amir, a deputy Amir, and a military and Shura council, the Saudi and Yemeni affiliates have joined together as al-Qaeda in the Arabian Peninsula (AQAP).

On the war in Gaza, al-Wuhayshi said that the Muslim nation is longing for jihad, as is evident from the protests that broke out everywhere, but accused Hamas of refusing to receive the Salafi-jihadis that tried to aid Palestinians in the fighting. The Arab mujahideen went to Afghanistan only to prepare for jihad in Palestine, but before the mujahideen can go to Palestine, the blockade imposed by Arab regimes should be broken - an implicit call to topple Arab regimes, or what al-Qaeda identifies as "the near enemy." In the meantime, al-Wuhayshi believes it is necessary to also attack the interests of the supporters of Israel, the United States and Europe in the Arabian Peninsula: "The Crusaders' campaign on our people in Palestine, Somalia and Afghanistan uses the Arabian Peninsula as a launching pad. The U.S., British and French fleets in the region are only there to protect the Jews in Palestine. The Arab leaders, among them the Yemeni leader [President Ali Abdullah Saleh], vigorously contribute military and logistical aid to the Crusaders' campaign."

Al-Wuhayshi further asserts that until the mujahideen are able to infiltrate into Palestine and fight the Jews, Western tourists are a legitimate target for the mujahideen, as the tourists are part of the Crusaders' campaign. Western tourists are either Christian missionaries, depraved individuals, or Western government agents spying on Muslims. Al-Wuhayshi justifies killing Muslims who protect Christian and Jewish interests such as embassies and cultural centers, referring to al-Qaeda's attack on the U.S. embassy in Sana'a in September 2008 in which six Yemeni security personnel, six attackers, and four bystanders were killed. "Shame on those who protect the embassies of the Crusaders' countries. Shame on them to watch U.S. rockets and Israeli white phosphorus shells tearing up and burning Gaza children and still protect their interests," says al-Wuhayshi.

Asked why al-Qaeda targets the oil industry infrastructure that serves the economy of a Muslim country when the majority of employees in that industry are Muslims, al-Wuhayshi insisted that Muslims do not benefit from Yemeni oil. On the contrary, it only sustains the lifeline of the Crusaders and Zionists who are attacking Muslims, thanks to President Saleh. On the topic of tourism, al-Wuhayshi insists Muslims should not allow infidel Jews and Christians into the Arabian Peninsula in the name of tourism or any other purpose.

On the Yemeni leadership, al-Wuhayshi refuses to recognize the authority of the Yemeni president, alleging that he came to power through sham elections: "Democracy is a religion invented and imposed on Muslim nations by the United States to create grudges and animosity among them. Democracy drains the energy of Muslim youths by keeping them occupied with elections and leaves the nation powerless and acquiescent to the Crusaders' campaign."

Refuting President Saleh's declaration that al-Qaeda extremists have no vision and only blow up and kill innocent people, al-Wuhayshi said the Yemeni president has been stealing government funds and destroying the country for years without a vision or plan for the well being of the country and its people. Al-Wuhayshi claims Yemen's president has turned Yemen into a base for Crusaders and Zionists. Al-Qaeda therefore aims to replace the current regime with a just and secure Islamic Shari'a government in Yemen that will end U.S. influence in the region. The Amir adds that mujahideen attacks on U.S. interests have weakened the U.S. economy, as seen in the current world economic crisis. Finally, al-Wuhayshi claims al-Qaeda possesses a nuclear weapon and only refrained from using it in the 9/11 attacks because those attacks were only al-Qaeda's "first message" to the Americans.

Many ordinary Yemenis believe the nation's "enemies" are propagating false allegations that Yemen is becoming a regional base for al-Qaeda in order to damage its relations with Saudi Arabia (al-yemen.org January 25, 2009). Others anticipate more international support for the Yemeni government in its fight against AQAP in Yemen in response to AQAP's formation. Answering AQAP's threats, Yemen's Interior Ministry said the Yemeni security apparatus is on high alert and is conducting security sweeps of all possible AQAP hideouts, adding that Yemen and Saudi Arabia are cooperating fully to apprehend AQAP members (*Dar al-Hayat*, January 31, 2009).

[Original Publication: *Terrorism Focus* 6 (4) – February 6, 2009]

The Jihadis and the Cause of South Yemen: A Profile of Tariq al-Fadhli

By Rafid Fadhil Ali

In 2009, Tariq al-Fadhli, the prominent jihadist leader from South Yemen, broke his 15-year alliance with the Yemeni government of President Ali Abdullah Saleh. Al-Fadhli, who was a member of the anti-Soviet Mujahideen movement in Afghanistan, is often described as the founder of the jihadi movement in Yemen. His break with the government was reported in the mainstream Arab and Yemeni media but was also noted on pro-jihadist websites (Alflojaweb.com, April 18, 2009). Al-Fadhli's new position provided momentum to the Southern Movement (SM) and its struggle for secession and he soon became a leading figure in the alliance.

Tariq al-Fadhli's father, Nasir bin Abdullah al-Fadhli, was the leader of the powerful al-Fadhil tribe and a sultan who owned and ruled wide areas of the southern province of Abyan. After the British pulled out of South Yemen in 1967, the elder al-Fadhli lost his lands and power to the new rulers of South Yemen, the Marxists of the Yemen Socialist Party (*Al-Hizb al-Ishtiraki al-Yamani* – YSP). Tariq's family moved to Saudi Arabia where he grew up. In the late 1980s, he abandoned his education and joined the mujahideen movement in Afghanistan fighting against the Soviet forces (Yemen-Sound, July 29, 2009).

Since joining the SM, al-Fadhli has presented himself as a nationalist from the south calling for the rights of South Yemenis. The terminology he uses in his statements and speeches is more patriotic than Islamist. He talks about his time in Afghanistan as something from the past. About a month after he joined the SM, al-Fadhli was interviewed by a pan-Arab daily. In response to a question about his experience in Afghanistan, he stated, "You are talking about something from 20 years ago… We now live on our lands and have no links with Afghanistan. Let anyone who accuses us of terror present his accusation in front of the whole world and the international community. I will be ready to take responsibility if anything was proven against me. Otherwise those who accuse me should be held responsible… We [in South Yemen] have been invaded 15 years ago and we are under a vicious occupation. So we are busy with our cause and we do not look at any other cause in the world. We want our independence and to put an end to this occupation" (*Asharq al-Awsat*, May 14, 2009).

133

On the same day al-Fadhli's interview was published, the regional organization of al-Qaeda declared its support for the people of South Yemen. In an audiotape released on the internet, Nasir Abdul Kareem al-Wuhayshi (a.k.a. Abu Basir), leader of al-Qaeda in the Arabian Peninsula, expressed his sympathy with the people of the southern provinces and their attempt to defend themselves against their "oppression." Al-Fadhli declared that what the people of the South need is not a call for secession but a call for ending the oppression. "What is happening in Lahaj, Dhali, Abyan and Hadramaut and the other southern provinces cannot be approved. We have to support and help [the southerners]," said al-Wuhayshi. He went on to address the South Yemenis, promising retaliation. "The oppression against you will not pass without punishment... the killing of Muslims in the streets is an unjustified major crime" (al-Jazeera.net, May 14, 2009).

Al-Fadhli and Bin Laden

In his book *Da'wat al-muqawamah al-islamiyyah al-'alamiyyah* (The Call of the Global Islamic Resistance), Syrian jihad strategist Abu Musa'ab al-Suri indicated Osama bin Laden intended to initiate a major jihadist movement in southern Yemen, taking advantage of the internal rivalries of the YSP leaders. According to al-Suri, Tariq al-Fadhli was chosen and trained by bin Laden to practice jihad in Yemen, but President Saleh managed to convince him to join the government (Minbaralhurriyya.org, September 16, 2009). Al-Fadhli denies any special relationship with bin Laden. "Osama was not as famous at that time [in 1980s Afghanistan] as he is now. We were with Gulbuddin Hekmatyar, whom many Arabs were comfortable to fight with. I was in an area west of Kabul called Maidan Warda. I did not meet bin Laden till the last battle of Jalalabad and only for short and staggering times. My relationship with him was like any other one in the field, very normal with nothing special" (*Asharq al-Awsat*, May 14, 2009).

After the Soviet withdrawal from Afghanistan, al-Fadhli returned to Saudi Arabia and then to North Yemen. When the unification of Yemen was declared in 1990, al-Fadhli saw his socialist enemies becoming partners in the power structure. The YSP accused him of being behind the assassination of one of their leaders. He was arrested after the attacks on two hotels in Aden where American soldiers participating in Operation Restore Hope in Somalia were staying. Al-Fadhli denies any involvement in the attacks or the assassination. He spent three years in jail on the charges.

The Civil War

By the time the fourth anniversary of unification arrived, relations between President Saleh and the YSP were at their worst. The YSP leaders waged a war in the south calling for secession. They accused the north and president Saleh of dominating the government. Upset by President Saleh's support for Iraqi president Saddam Hussein during the first Gulf War, Kuwait and Saudi Arabia supported the South [1].

President Saleh turned to the YSP's ideological enemies, the jihadis, for help. Who else but Tariq al-Fadhli could provide the best assistance against the socialists? According to al-Fadhli's account, he was released at 2:30 in the morning and asked to join the fight immediately (*Asharq al-Awsat*, May 14, 2009). The role of the jihadis led by al-Fadhli was vital in winning the war for the north (see *Terrorism Monitor*, July 13, 2006). Al-Fadhli was then rewarded by becoming a senior member of President Saleh's ruling party, the General People's Congress (*al-Mo'tamar al-Sha'by al-'Am*). He also got part of his father's lands back (Albaisanews.com, May 14, 2009).

Yemen has been, and will always be, a country of symbolic importance for the Islamists, especially its southern part. The family of Saudi-born Osama bin Laden is originally from Hadramaut province in South Yemen and he once aimed to eventually settle there. Yemen is also mentioned in an apocryphal hadith as a place for believers to go when there is a threat. Aden-Abyan is specifically mentioned in the hadith as the place where an army of 12,000 men will arise to fight for the religion of Allah in the last days (see *Terrorism Monitor*, February 23, 2006; May 4, 2006; July 13, 2006). Yemen is also of crucial strategic importance. Its geographic location places it close to vital shipping lanes, as well as Sudan, Somalia and Saudi Arabia, countries of high interest for al-Qaeda.

The unification of Yemen denied jihadis the battle they wanted to fight – a pure battle against the deteriorating pro-Soviet YSP, a scenario that would be similar to Afghanistan. When the 1994 civil war broke out, they fought for Saleh against the YSP, whom they considered to be unbelievers.

The defeat of the south in 1994 did not end the secessionist cause of its people. Frustration led to the emergence of the SM, formed by secular groups and led by the YSP. The deterioration in south Yemen has reached a point where ideological enemies have put their differences behind them for a common cause. Tariq al-Fadhli became a leading figure in the SM and recognized the former president of

South Yemen, Ali Salem al-Beedh, as the legitimate leader of the south Yemeni people. Al-Fadhli also claimed that he continues to maintain his influence over the jihadis, but tries to separate this role from al-Qaeda, whose existence postdates the anti-Soviet Afghan jihad. "It is impossible that I let [the jihadists] down. Al-Qaeda is new. These are jihadists who fought in Afghanistan and I was with them fighting the Soviets in the 1980s. I have strong relations with all of the jihadists in the north and the south and everywhere, but not with al-Qaeda" (Albaidanew.com, May 14, 2009). President Saleh's old tactic of manipulating competing groups seems to be of diminishing value. In his last meeting with President Saleh, al-Fadhli refused to cooperate with the government on the jihadi issue or the southern issue.

The situation in the south is of interest to al-Qaeda as well. After the declaration of al-Qaeda in the Arabian Peninsula (formed by the Saudi and Yemeni branches of the organization), the 33-year-old al-Wuhayshi emerged as the leader of the new organization. His statement expressing support for South Yemen came from a man who knows the area and its people. Like al-Fadhli, al-Wuhayshi comes from the southern province of Abyan. The link between al-Fadhli's and al-Wuhayshi's support for the people of the south has not been proven yet, but the pro-government media has already put both men in one basket as leaders of al-Qaeda (*al-Thawra*, October 17, 2009). With his senior position among jihadis and tribesmen, al-Fadhli's loyalties and policies will play an important role in shaping the future of South Yemen.

[Original Publication: *Terrorism Monitor* 7 (35) – November 19, 2009]

Notes

1. See *Harb al-Yamen 1994 al-Asbab wal Nata'ij* (The Yemen War: The Causes and Effects), Emirates Center for Strategic Studies and Research, 1995.

Ibrahim al-Rubaish: New Religious Ideologue of al-Qaeda in Saudi Arabia Calls for Revival of Assassination Tactic

By Murad Batal al-Shishani

The Mufti, or religious leader, plays an essential role for al-Qaeda and affiliated Salafi-Jihadi groups, particularly in Saudi Arabia, where the government's counterterrorism strategy involves denouncing al-Qaeda's religious credentials. There have been several al-Qaeda Muftis since the group began attacks on the Saudi establishment in 2003. Issa bin Sa'ad al-Oshan was killed by Saudi forces in Riyadh on July 21, 2004; Abdullah al-Rashoud was declared dead in Iraq on June 23, 2005 by the late Abu Musab al-Zarqawi (then-leader of al-Qaeda in Iraq); and Faris Shuwayl al-Zahrani (a.k.a. Abu Jandal al-Azdi), who has been in a Saudi prison since August 2004.

Since the Saudi al-Qaeda movement shifted to Yemen after the government crackdown of 2003-2006, the religiously trained Ibrahim al-Rubaish has been presented as the new religious ideologue of al-Qaeda in the Arabian Peninsula, responsible for issuing the latest statements of the organization, especially those related to Saudi Arabia. Most significant was an audiotape that addressed the attempt last August on the life of Saudi Prince Muhammad bin Nayif (see *Terrorism Monitor*, September 17, 2009).

Al-Rubaish justified the assassination attempt in a tape entitled, "Why Muhammad bin Nayif?," stating that bin Nayif is responsible for a war against the Mujahideen and wages that war against them on behalf of the United States. Al-Rubaish considers assassination to be a legitimate tactic as it was used in the early history of Islam. He cites a Sunnah authorizing the murder of "polytheists" and several examples of the Prophet Muhammad calling for the assassination of "enemies of Islam":

We are in dire need of reviving this Sunnah against the enemies of Allah, for it instills terror and fear in the ranks of the enemy. It also is a factor which leads the mercenaries in the ranks of the enemy to re-evaluate their work, for even though they are slaves of money, their lives are more important to them than their salaries. It also makes those given orders amongst the soldiers think about the assassination teams before they think about fulfilling their commands. Through them, the enemies live in fear, even in their own houses amongst their families, for they do not know when they will be attacked by the predator lions. They know that they are doing their best to seek revenge, even if it leads to their own death, making the matter even more fearful and terrorizing.

Al-Rubaishi went on to describe the reasons behind the failed assassination attempt against Prince Muhammad bin Nayif, the Deputy Minister of the Interior for Security Affairs and the leader of Saudi Arabia's counterterrorism campaign since 2003:

Why Muhammad bin Nayif? Allah has favored me in the fact that I have never met Muhammad bin Nayif, may Allah deal with him as he deserves, but I have been in his prisons, I have dealt with his wardens and I have lived with those charred by the fire of his tyranny. I along with others have witnessed, while we are the witnesses of Allah on His earth, how he has waged war against jihad and the Mujahideen, something that even the media affirms. Muhammad bin Nayif stood alongside his troops guarding and protecting the Americans, preventing the Mujahideen from reaching them. He could have assumed the role of a bystander, but instead defended them, just as a good child defends his father's possessions [1].

Al-Rubaish was born in the ultra-conservative region of Buridah in al-Qasim in 1980, where he studied until graduating from Imam Muhammad bin Sa'ud University with a B.A. degree in Shari'a. He then moved to Afghanistan, where he was arrested by American troops and shipped to Guantanamo Bay, where he spent five years in prison (*Okaz* [Jeddah], October 10, 2009; Al-Riyadh.com, February 4, 2009). A poem he wrote about his imprisonment was published by *al-Hayat* newspaper and reprinted in a variety of Arabic language websites [2].

In December, 2006, al-Rubaish and a number of other Saudis were released from Guantanamo Bay prison and enrolled in the Saudi rehabilitation program. He decided to complete his Master's degree, but suddenly disappeared. Eventually his name was included in the so-called "85 Most Wanted" list released by Saudi authorities in February (Al-Riyadh.com, February 4, 2009).

In the meantime, al-Rubaish left his wife and three children behind to join al-Qaeda in Yemen in April 2008, along with 11 other Saudi ex-Guantanamo prisoners leaving the Kingdom (*Okaz*, October 10, 2009).

To demonstrate his religious abilities, al-Rubaish released a book criticizing Sheikh Salman al-Ouda because of the latter's "alliance" with the Saudi regime.

The sheikh, who directs the website *Islam Today*, has condemned the 9/11 attacks and used his media access to rebuke Osama bin Laden as a killer of innocent people. Al-Rubaish stated that al-Ouda has revised his ideas since inspiring young Saudis in the mid-1990s (almedad.com, October 12, 2009).

In early November 2009, al-Rubaish released an audiotape entitled "And the Mask Falls Down," criticizing Saudi King Abdullah's decision to allow mixed-sex education at the new King Abdullah University of Science and Technology near Jeddah (hanein.info, October 24, 2009). Al-Rubaish wrote an article in the latest issue of al-Qaeda in the Arab Peninsula's journal *Sada al-Malhim* warning about Shiites (*Rafidha*, or "rejectionists" as the jihadis refer to them) who are fighting Sunnis everywhere and who are supported by Iran. Al-Rubaish also warned of the consequences of a victory by the Zaidi Shiite Houthis who are fighting the Yemeni government, suggesting that they will fight against Sunnis if they finish with the government (hanein.info, March 20, 2008).

The emergence of al-Rubaish and the ideas he promulgates show that al-Qaeda, through propaganda and media vehicles, can generate new leaders to serve in its continuing battle against "infidels and hypocrites." At the same time, the work of a religious ideologue like al-Rubaish reveals that al-Qaeda still cares about Muslim public opinion, especially in areas of religious significance like Saudi Arabia.

[Original Publication: *Terrorism Monitor* 7 (36) – November 25, 2009]

Notes
1. See the English transcript of the audio: forums.islamicawakening.com/f18/why-muhammad-ibn-naif-shaykh-ibrahim-al-rubaish%7Ballah-preserve-him%7D-28847
2. See www.al-asra.com/f6/p6_15.htm

Anwar al-Awlaki: The Radical Source for Non-Arabic Speaking Muslims

By Murad Batal al-Shishani

In November 2001, an American Muslim cleric told the *Washington Post* that he had no sympathy for the perpetrators of 9/11, that Muslims and non-Muslims needed "more mutual understanding," and that the Taliban had no right to impose the burqa on women (*Washington Post*, November 19, 2001). The cleric, Sheikh Anwar al-Awlaki, is the same man who is now believed to have played a major role in radicalizing Major Nidal Malik Hasan, the U.S. army psychiatrist who killed 13 American soldiers at Fort Hood last November, and 23-year-old Nigerian Umar Farouk Abdulmutallab, who tried to detonate explosives aboard an airliner over Detroit on Christmas Day.

In an exclusive interview, al-Awlaki told Yemeni journalist Abdulelah Hider Shaea (the only journalist to interview the leader of al-Qaeda in Yemen, Nasir al-Wuhayshi), that Major Hasan contacted him on December 17, 2008, to inquire about the legitimacy of killing American soldiers and officers. Further correspondence discussed Shari'a-based justifications for killing Israeli civilians. Al-Awlaki considered the Fort Hood attack a legitimate act of jihad as it was a military target and described Hasan's attack as a "heroic act." At the same time, al-Awlaki said that he has not recruited Hasan. "America did with its crimes and injustices" (al-Jazeera, December 23, 2009). A Yemeni official stated that Nigerian terror suspect Abdulmutallab met al-Awlaki in Shabawa, east of Sana'a. (AFP, January 7, 2010).

There is a huge difference between the moderate statements al-Awlaki made in the period between 2001-2002 and the radical views he has expressed since 2007. In the intervening period, al-Awlaki moved to Yemen, where he was banned from re-entering the United States and detained without charge in a Yemeni prison for over a year. Al-Awlaki believes he was imprisoned at the request of the United States, but describes his detention as "a chance to review the Quran and to study and read in a way that was impossible out of jail. My time in detention was a vacation from this world" (Interview with Infocusnews.net [Anaheim], September 17, 2008). The sheikh says he was interrogated in prison by the FBI about his connections to the 9/11 terrorists (Interview with cageprisoners.com, December 31, 2007).

After his release, al-Awlaki translated and summarized the works of Yusuf al-Ayiri, an al-Qaeda ideologist who was killed in a security operation in northern Saudi Arabia in 2003 (muslim.net, Jan 15, 2009; *Asharq al-Awsat*, April 30, 2007). He then went on to write the guide *44 Ways to Support Jihad*, in which he says, "Jihad today is obligatory on every capable Muslim. So as a Muslim who wants to please Allah it is your duty to find ways to practice it and support it." The 44 ways of supporting jihad include giving the mujahideen money, praying for them, preserving their secrets, sponsoring their families, providing moral encouragement and urging others to join the jihad.

In the same book, al-Awlaki encourages followers to be "Internet mujahideen" by, among other things, "setting up websites to cover specific areas of jihad, such as: mujahideen news, Muslim POWs and jihad literature." Al-Awlaki also offers some advice to potential mujahideen: "Sheikh Abdullah Azzam used to say: 'Luxury is the enemy of jihad.' Jihad is difficult and demands sacrifice. Therefore avoiding the life of luxury removes some of the obstacles that may stand between a person and Jihad. You need to be able to sleep on the floor, eat food different than what your mother or wife cooks for you, use cold water for [ablutions] and not mind being unable to take a shower everyday." The would-be jihadist is also advised to learn Arabic, he argues, saying, "Arabic is the international language of jihad. Most of the jihad literature is available only in Arabic and publishers are not willing to take the risk of translating it. The only ones who are spending the money and time translating jihad literature are the Western intelligence services...and too bad, they would not be willing to share it with you" [1]. The book was published on the sheikh's blog, www.anwar-alawlaki.com, currently offline.

Furthermore, in a lecture entitled "Allah is Preparing us for Victory" (recommended reading by many jihadi forum contributors), al-Awlaki says, "Some Muslims say the way forward for this Ummah [community] is to distance itself from terrorism and spend their time in becoming good in business, good in technology, agriculture, and the rest; and this is how we can compete with the rest of the world. The Prophet of God (p.b.u.h) said that this is wrong and Allah will dishonor us if we do that" (salaattime.com, n.d.; see also muslim.net November 9, 2009).

Al-Awlaki was born in New Mexico in 1971, when his father, Nasser al-Awlaki, a former government minister before the 1994 unification of North and South Yemen, was studying there. Anwar spent his childhood in Yemen, returning to the United States in 1991 to obtain a Bachelor's degree in engineering from Colorado University and a Master's degree in education from San Diego University. Al-Awlaki then served as Imam of a San Diego mosque, where he met Khaled al-Mihdar and Nawaf al-Hazmi, two of the 9/11 hijackers. In 2001 he became Imam of Dar al-Hijrah mosque in Falls Church, Virginia, near Washington, before leaving the United States in 2002. His next stop was London before leaving for Yemen, where he spent 18 months in prison, for reasons that remain unclear (hanein.info, November 13, 2009; albidaweb.com, December 26, 2009). Currently he is based in Shabawa, east of Sana'a, and is associated with Sheikh Abdul Majid al-Zandani's al-Iman University. He is apparently living among his tribal relatives as he belongs to one of the largest tribes in southern Yemen. His relatives have warned against targeting him, saying it would escalate the tension the country is already experiencing instead of calming it down (albidaweb.com, December 26, 2009).

It is worth noting that al-Qaeda in the south of Yemen is uniquely combined with the tribal structure (explaining the protection al-Awlaki is being offered), but it is worth noting that al-Awlaki's influence is greater among non-Arabic speakers. In Arabic language jihadi forums, Anwar al-Awlaki's writings are very rare as most of them are in English and more Western-oriented. They are made available in different e-libraries and Islamic e-bookshops in the United States and the UK, where his radical views form a major resource for non-Arabic speaking Muslims, especially in the West.

[Original Publication: *Terrorism Monitor* 8 (2) – January 14, 2010]

From Yemen to Detroit: The Expanding Influence of AQAP's Sa'id al-Shihri

By Murad Batal al-Shishani

In the Saudi state television broadcast of a recorded conversation which took place on August 27, 2009 between Saudi Prince Muhammad bin Nayef and Abdullah Hassan Tali al-Assiri – moments before al-Assiri attempted to assassinate the prince via suicide bomb – bin Nayef made mention of a woman and her children whose safety he claimed was a top priority. The woman to whom Bin Nayef was referring is Wafa'a al-Shihri. She had fled to Yemen from Saudi Arabia to be with her husband, Sa'id al-Shihri, a fugitive and the deputy leader of al-Qaeda in the Arabian Peninsula (AQAP), and someone that bin Nayef – as Deputy Interior Minister in charge of Counterterrorism – was hoping to convince into surrender. Meanwhile, al-Assiri – equipped with a body-borne suicide bomb – sat down with bin Nayef under the false pretense of coming forward himself. When a cell phone rang during the meeting, al-Assiri answered and explained to bin Nayef it was al-Shihri on the line and that he should speak with him. The cell-phone that bin Nayef naively intercepted sent a signal from al-Shihri that detonated al-Assiri's explosive, killing the bomber, and leaving bin Nayef largely unharmed. This narrative indicates that al-Shihri (a.k.a. Abu Sufyan al-Azdi) was in charge of the plot to assassinate Muhammad Bin Nayef, operating from Yemen. Ultimately the assassination attempt was a failure; but AQAP sent a clear message that the ruling personalities of the oil-soaked, desert kingdom were clearly in their sights, and now, firmly within their reach. Saudi reports confirmed that the prince was in fact speaking to Sa'id al-Shihri on the phone at the time of the detonation. Several days later, AQAP released its own video about the assassination attempt and broadcasted the phone conversation between bin Nayef and al-Shihri, comprising part of this dueling narrative between the Saudi state and AQAP.

From Afghanistan to Yemen by way of Guantanamo Prison

Sa'id Bin Ali Bin Jabir al-Khothim al-Shihri was born in Riyadh on September 20, 1973 to a retired lieutenant of Saudi Army. He grew up in Khamis al-Mushayt in the Kingdom's southern Asir province, birthplace of several 9/11 hijackers. According to Saudi reports, al-Shihri failed to complete his schooling. He

143

travelled to Afghanistan two weeks after the 9/11 attacks via Bahrain and Pakistan. According to some reports he was trained in 2000 on urban warfare in a Libyan jihadi training camp in north of Kabul. There were also reports which advised that he spent time in Iran. Although he was arrested later along the Pakistan-Afghanistan border following an injury he sustained from a missile strike, he claimed that he was there to participate in philanthropic activity. Al-Shihri spent a month and a half in a Pakistani hospital, before he was transferred to Guantanamo Bay.

In the Guantanamo detention facility, al-Shihri was prisoner number 372, and was one of the Saudi prisoners whom, in 2006, Riyadh lobbied for release. He was one of eleven released Saudis from Guantanamo that Riyadh has currently listed as having fled the country and returned to terrorism. His brother in arms, Abu Hareth Muhammad al-Awfi, was with al-Shihri on the flight that ferried the detainees back to Saudi Arabia. Both men, along with several others linked to jihadi activities, were enrolled in a rehabilitation program that was being run by Saudi security. Disappearing from the Kingdom, al-Awfi and al-Shihri appeared in an AQAP video emanating from Yemen. A few months later, al-Awfi resurfaced in Saudi Arabia and surrendered to Saudi authorities, returning to his family in Riyadh. Several Saudi jihadists released from Guantanamo, such as al-Awfi and al-Shihri, turned up in Yemen and the majority of them are named on a Saudi most wanted list (now minus al-Assiri) known as "the 85 list."

The Saudi daily *Okaz* quoted a specialist working in the Prince Muhammad bin Nayef Centre for Care and Counseling where al-Shihri resided, describing his life after his release from Guantanamo. "He returned to Saudi Arabia, from Cuba, on the 29th of Shawal 1427 (November 21, 2006). He was incarcerated in al-Ha'ir prison for several months during which he was 'advised' at least for an hour and a half per day, while he was subject to daily classes in the care centre no less than three hours a day, with an aim to [rehabilitate and reintegrate into Saudi society]. On one occasion [al-Shihri] asked the psychology specialists [in the centre for their help] because of the lack of acceptance [he was receiving] from [the] daughter [of] his first marriage, Asmm'a, a student at the primary level. [He] asked them to assist him in [finding a way to gain his daughter's acceptance as a father], as he had been absent [from her for] about seven years in Guantanamo. After undergoing rehabilitation, he left the [rehabilitation] center to the dismay of his family [and made an appearance] in Yemen, accompanied by his colleague Mohamed al-Awfi." The same report quoted al-Shihri's father talking about his son before he left for Yemen. "Sa'id after his release from the care centre came back to Khamis al-Mushayt, and [I] prepared [for] him accommodations and proceeded [to make his arrangements] to marry Wafa'a al-Shihri."

Ideology

While the majority of reports on al-Shihri in Saudi newspapers were written with the aim of undermining him and his charisma, his own writings in AQAP's journal *Sada al-Malahim* ("The Echo of Battles") convey a personality of a man that subscribes deeply to his own Salafi-jihadi ideology. For example, he considers establishing a caliphate on earth a high priority. He writes: "... September [11, 2001], was the beginning of the epics and was the reason [behind] preparing the ummah for these great enduring fronts in Iraq, Afghanistan and Somalia, where the greatest power in the world, the damned America failed, and which by Allah [will] rebirth the spirit of jihad among our ummah's youth, who has become [adept at] carrying the greatest elements for victory, empowerment [will] inherit the earth to establish [an] Islamic caliphate and [apply] the law of Allah on the earth. These elements are faith, immigration and jihad."

Furthermore, in an article entitled "Haqiqat al-Jahilyyah fi A'adam Tahkim al-Shari'a" ("the real ignorance is in not ruling by sharia"), he criticized contemporary Muslim clerics because they have forgotten the fundamentals of their religion, Shari'a rule, and the duty to wage jihad against the tyrants for the sake of their own mundane interests. Also, in demonstration of his Salafi-jihadi ideological credentials, he penned an article warning readers that he considered the Shia more "dangerous than others." His text went on to say that the Shiite aim to control the Arabian peninsula as proxies of the United States and Western interests. Al-Shihri then stated forebodingly that "our sympathizers [are] awaiting our orders for the next war."

Influence

The influence that al-Shihri has had on AQAP, apart from being the second man organizationally, seems to be significant on two levels: he is responsible for the funding channels of AQAP and for defining the organization's offensive strategy. On September 27, 2009, al-Arabiya reported a mobile message showing al-Shihri and another man pictured beside him calling on their followers to donate money to the cause of AQAP. He claimed, "The blessed jihad of your brothers in Yemen against the enemies of religion and the [enemies] of [the] people – the Jews and the Christians – needs lifeblood and the lifeblood of jihad is money…this is our brother, who is carrying this letter, [he] is [a] trusted man by us." Al-Arabiya revealed that the man who appeared with al-Shihri was Mohammed Abdulkarim al-Ghazali, a Yemeni jihadist wanted in Saudi Arabia, who is believed to be the same operative who facilitated the meeting of Abdullah al-Assiri and Prince Muhammad Bin Nayef in August 2009.

Furthermore, when the U.S. government arrested him, they charged al-Shihri with working for charities that had been designated as fronts for al-Qaeda. Also, the government's unclassified files on al-Shihri note that he was an "al-Qaeda travel facilitator" who would brief "others in Mashad, Iran on entry procedures into Afghanistan utilizing a certain crossing."

Regarding AQAP's hierarchy and mission, al-Shihri stated in his latest video message that the botched Christmas day suicide attack by 23 year-old Nigerian Umar Farouk Abdulmutallab on Northwest Airlines flight 253 that was flying between Amsterdam and Detroit was coordinated directly with Osama bin Laden. Furthermore, al-Shihri proclaimed in the same recording that AQAP has a strong desire to gain control over the Bab al-Mandab strait in coordination with the (al-Shabaab) mujahideen in Somalia in order to create an international incident by restricting the flow of oil with an aim to choke Israel, "because [the] USA [is] supporting [the Israelis] from there through the Red Sea."

These incidents indicate the level of influence that al-Shihri has had among al-Qaeda's new leadership. If the leader of AQAP, Nasir al-Wuhayshi, were to be captured or killed, al-Shihri is readily available to take his place far from the reach of the rule of law. In addition to his own jihadi credentials, it seems that al-Shihri's importance is steadily growing as he is in charge, operationally, of one of the most important branches of al-Qaeda. The fact that Yemen has recently gained notoriety as one of the most crucial areas where al-Qaeda is freely operating and aiming to create a safe haven can be largely credited to Sa'id al-Shihri. In less than one year, AQAP was able to prepare attacks outside of Yemen's borders either regionally (as the clever bin Nayef assassination attempt showed) or internationally, as the crude attempt by a young AQAP-trained Nigerian operative on Northwest 253 demonstrated.

[Original Publication: *Militant Leadership Monitor* 1 (2) – March 1, 2010]

Notes

1. The biography of Wafa'a al-Shihri (a.k.a. Um Hajer al-Azdi), who is described by Saudi media as "the first Saudi woman to join al-Qaeda," reflects how the Salafi-jihadist groups desire to create their own sub-communities in the societies they live in. Al-Shihri, after her divorce from her first husband, married one of Saudi security's most wanted, Abdul Rahman al-Ghamdi, who was killed in a confrontation with Saudi security forces in 2004 in the city of Taif. Then, her brother, Yusuf al-Shihri convinced her to marry his prison-mate in Guantanamo, Sa'id al-Shihri. Yusuf was killed by Saudi security forces in October 2009 while trying to sneak into Saudi Arabia from Yemen. Wafa'a al-Shihri left Riyadh in 2009 to reconnect with her husband, and her three children (one from each husband), in Yemen, where Sa'id received her, accompanied by her nephew (Yusuf's son) Abdulelah al-Shihri, the youngest member of al-Qaeda in Yemen. For further details see, Arabian Business, September 4, 2009. www.arabianbusiness.com/arabic/566763, also Saudi daily *al-Watan* [Riyadh], September 2, 2009. www.alwatan.com.sa/news/newsdetail.asp.

2. *Al-Watan*, September 7, 2009

3. Okaz [Jeddah], October 24, 2009. www.okaz.com.sa/new/Issues/20091024/Con20091024311434.htm

4. Ma'arb Press, February 16, 2010. marebpress.net/articles.php

5. For a description of his family's celebration upon his release, see al-Khothim's forum: kothimy.com/vb/showthread.php

6. Ma'arb Press, Op. Cit.

7. *Okaz*, October 24, 2009, www.okaz.com.sa/new/Issues/20091024/Con20091024311434.htm.

8. *Sada al-Malhim*, Issue 8, March/April, 2009.

9. *Sada al-Malhim*, Issue 10, June/July, 2009.

10. *Sada al-Malhim*, Issue 12, January/February, 2010.

11. Alarabiya.net, September 27, 2009.

12. Thomas Joscelyn,"Return to Jihad,"The Long War Journal,January 25, 2009, www.longwarjournal.org/archives/2009/01/return_to_jihad.php.

13. His speech can be found in this link 202.71.102.68/~alfaloj/vb/showthread.php February 8, 2010.

Back From the Grave: The Re-emergence of Houthi Rebel Leader Abdul Malik al-Houthi

By Michael Horton

Abdul Malik al-Houthi, the resilient leader of the Houthi rebellion in northwestern Yemen, was reported dead by a number of regional newspapers in the Arab realm as well as the Yemeni government in December 2009. However, recent reports indicate that Abdul Malik al-Houthi is alive and recovering from injuries suffered during an air raid (al-Jazeera, December 2009; *al-Thawra*, December 2009). Shortly after the Yemeni government claimed that Abdul Malik was dead, the Houthis, via their website "Sadahonline," released a video showing Abdul Malik alive and not obviously injured, though Iranian state media speculated that his left arm appeared immobilized (Press TV, January 23, 2010). The Yemeni government maintains that Abdul Malik was seriously injured and that Abdul Malik's deputy, Youssef al-Midani has assumed leadership of the Houthi movement. However, both the Yemeni and wider Arab and international press have reported that Abdul Malik was directly involved in the negotiation of the recent ceasefire and exchange of prisoners between the Yemeni government and the Houthis (*The Guardian*, March 19, 2010; *Asharq al-Awsat*, February 6, 2010).

The February-March 2010 ceasefire between the Houthis and the Yemeni government ended the sixth and most protracted round of fighting between the two belligerents. The most recent bout of fighting drew in the ground and air forces of Saudi Arabia (*Yemen Times*, November 9, 2009). The Houthi rebellion has its roots in the economic and cultural marginalization of the Zaidis inhabiting northern Yemen. Zaidism is a branch of Shiite Islam, although it is sometimes referred to as the fifth school of Sunni Islam due to its similarities with Sunnism. Zaidis make up roughly 35 percent of the Yemeni population. The movement now commonly referred to as the "Houthis" is a group of clans and tribes aligned with the Houthi clan, a prominent Hashemite family that traces its lineage back to the Prophet Muhammad. In June 2004, under the leadership of Hussein Badr al-Din al-Houthi (Abdul Malik's brother) an armed rebellion that centered around the northern town of Sadah broke out. Hussein Badr al-Din founded a group that called itself *al-Shabab al-Muminin* (*The Believing Youth*).

The group's agenda, never particularly well articulated, focused on defending Zaidi traditions against a perceived encroachment of Sunni and Salafi beliefs. The group claimed that the Zaidis in northern Yemen were the victims of prejudice and that their traditions and way of life were under attack by the Yemeni government led by President Ali Abdullah Saleh who is himself a Zaidi (al-Jazeera, November 16, 2009). The group also criticized the Saleh government for having close relations with the United States and for having deployed Salafi aligned groups against them. In response to the armed rebellion, the Yemeni government launched a punitive campaign against the Houthis resulting in the death of Hussein Badr al-Din in September 2004. Hussein Badr al-Din's octogenarian father, Badr al-Din al-Houthi, who has long been the group's spiritual leader, took over as titular head of the movement. Abdul Malik is thought to have taken over as military head of the movement in early 2005 (Jane's Intelligence Review, January 2010).

Abdul Malik al-Houthi is something of an enigma even to the Yemeni security services. Very little is known about his personal life or his origins other than the fact that he is 29 and has a reputation as a charismatic and thoughtful leader. He, like many senior members of the Houthi clan, is well schooled in Zaidi theology and more broadly in the Islamic sciences. In video and audio postings, Abdul Malik comes across as articulate and controlled (Sadahonline.com). After his brother's death in September 2004, Abdul Malik, who was already a senior military commander within the Houthi movement, took on a more direct leadership role. It is thought that he initially shared power with Abdullah Ayed al-Ruzami. However, due to his ability to plan and execute military operations, demonstrated in the successive campaigns from 2005-2008, he quickly assumed full command of the Houthi movement (*The National* [Abu Dhabi], August 21, 2009; author interviews in Yemen, December 2009). After a Qatari-brokered ceasefire crumbled in 2008, the Yemeni government launched an all out offensive against the Houthis. The Yemeni Army deployed more than 20,000 troops and an unknown number of men drawn from tribal levies. The Houthi fighters, who are thought to number no more than six thousand in 2008, were able to fight the Yemeni Army to a standstill yet again. Abdul Malik's ability to rally his followers and to rapidly deploy small groups of motivated well-trained fighters is credited with bringing the 2008 offensive to an end. In June 2009, nine expatriates working at the Jumhori hospital in Sadah province were kidnapped by unidentified gunmen that Sana'a labeled as Houthis (Yemen News Agency, June 14, 2009).

Ostensibly in response to the kidnapping, the Saleh government launched a campaign ominously entitled "Operation Scorched Earth" in August 2009 (al-Arabiya, August 29, 2009). The 2009 offensive involved as many as 40,000 regular Yemeni Army troops. On November 4, 2009, Saudi Arabia became officially drawn into the hostilities against the Houthis. Responding to an attack on a border post, the Saudi Air Force and Royal Saudi Land Force began operations along the Saudi-Yemeni border with the aim of securing the border and creating a *cordon sanitaire* (Jane's Intelligence Review, January 2010). Despite the involvement of significantly better-armed Saudi forces in addition to tens of thousands of Yemeni troops, the Houthis were able to largely fight both forces to another standstill. The Houthis captured and killed a number of Saudi troops and were able to capture significant amounts of material (BBC News, February 15, 2010; *Asharq al-Awsat*, November 27, 2009). However, the protracted offensive against the Houthis is thought to have significantly weakened their war-fighting capabilities. Abdul Malik's latest uprising plunged the region into chaos and displaced approximately 250,000 people from the Sadah region (*Gulf News*, February 19, 2010).

Conclusion

The bitter 2009-2010 campaign against the Houthis has only strengthened Abdul Malik's position as the movement's paramount chief. The Houthis' impressive performance against both Yemeni and Saudi conventional forces confirms that Abdul Malik has the ability to plan and implement complex guerrilla operations. The recent ceasefire and prisoner exchange have only added to Abdul Malik's reputation as both a military and political leader. Even the Yemeni ground troops that have been deployed against him acknowledge his prowess as a fighter and a leader (Author's interviews in Yemen, December 2009 and January 2010). As of this writing, President Saleh has declared his latest battle with Abdul Malik al-Houthi to have ended (*Yemen Times*, March 23, 2010) though locals remain skeptical after having seen several truces crumble in recent years (al-Jazeera, March 19, 2010), and with the Houthis, led by Abdul Malik, ready to return to the battlefield.

[Original Publication: *Militant Leadership Monitor* 1 (3) – March 31, 2010]

Adel al-Abbab: Al-Qaeda in the Arabian Peninsula's Religious Ideologue

By Murad Batal al-Shishani

Al-Qaeda in the Arabian Peninsula (AQAP) consists of several divisions: the *Shura* council, which is the highest authority of the organization; the Media division; the Military division; and the Sharia committee. Currently, it seems that AQAP relies on consensus rather than individuals in legitimizing its activities in Yemen. This committee includes individuals such as Ibrahim al-Rubaish, Khaled Batarfi (a.k.a. Abu Miqdad al-Kindi), and Adel al-Abbab (a.k.a. Abu al-Zubair) who is described as the pre-eminent figure concerned with the implementation of *Sharia* issues in AQAP's organizational hierarchy. This article represents a short biography of Adel al-Abbab and aims to highlight some of his ideas which seek to legitimize the deeds of AQAP in the eyes of his fellow travellers.

Background

Adel al-Abbab, whose full name is Adel Bin Abdullah Bin Thabit al-Abbab, is the son of a Yemeni preacher who was formerly an imam of a Sana'a mosque. As with most salafi-jihadist movements' ideologues or Sharia interpreters, Sheikh Abu al-Zubair al-Abbab, as he signs his statements, ironically studied at The Scientific Da'awa Centre for Sharia Sciences in Sana'a [1]. The Da'awa Center represents the traditional Salafi ideology in Yemen and holds strong disagreements with al-Qaeda and affiliated Salafi-jihadist movements. Although the fundamental ideas of both parties are the same, in the understanding of traditional salafis the involvement in earthly politics is forbidden and waging jihad is put off and permitted solely for defensive purposes. After his graduation from the Da'awa Center, Adel al-Abbab, stayed on working as a librarian [2]. He regularly took part in vigorous debates and became known for having strong disagreements with instructors and students at the Center [3]. Al-Abbab left his work in the months following a February 2006 jailbreak when 23 jihadists escaped from the central prison in Sana'a. Al-Qaeda in Yemen (later AQAP) was regrouping at that time. In July 2007, Yemeni authorities arrested al-Abbab's father (who was later released) and his three brothers in order to put pressure on him to surrender [4].

151

Since then, al-Abbab began to feature in AQAP's videos and his articles were published in *Sada al-Malahim* (The Echo of Battles), AQAP's journal. It is worth noting that al-Abbab, in both his written statements and disseminated messages, is looked upon as an authority as he always focuses on practical issues such as the judicial system in the Islamic state as jihadis understand it, how to impose Shari'a rule, and dispensing guidance to those wishing to partake in holy war.

The Importance of Shari'a Rule

Al-Abbab devotes a considerable amount of his writing to the importance of his notion of the dictatorial infidelity of Arab regimes, casting particular scorn on the Yemeni and Saudi regimes, as a method of questioning their legitimacy. In his widely circulated video speech entitled "Haqiqat al-Hukkam" (the Reality of the Rulers) [5], al-Abbab said, "The issue that no two persons will not disagree on, is that any [ruler] who places the law of *compassionate [Allah] by man's law* is a *Kaffir* committing the *Kufr al-Akbar* [6] …today, we see the rulers of the [Arabian] Peninsula have replaced Islam with secularism, and this by itself is *kufr* (unbelief) and apostasy…The United Nation's system is based on the abolition of *Sharia*, and abolition of *Hudood* (Islamic punishments for serious offenses) which [when implemented] save lives."

In the same message, al-Abbab lists five reasons why it's legitimate to name Arabian Peninsular rulers as Kaffirs:

1. Their alliance with the West against mujahideen, which is considered to be "taking part in the so-called War on Terrorism." Al-Abbab considered this alliance *walla'a* (allegiance) to "crusaders" and *bara'a* (disloyalty) to Muslims.

2. The opening of "spying" offices to monitor mujahideen and all Muslims through CIA and FBI offices in the Gulf states such as Qatar, UAE and Yemen.

3. Their promotion of "infidel" sects and secularism.

4. Protecting and advocating American and Western troops on the Red Sea coast as well as opening bases for non-Muslim troops everywhere in the Gulf.

5.   Finally, al-Abbab considers Gulf state rulers *Kaffirs* because of their tolerance of newspapers and global satellite channels that al-Abbab claims curse Allah and mock the Prophet Muhammad.

The Infidel Regimes

In this context, al-Abbab, wrote an article on *Sada al-Jihad* (Echo of Holy War) magazine (Issue 10, Rajab 1430), offering practical steps on how to establish Shari'a rule when confronted with a regime of infidels seeking to avoid it, and in particular the kinds of acts which legitimate waging jihad against them. Al-Abbab lists thirteen ways to advance the establishment of Shari'a rule:

First: Believe in Allah and propagate monotheism.

Second: Jihad in the sake of Allah.

Third: Increase awareness of Allah's rule among people in the Arabian Peninsula.

Fourth: Isolate the Arabian Peninsula's rulers.

Fifth: Prepare by [acquiring] weapons and power.

Sixth: Secure funding through means that are accepted by Islam   such as spoils and *Zakat*, etc., and send them to the mujahideen in order to facilitate their fight to establish Shari'a rule.

Seventh: Activate the role of preachers and imams in educating people of the benefits of Shari'a rule using all possible platforms such as the Jumma'a speech (the sermon that follows Friday prayer sessions), seminars, lectures and other means.

Eighth: Direct Quranic teachers to implement Shari'a rule and fight to imbue the importance of it in the minds of young pupils.

Ninth: The proper Muslim family must take better care to raise their children knowing that establishing Shari'a rule is a must, and indoctrinate them with the urge to establish the Caliphate.

Tenth: Each Muslim has to support the mujahideen in waging jihad to establish Shari'a rule, and must respond to Western media by circulating the mujahideen publications, audios and videos.

Eleventh: Fulfilling the duty enjoining good and forbidding evil.

Twelfth: Expanding the circle of sympathizers of Shari'a rule.

Thirteenth: Calling for Shari'a rule in all manner of social and religious occasions.

Al-Abbab justifies targeting embassies in the Arab world on the basis of the same argument. He considers these embassies to be "dens of conspiracy", operating against the mujahideen. In a video seminar about the September 17, 2008 attack on the U.S. Embassy in Sana'a, he rationalized the killing of Muslims employed as guards for theses embassies, singling out the U.S. embassy in particular. He stated that the U.S. embassy in Yemen has CIA and FBI offices that are waging war against mujahideen and that the embassy is actively recruiting Yemenis to work against the mujahideen in selecting specific people in Yemen for targeted assassination. Furthermore, in aiming to mobilize culturally conservative Yemenis, al-Abbab alleged that the American Ambassador to Yemen at the time, Thomas Krajeski, said that he will focus on Aden and had observed beautiful women there [7].

Conclusion

It is clear that al-Qaeda and like-minded Salafi-jihadis started to go about relying on committees rather than on individuals for the issuing of fatwas and religious justifications of their activities. This seems to indicate that AQAP has begun to pay closer attention to the importance of religious justification for their actions. In this context, al-Abbab is a key personality within the clerical quarter of AQAP. What makes him significant is that he neatly presents a well-packaged Islamist opinion in a way that is easy to grasp for those less educated in the rigid Sunni jurisprudence that he is adept at promulgating in both his writings and media statements.

Al-Abbab is trying to differentiate his view on the importance of the establishment of Shari'a rule from the elite's version of the debate by taking large sections from the Quran as well as the Hadiths (statements attributed to the

Prophet Muhammed) and putting them into an easily digestible rhetoric for the public's consumption. This simplified jihad-speak displays and emphasizes the importance that al-Qaeda is putting on Yemen as a potential safe haven for their ranks and also why they are appealing and directing their rhetoric to the broader public in the region.

It is obvious that the mufti or religious leader has become an essential role for al-Qaeda and other Salafi-jihadi groups, particularly in Arabian Peninsula. The Saudi regime, itself as an outwardly conservative *wahabbi* institution, maintains a policy of rebuffing al-Qaeda thought in the Kingdom based on denouncing the organization's religious credentials or lack thereof and now al-Qaeda's ideologues. This could explain why, perhaps, al-Qaeda and affiliated groups insist on attracting and then posting religious educated graduates in their leadership milieu. Issa bin Sa'ad al-Oshan, who was killed by Saudi forces in Riyadh on July 21, 2004; Abdullah al-Rashoud was declared dead in Iraq on June 23, 2005 by the late Abu Musab al-Zarqawi; Faris Shuwayl al-Zahrani (a.k.a. Abu Jandal al-Azdi) who has been in a Saudi prison since August 2004; and al-Abbab's colleague in Yemen, the Saudi Ibrahim al-Rubaish (*Terrorism Monitor* November 25, 2009) were all schooled in Shari'a law. This indicates that al-Qaeda requires a specific Islamic pedigree for the men responsible for Shari'a issues inside the movement. It is thought these credentials may help to bolster al-Qaeda's religious *bona fides* and Adel al-Abbab appears to be playing a major role in the simplification of al-Qaeda's sometimes convoluted rhetoric in order to attract more Yemenis and Saudis from the peninsula.

[Original Publication: *Militant Leadership Monitor* 1 (3) – March 31, 2010]

Notes

1. See the Dawa Center's Arabic-language website: http://www.dawacenter.net/
2. For the original Arabic, see: http://www.muslm.net/vb/showthread.php?t=344678 May 5, 2009.
3. For the original Arabic, see http://www.majahden.info/showthread.php?t=20573 November 4, 2009.
4. Ibid
5. For the original Arabic, see: http://www.ukht-benladn.net/news-14.html Thow al-Qi'ida 1430 (October 2009)
6. The major *kufr* who is excluded from the fold of Islam.
7. For the original Arabic see: http://www.al-yemen.org/vb/showthread.php?p=5271142 November 29, 2009.

AQAP's Man in the South: Nasir al-Wuhayshi

By Rafid Fadhil Ali

In January 2009, Nasir al-Wuhayshi (a.k.a. Abu Basir) appeared on a video to announce the merger between al-Qaeda branches in Saudi Arabia and Yemen under his command. The new organization was given the name Qaedat al-Jihad in the Arabian Peninsula, or al-Qaeda in the Arabian Peninsula (AQAP). Al-Wuhayshi was surrounded by three leaders of AQAP, his fellow Yemeni Qasim al-Raymi, who was reportedly killed in an airstrike in January 2010 (*Yemen Observer*, January 16, 2010) and the Saudis Said al-Shihri and Mohammed al-Ofi. Each of the four men made a statement about the evolution of their group (Al-Jazeera, January 29, 2009) [1]. The leadership of AQAP made it clear that, in addition to targeting the near enemy in Sana'a and Riyadh, it would target Western interests and ultimately the West itself. But before the end of 2009, the organization went even further, conducting the most serious terrorist operation to affect the American homeland since 9/11.

Nasir Abdul Kareem al-Wuhayshi was born 34 years ago in the town of Mukayris, which was part of the South Yemeni governorate of Abyan. The area is now part of the northern governorate of al-Bayda after Yemen was united in 1990. In a rare interview with the Yemeni journalist Abdulelah Hider al-Shaea [2], al-Wuhayshi talked about his personal history after he decamped from his native Yemen and traveled to Afghanistan in the mid-1990s:

I stayed in the Taliban's Afghanistan for about five years. With Allah's grace we lived under that state... After we withdrew from Torah Bora in 2002, I left Afghanistan and went to Iran. I stayed in the areas of the Sunni community inside Iran until the rafidah [2] arrested me. The Iranians kept me in custody for about one month and a half and then turned me over to the Yemeni government.

During those five years al-Wuhayshi was Osama bin Laden's secretary. But this fact remained hidden until al-Wuhayshi assumed his position as the leader of al-Qaeda in Yemen. He became the head of the group (amir) while in prison in 2006.

While the group was struggling after a series of setbacks between 2003 and 2006, al-Wuhayshi and 22 other inmates escaped from their prison in Sana'a in

February 2006 (*Asia Times*, January 8, 2010). Although many of the runners surrendered, were captured or killed, al-Wuhayshi and his most trusted lieutenant Qasim al-Raymi (a.k.a Abu Hurayrah al-San'ani) stayed on the run and managed to rebuild the organization. The group developed significantly under al- Wuhayshi. (see *Terrorism Focus*, March 18, 2008), launching a number of attacks, mainly on tourists and Yemeni forces but also on the American embassy in Sana'a, which it attacked twice in 2008 (Alwasatnews.com, September 18, 2008).

As a leader of al-Qaeda's branch in Yemen, al-Wuhayshi has been very ambitious. In 2008, the group changed its name to al-Qaeda in South Arabian Peninsula. The escalating economic and military difficulties the Yemeni government of President Ali Abdullah Saleh was facing created the circumstances that al-Wuhayshi needed to consolidate the presence of his group; Yemen was under pressure from the Houthi rebellion in the north and the secessionist movement in the south.

Under al-Wuhayshi, AQAP has been very adept at producing its own brand of literature and propaganda. The group started its bi-monthly magazine *Sada al-Malahim* (The Echo of Battles) in late 2007. In addition to al-Wuhayshi, many leaders, scholars and activists of AQAP contribute to the online publication, which can be found on various Islamist websites. The content propagates AQAP's views on contemporary and theological issues facing those in the convoluted jihadist landscape.

Al-Qaeda's New Weapon

The failed assassination attempt on the Saudi Deputy Interior Minister Mohammed bin Nayef was executed using a bizarre a new weapon. The assassin, Mohammed al-Assiri (a.k.a Abu al-Khair) was able to pass through the security search with explosives planted inside his body. When he met with bin Nayef, in the Prince's own house, he looked clean and clear to the guards (see *Militant Leadership Monitor*, February 2010).

Al-Wuhayshi then urged his followers to use the new formula and tactic. In the eleventh issue of *Sada al-Malahim*, published in September-October 2009, al-Wuhayshi's wrote an article entitled "War is deception." It centred on lauding the assassination attempt on bin Nayef. But al-Wuhayshi also outlined the new tactic, to be used again about two months later in a failed attack by Omar al-Farooq Abdulmutallab, a young Nigerian student trained in Yemen, who, on Christmas

157

Day 2009, tried to blow up an airplane traveling between Amsterdam and Detroit just minutes before it landed. Al-Wuhayshi wrote:

You do not need to make a big effort or a huge amount of money to manufacture 10 Grams or so of these explosives. And do not waste much time looking for the raw material, they are in your mother's kitchen. Manufacture it as a bomb to throw, a time bomb, an electric device, a picture, a paper folder or an envelope.

More significantly, al-Wuhayshi went on to list the favorite targets for such attacks including airplanes and airports:

Blow it up on any target of evil; intelligence headquarters, a prince, a minister, a crusader (Christian especially Western) wherever you find those. Also explode them in the airports or the airlines of the western crusade countries which participated in the war against Islam. Or target residential compounds or underground trains of those countries. You will find the way if you think and depend on Allah. And do not worry that those explosives could be discovered after you hide them properly. It is impossible to discover them.

AQAP refuses to label the two attacks as thwarted efforts. They argue that they both succeeded on the grounds that they shocked aviation security and returned America to the atmosphere of anxiety and fear spawned by 9/11, despite the untold sums of taxpayer funds and manpower efforts that have been spent since that era to consolidate the security situation.

The Palestinian Question

Long before the emergence of al-Qaeda, the Palestinian question has been a central challenge within circles of Salafi-jihadi thought in the Muslim world. They frequently had to answer fellow Muslims asking different versions of the same question: why do you not fight the Israelis in Palestine?

Al-Wuhayshi has placed the ongoing Palestinian crisis at the centerpiece of his propaganda campaign. A video accnouncing the merger of the Saudi and Yemeni branches of al-Qaeda to form AQAP contained the wording, "From here we will begin and in al-Aqsa we shall meet," referring to al-Aqsa mosque in heavily disputed Jerusalem. In the video, he stressed that Palestine has always been the cause that al-Qaeda has fought for, even when it was waging jihad on differing fronts. He echoed Abu Musab al-Zarqawi's words that while fighting in Iraq, he never took his eye off of Jerusalem (*al-Quds* in Arabic), and stressed that Osama bin Laden swore that America will remain unsafe until the people of Palestine are safe. But al-Wuhayshi's vision for his group's involvement in the Israeli-Palestinian conflict is typical of the indirect approach of the wider al-Qaeda grand strategy:

> *We went to Afghanistan in order to prepare for the liberation of Palestine but, before we enter Palestine, we have to break the blockade that the Arab rulers, the betrayers, are imposing on it…. Also, the actual supporters of the Israeli occupation are America and Europe. So we have to destroy the Crusaders' interests in the Arabian Peninsula, including Yemen, and prepare the generation that the Prophet Mohammed said would come out of Yemen to liberate al-Aqsa mosque.*

South Yemen

AQAP is more active and operative in the eastern and southern governorates, which historically made up the People's Democratic Republic of Yemen (otherwise known simply as South Yemen or PDRY) until the unity of Yemen in 1990. The frustration and resentment of the population in those governorates, against what they consider a northern domination by President Saleh's regime, provided AQAP with the population-centric *raison d'etre* that they needed to operate against Saleh. Al-Wuhayshi, who is from the south himself, supported the struggle of the South Yemenis but condemned both Saleh and the former Marxist rulers of South Yemen, the leaders of the Yemeni Socialist Party who currently lead the secessionist movement (see *Terrorism Monitor*, November 19, 2009). Future developments in Yemen's southern governorates will play a major role in the future of al-Wuhayshi's organization. While President Saleh still has a considerable amount of support from the tribes in the north, minus those supporting the Houthi rebellion in the Saada governorate, his southern support has been on the wane for some time as evidenced by the increase in north-south agitation by southern political actors.

Conclusion

After the attempt made by Abdulmuttalleb and the shooting spree of Nidal Malik Hasan [3], particularly the AQAP link with both, al-Wuhayshi and his group have found themselves at the center of the international conflict between America and the salafi-jihadists. The impact of the three airstrikes last year on Abyan, Arhab and Shabwa have yet to be completely understood [4]. AQAP denied that al-Wuhayshi was killed in one of them but he did not release a statement and he did not compose his usual editorial in *Sada al-Malahim's* January-February 2010 issue. Al-Wuhayshi succeeded in rebuilding and reordering al-Qaeda in Yemen, benefiting from the difficulties that President Saleh's regime faces on the economic and security fronts. He also can be credited for the successes of a major regional organization by unifying the Yemeni and Saudi branches of al-Qaeda. But this honeymoon phase is now over and Nasir al-Wuhayshi and his group are facing more direct challenges by virtue of increased American, Saudi and international support for the Yemeni government. The capacity and developments of this conflict will be of critical importance to the regional and international scene for years to come.

[Original Publication: *Militant Leadership Monitor* 1 (4) – April 30, 2010]

Notes

1. Video footage available on Youtube.
2. A derisive term denoting Shi'ites used by Sunni militants; in this case implying the Iranian authorities.
3. The interview was placed on al-Shayea's blog on May 14, 2009, Abdulela.maktoobblog.com.
4. On November 5, 2009, the American Major Nidal Malik Hasan opened fire on the Fort Hood camp in Texas, killing 13 of his colleagues. Hasan, a Muslim of Palestinian descent, is believed to have had contacts with the Yemeni-based radical cleric Anwar al-Awlaki.
5. On December 17, 2009, an airstrike by the United States followed by a raid by the Yemeni ground forces was launched on a suspected al-Qaeda target in Abyan. Another airstrike hit a target in the city of Arhab in the Sana'a governorate. On December 23, 2009, yet another strike occurred on targets in Shabwa. Dozens were killed in those offensives including women and children according to both Arab and international media. (al-Jazeera, December 18, 2009, AFP, December 23, 2009). AQAP claimed that the Christmas day attempt by Umar Farouk Abdulmuttalab was launched in response to these air strikes.

Chapter Four
The Houthi Rebellions

Shiite Insurgency in Yemen: Iranian Intervention or Mountain Revolt?

By Andrew McGregor

In the midst of growing political tensions between Iran and the United States a Shiite rebellion in the remote mountains of northwest Yemen has created suspicions that Iran may be attempting to open a new anti-American front to weaken U.S. efforts in the region. Yemen's president, Ali Abdullah Saleh, has been a resolute ally of the U.S. in the War on Terrorism, but has used the alliance to reverse a once-promising democratic reform process. After a short truce fierce fighting has resumed, as President Saleh sought to eliminate resistance from the radical Shiite movement. This new conflict follows similar expeditions in the past few years against well-armed groups of Sunni militants.

The Zaidi Shiites

Yemen's Zaidi Shiites are well known for passionate loyalty to their Imams (traditional dual religious/political leaders) but are regarded as moderate in their practice of Islam. With the reported growth of the rabidly anti-Shiite al-Qaeda organization in Yemen, it has been suggested that Iran may intervene in support of the Zaidi Shiite. In the past, Sunni veterans of the anti-Soviet jihad in Afghanistan were used to control any resurgence of the Zaidi Shiite, from whom the old royal family was drawn [1]. Zaidi Shi'ism is one of three main branches of the Shiite movement, together with Twelver Shi'ism and the Isma'ili branch. Unlike the other branches, the Zaidis are restricted almost solely to the Yemen area. Their form of Shari'a law follows the Sunni Hanafi school, which aids in their integration with the Yemeni Sunnis.

The Saada uprising has a more traditional character than most of the modern Islamist militant organizations, which are led largely by military veterans and

161

professionals such as doctors and engineers. The mountain revolt is led by a Zaidi religious figure, Hussein al-Houthi, who leads a student movement committed to Islamic reform called the *Shabab al-Muminin* ("The Believing Youth"). Al-Houthi was a member of Yemen's parliament from 1993-97. Unconnected to the mainstream of Sunni radicalism, al-Houthi is a fierce opponent of al-Qaeda, which cemented its anti-Shiite reputation by participating in the Taliban's massacres of Afghan Shiites. Like the Sunni militants, however, al-Houthi's most scathing invective is reserved for America and Israel, whom al-Houthi alleges are conducting an anti-Muslim campaign throughout the Middle East. Al-Houthi has urged his followers to prepare for a U.S. invasion of Yemen. Democracy is viewed as a trick to complete the Zionist domination of the Arab world. Even among the Zaidis, support for al-Houthi is far from universal; while refuting charges of Iranian support for the insurgency, al-Houthi's brother, a member of parliament, called the religious leader a "criminal" and an international embarrassment [2].

Al-Houthi's insurrection is not aimed at spreading Zaidi Shi'ism, but is rather an expression of dissatisfaction with President Saleh's pro-American policies. Al-Houthi describes President Saleh as "a tyrant… who wants to please America and Israel, by sacrificing the blood of his own people," [3] while the President describes al-Houthi as "sick and mentally abnormal" [4].

War in the Mountains

The insurgency began June 18, 2004. Since then the government has unleashed the full force of its arsenal of jets, armour and artillery to pound the lightly armed "Believers." On July 23, 2004, operations were suspended to allow religious scholars a last chance to cross the lines and convince al-Houthi of the mistakenness of his rebellion. Negotiations with al-Houthi have failed in the past, but with Yemen's existence relying on a delicate balance of tribal allegiances there is usually a preference for negotiated settlement. Many believe that the President's insistence on a military solution derives from the rude reception he received on a visit to the mountains earlier this year.

The campaign against al-Houthi was expected to be quick, but the Shiite fighters have lived up to their warrior reputation, giving fierce resistance to what should have been an overwhelming government force. Government troops have had to struggle up passes similar to the one where a well-equipped column of 10,000 Saada-bound Ottoman troops was wiped out by the Zaidis in 1904. The savagery of the fighting and the number of casualties on both sides (300-400 dead so far) has been a shock to many Yemenis. Though the Shabab al-Muminin are only somewhere between 1,000 to 3,000 in number, many Yemenis believe that al-Hourthi is only giving voice to opinions widely shared in Yemen.

In urban areas like Sana'a, however, there is some disdain for yet another Mahdist-style movement that will come to a bad end for its superstition-fed adherents. Even Abdul Majid al-Zindani, leader of the radical wing of the Islamist Islah party, has warned against the "serious consequences of extremism and all forms of fanaticism, which are the major reason behind the civilizational decline and backwardness of the Muslim nation" [5]. A powerful political figure and a former comrade of bin Laden during the Afghanistan war against the Soviets, al-Zindani has recently been accused of collecting funds for al-Qaeda, only to be strongly defended by President Saleh. Like many of Yemen's clerics, al-Zindani called for a Muslim jihad against American and British troops in the early days of last year's Iraq campaign.

The ruling General People's Congress Party has accused Iran of direct support for the Saada uprising as an effort to create a new front to drain U.S. resources in anticipation of American attacks on Iran and the Hezbollah of southern Lebanon. The President has personally avoided naming Iran, but left little doubt to whom he was referring in making charges of interference by 'foreign intelligence agencies.' There have also been suggestions that al-Houthi has received financial assistance from the Shiite communities of Kuwait and the United Arab Emirates. The insinuation of Iranian involvement came only days after the signing of several new economic agreements between Iran and Yemen and the extension of a 10 million Euro credit by Iran following the conclusion of the 7th meeting of the Yemen-Iran Committee, a forum for bilateral relations.

In Yemen's long civil war of the 1960s, Iran gave financial aid and a small quantity of arms to the Royalist government of the Zaidi Imam, though its contribution was small compared to that of Sunni Saudi Arabia. The Shah's help had less to do with Shiite fellowship than with hindering the regional ambitions of Gamal Abdel Nasser, who had already deployed the United Arab Republic army on the Republican side. The Republicans were themselves dominated by a mainly Zaidi officer corps and most Shiite and Sunni tribes were usually just a bribe away from changing sides. For the most part, the Arab Zaidis of Yemen have continued to evolve in isolation from their Shiite brethren in Iran.

Then outgoing U.S. Ambassador to Yemen Edmund Hull recently expressed satisfaction with Yemen's anti-terrorist efforts while suggesting that conditions in Saada province made it rife for penetration by elements of al-Qaeda. Hull's critics in Yemen accuse the ambassador of running autonomous counterterrorism operations within Yemen, though both the ambassador and the government insist that their operations are fully coordinated. Hull, the survivor of several assassination attempts, was recently described by a Yemen columnist as "the ambassador who did not give a damn for diplomacy" [6].

Alliance with Saudi Arabia

Efforts have been made to cooperate with Saudi forces in securing the poorly defined and largely unpopulated Yemen-Saudi border in order to prevent the infiltration of Islamist militants fleeing Saudi Arabia's own crackdown. Saudi Arabia has also long complained of the traffic in arms from Yemen. The Saudis' construction of a security barrier along the border has outraged opposition groups in Yemen, who compare it to Israel's wall in the West Bank. Official relations between the Saudi kingdom and Yemen have rarely been closer than they are now. In July 2004, Saudi Arabia returned to Yemen over 40,000 square kilometers (mostly in eastern Hadramaut province) in accordance with the border treaty of 2000. On July 24, 2004, both nations exchanged 15 suspected terrorists for prosecution. Questions have arisen over just how far the new Saudi-Yemeni cooperation extends. The Saudis denied charges last month from al-Houthi's camp that the Saudi Air Force was involved in a joint Yemen-Saudi bombing campaign that destroyed several villages. The death of numerous Zaidi civilians in air and artillery attacks has brought the attention of Amnesty International, which has asked the Yemen Interior Ministry for an investigation.

Conclusion

By summer 2004, a movement appeared growing within some parts of the U.S. administration to identify Iran as a growing threat to U.S. interests, alleging Iranian aid to al-Qaeda before and after the 9/11 attacks. In making links between Iran and the Zaidi insurgency there is a tendency to integrate Shiite movements within a vertical command structure (with Tehran at the top) that does not accurately reflect historical, social, linguistic, ethnic and even religious differences between the branches of Shiite Islam.

Iran weathered similar political storms during the invasions of Afghanistan and Iraq with surprising patience, perhaps expecting the U.S. to exhaust itself before it can strike Iran. Despite the encouragement of Israel, the U.S. is unlikely in the short term to take military measures against Iran, a much larger and formidable adversary than Iraq. The usefulness of the Saada rebellion as an Iranian counter-strategy is questionable; the uprising is not large enough to influence the balance of power in the region or to draw away significant American resources in the way a general Sunni rising would. The attractions of militancy to a traditionally conservative and moderate community should sound a warning that the Saleh government may be leading Yemen into a period of renewed civil conflict that may easily spill into the international arena.

A more important threat remains from Yemen's Sunni extremists. On July 1, 2004, the Abu Hafs al-Masri Brigade threatened to drag the United States into 'a third quagmire' in Yemen (after Afghanistan and Iraq) with the cooperation of local Islamist groups. Yemen's Sunni radicals played a prominent role in the growth of al-Qaeda; the region may continue to provide an important source of manpower for international terrorist operations. Homegrown militant groups like the Islamic Army of Aden also continue to provide military challenges to the Saleh government. With U.S. forces unexpectedly overextended in Iraq, the U.S. has so far avoided a large-scale military commitment in Yemen, preferring to aid the Yemen regime in its own local war against Islamist extremism.

Yemen's experiment with democracy is withering as Saleh, president since 1978, attempts to create dynastic rule at the head of a one-party state. Lately Saleh has attempted to reverse the process of integrating Islamists into the government. The pro-U.S. position of the President (and its offer of troops for service in Iraq) is hardly a representation of popular sentiment in Yemen. Saleh's control of Yemen will be sorely tested in the days ahead as the government simultaneously tries suspects in the 2000 bombing of the U.S.S. Cole and the 2002 attack on the French tanker Limburg.

Saleh has established a pattern of playing off Islamists against Socialists, with the intention of eliminating both as potential opponents of the GPC. While Saleh grooms his son as his successor, Yemen threatens to become a replica of the hereditary Ba'athist presidencies of Iraq and Syria. The stifling of democracy and the alienation of Islamists from the political process are contributing factors to the radicalization of Yemen's Sunni majority. With new challenges from a revival of Southern separatism and the unexpected insurgency in the Zaidi heartland, Yemen has become a new Middle Eastern tinderbox.

[Original Publication: *Terrorism Monitor* 2 (16) – August 12, 2004]

Notes

1. The Zaidi Imams ruled Yemen from the ninth century until 1962, with interruptions. The Shiites represent roughly 40% of Yemen's 20 million people.

2. John R Bradley: "A warning from Yemen, cradle of the Arab world," *Daily Star* (Beirut), July 13, 2004.

3. "Yemeni preacher speaks out against Saleh," Agence France Press, July 22, 2004.

4. "Yemeni President: al-Houthi is an ill man, mentally abnormal," *Arab News*, July 9, 2004, arabicnews.com/ansub/Daily/Day/040709/2004070905.html

5. Mohammed al-Qadhi, "Islah warns of Sa'ada events consequences: Criticism of U.S. accusations against al-Zindani," *Yemen Times*, July 23, 2004

6. Hassan al-Zaidi, "Yemen bids farewell to Ambassador Hull," *Yemen Times*, July 26-28, 2004, yementimes.com/article.shtml

Yemeni Rebel Leader Al-Houthi Slain

By Stephen Ulph

Yemeni government sources formally announced on September 10, 2004 the end of the rebellion under Zaidi Shiite tribal chief Hussein Badr al-Din al-Houthi. This follows the killing of al-Houthi and his brother as the result of an attack on their hideout in the region of Sha'ab Salman in Saada province near the Saudi border, 150 miles north of the capital Sana'a. Their deaths mark the termination of a three-month punitive campaign, which has killed up to 600 civilians, rebels and troops.

Since the outbreak of the rebellion on June 18, 2004, al-Houthi had directed his followers, the *Shabab al-Muminin* ("The Believing Youth"), in a vigorous guerrilla campaign characterized above all by its anti-U.S. sloganeering, and rejection of Washington's policies in Iraq and the wider region. As a Yemeni local issue and – due to doctrinal antagonism – unconnected with al-Qaeda inspired groups in the country, the rebellion looked to the Lebanese Shiite Hezbollah for an operational model, and has been suspected of Iranian support. Its military muscle was trained and indoctrinated in unauthorized religious schools where, according to Sana'a, a policy was taught of armed resistance to central authority and a program for the restoration of the long-abolished monarchy.

While the government of Ali Abdullah Saleh is counting on exploiting a significant boost to prestige, which may enable it to promote further the disarmament program in a country where weapons outnumber population three to one, the potential for further conflict remains. Al-Houthi's scattered supporters vow to fight on. "The issue will not be ended by the death of Sheikh Al-Houthi" a source close to al-Houthi said, "Many will adopt the cause for the sake of which Al-Houthi was martyred...War will continue endlessly, and the authority will not find rest unless it answers their crucial and lawful demands" (September 13-15, 2004, *Yemen Times*). Despite such comments, the likelihood of a reprise of the fighting soon on this scale is small. However, a three-month armed rebellion of up to 3,000 insurgents building its momentum on little more than vaguely defined antagonism to the U.S. (which is not an occupier of the country) should give some pause for thought.

[Original Publication: *Terrorism Focus* 1 (4) – September 16, 2004]

Understanding the Second Houthi Rebellion in Yemen

By Shaun Overton

The year 2004 witnessed a lengthy battle between *Shabab al-Muminin* ("The Believing Youth"), a Shiite religious organization, and the Yemeni government. Shabab al-Muminin's leader and inspirational figure, Hussein Badr al-Din al-Houthi, was killed in early September 2004 and his death marked the end of that conflict. The fighting, however, staged a short-lived comeback in March-May of 2005.

Tensions between Shabab al-Muminin and the government renewed when al-Houthi's father, who shares the name of his son, returned to Saada from Sana'a in mid-March 2005. He cited the president's refusal to meet with him over the release of prisoners as the reason for his return [1]. In a March 9, 2005 interview, al-Houthi made a public appeal for the president to "make good on his promises," chief among them the release of al-Houthi followers from prison [2]. Later, on March 19, 2005 al-Houthi claimed that after the first war, the president invited him to Sana'a promising that if he came, he would release all prisoners and cease military and legal action against all of his followers. Al-Houthi first arrived in Sana'a in January 2005.

The fighting broke out on March 20, 2005 between Shabab al-Muminin and the Yemeni government at Souk at-Talh, 14 kilometers outside of Saada. The fighting quickly escalated, spreading to Wadi Nashoor, Razamat and al-Shafa'a, all of which are rural areas surrounding the city of Saada. The government brought in heavy equipment, including tanks and artillery. The fighting largely culminated from March 29, 2005 to April 3, 2005, where the dead numbered well over 100, and a major firefight occurred within the actual city of Saada [3]. By April 7, 2005, Yemeni forces had the second in command surrounded. He died five days later [4].

A week after the government announced the end of hostilities on April 14, 2005, al-Houthi supporters continued sniper attacks in scattered areas around Saada province. The rebels managed to disperse their attacks, moving into the tribal area of Khowlan and within the capital city of Sana'a. There they conducted a series of drive-by grenade attacks and assassination attempts, the last of which was on May 13, 2005.

The end of the attacks in mid May 2005 fully coincides with the Political Security Organization's successful penetration of Houthi supporters in Sana'a.

Left without any further resources, al-Houthi sent a letter asking for pardon. President Saleh agreed in principle on May 14, 2005 [5]. Al-Houthi has yet to surrender, though negotiations continue.

Goals

Al-Houthi, despite his emphatic denials, seems to desire the establishment of an imamate in Yemen. He and his son are Hashimites, the family of the prophet Muhammad. While denying that the purpose of Shabab al-Muminin is to establish an imamate, al-Houthi the father clearly states his beliefs when responding to questions about democracy. According to him, there are two forms of legitimate government: an imamate ruled by Hashimites or rule by any pious Muslim. He made his views clearer when directly confronted, stating that an imamate is the most preferred form of government. Al-Houthi takes pains to distance himself from the idea of democracy, saying "We are for justice. We do not know this democracy you speak of" [6].

Whether Shabab al-Muminin has a coherent political program remains unclear. Aside from the imamate as the ideal form of government, it seems to encompass a general feeling of disenfranchisement against numerous causes. Hussein al-Houthi the son distributed a great amount of literature denouncing the role of America in the world and specifically the Yemeni government's newfound cooperation with it. Al-Houthi the father claims in his interview with *al-Wasat* that the entire purpose of the first rebellion was a defense of Islam against America. When directly prompted about the government's attitude to the Hashimite family, and by inference its Shiite members, al-Houthi responds that the authorities hate the Shiite. A multifaceted dislike of the government is perhaps the best explanation for the al-Houthi rebellions.

Iran

Concerns over Iran are related to al-Houthi the son's 1993 meeting with the Iranian president. Al-Houthi the father visited Iran in 2003 and is accused of fleeing to Iran during the first al-Houthi rebellion in 2004.

It is likely that there is some sort of a relationship between Shabab al-Muminin and Iran. It appears from al-Houthi's interview that he frames the conflict in terms of Shiite versus other. He clearly feels an affinity toward the Islamic Republic, as evidenced by his family's numerous visits. Knowing that he sees

America as an enemy of Islam, he likely identifies Iran as a Shiite pillar of strength actively combating their mutual enemy.

He knows, however, that actively and openly acknowledging Iranian support brings with it a host of difficulties. There is a traditional Arab-Persian antagonism. The idea of using Iranian support to bring down any Arab government would not play well among any Arab populace, especially in Sunni dominated Yemen. Open support would also entangle the Iranians, who are currently in a tense diplomatic situation with the U.S. and Europe over their nuclear program.

It is likely that Iran gives limited forms of support to Shabab al-Muminin in spite of the lack of clear benefits to the country. Iran has a lengthy history of supporting conflicts motivated by ideology, most notably Hezbollah in Lebanon. The power benefits in that conflict are clearer. By weakening Israel, Iran gains credibility among all Muslims and more influence in a contentious region of the world. In Yemen, however, supporting the al-Houthi rebellion brings a number of diplomatic risks with only minimal return. No oil exists in the Shiite areas of Yemen and the region has a long history of being irrelevant to world politics. The only clear benefit to Iranian support is proving its ideological commitment to itself and other Shiite.

Conclusion

The settlement appears to have only fractured the Houthi leadership without fully eliminating or uncovering its supporters. An article in *Asharq al-Awsat* dated May 15, 2005, notes that the security services have not fully uncovered all the cells of the Shabab al-Muminin. The security services claim the organization was formed in 1984. If true, the twenty-year duration of the organization would serve to discourage its members from simply abandoning its ideas, especially with the heavy casualties that have been inflicted on it recently.

On the surface the conflict is religious, but such a broad statement ignores the complex relationships that determine social and political life in northern Yemen. It is better understood as a balance of tribal affiliation with religious leadership. While the number of fighters supporting al-Houthi appears significant – at least in the hundreds judging from the number of dead – these military operations could never happen without the strong support of tribal leaders in the area. Ideology does play a limited role in their support, though their primary motivation stems from the opportunity to further diminish the government's limited influence in the region.

The current resolution merely removes a tribal means for active rebellion. The leadership and infrastructure for rebellion, the Shabab al-Muminin, has received a severe blow. What remains, however, is a strong willingness among the populace to fight whenever the opportunity presents itself. Whenever a new figure emerges, renewed conflict in remote regions of north Yemen is expected.

As applicable to al-Qaeda, the continuing rebellions weaken and embarrass the government. 2005 is the third consecutive year where the government was forced to confront Islamic conflicts (an al-Qaeda related revolt in Abyan in 2003, along with the 2004 and 2005 Houthi conflicts). All met with failure, but they amply demonstrate how easy it is to foment armed conflict against the government.

The greatest threat facing the government would be a Sunni rebellion, pitting thousands of tribesmen against the government in the Jawf and Marib provinces, where hatred of the government is near universal. The key ingredients are money, an opportunity to fight the government and organization. A multi-million dollar organization like al-Qaeda certainly has the financing and contacts necessary to implement such a rebellion. What offers the greatest challenge is organization. A rebellion with intra-organization communications could never happen due to innumerable rivalries between the tribes. What could happen, however, is a distribution of funds and an agreed upon start date between the tribes, leaving to their own judgment what to attack and how frequently. A revolt of the style mentioned above would only be limited by financing and its ability to keep the tribes focused on the government and not each other. A revolt on such a massive scale is not likely, but it is a threat that the government must consider.

[Original Publication: *Terrorism Monitor* 3 (12) – June 17, 2005]

Notes

1. "Al-Houthi Ya'oud Mughadhiban wa ar-Ra'ees Yutliq Sujana' min Atiba'a Hussein," *al-Wasat*, March 16, 2005.

2. "Al-'Alama Badr ad-Deen al-Houthi lil-Wasat: Hussein lam Yastallam min as-Sulta wa Ushakak bi Maqtalahi," *al-Wasat*, March 9, 2005. www.alwasat-ye.net/modules.php

3. Jarabani, Hussein, "al-Yemen: Atiba'a al-Houthi Yakhudhoon Harb Shawaria' ma'a Quwat al-Aman fi Sa'ada," *Asharq al-Awsat*, April 9, 2005, Volume 9629.

4., Hussein Jarabani, "al-Yemen: Anba' 'an Maqtal ar-Rajal ath-Thani fi Tantheem ash-Shabab al-Mo'min wa Harab al-Houthi al-Ab," *Asharq al-Awsat*, April 12, 2005, Volume 9632.

5. "Yemen President Pardons Rebel Chief," Alertnet, www.alertnet.org/thenews/newsdesk/L1295364.htm

6. "Al-'Alama Badr ad-Deen al-Houthi lil-Wasat: ar-Ra'ees Khafa an Ya'khuth Hussein minhu," *al-Wasat*, March 19, 2005.

Yemen Accuses Iran of Meddling in its Internal Affairs

By Gregory D. Johnsen

In late January 2007, a new round of fighting broke out between the *Shabab al-Muminin* ("The Believing Youth") and Yemeni forces in the northern governorate of Saada. Government sources put the combined death toll at nearly 100, although the actual numbers are likely far higher. Like much of what surrounds the lengthy conflict, the circumstances that led to this latest series of clashes are lost in a maze of half-truths and disinformation spread by both sides. Yet the spark seems to have been the decision by a group of roughly 50 Jews to seek refuge in a local hotel, where they would be protected from the Shabab al-Muminin. The government claims that the Shabab al-Muminin were harassing the Jews, while the Shabab counter with allegations that the Jews were selling wine to Muslims. In truth, little was needed to reignite the conflict, which has been raging since June 2004. If it had not been this incident, another excuse would have been found to justify the renewed fighting.

Yemen has also sought to strengthen regional and international opinion against the Shabab al-Muminin by stoking fears of Iranian involvement in the conflict. The Shabab, which are known in the official press as the al-Houthi rebels – an insulting term that is derived from the name of the group's first leader, Hussein Badr al-Din al-Houthi, who was killed in September 2004 – are comprised of Zaidi Muslims, a Shiite sect that has traditionally been closer to Sunni Islam than it has to the Twelver Shi'ism that is practiced in Iran.

Yemen has made similar allegations in the past, but given the current mood of anti-Shiite feelings among the country's neighbors in the Gulf Cooperation Council (GCC), it has stressed its claims much more in the early months of 2007 than it has in previous years. Part of this is a desire by Yemen to link its internal problems to regional issues in the hopes of securing financial aid.

Yemen has long been aware that any steps toward possible entry into the GCC and most aid from its member countries are contingent upon security issues. Not surprisingly, the current accusations were first made public during President Ali Abdullah Saleh's trip to the United Arab Emirates, where he was lobbying for more aid following the November 2006 donor conference in London. The charges were given more weight in the region following an al-Jazeera story that asked whether Iranian involvement in the conflict was real or imaginary (al-Jazeera, Feburary 6, 2007). Days later, Yemen's Supreme Defense Council met under Saleh's leadership and threatened to reduce ties with Iran and Libya to their barest essentials if the two countries did not cease meddling in Yemen's internal affairs (al-Jazeera, February 11, 2007).

Yemen has asked Libya to extradite Yahya al-Houthi, the brother of both the current leader of the Shabab al-Muminin, Abdul Malik al-Houthi, as well as its founder, Hussein al-Houthi (al-Jazeera, February 16, 2007). Saleh has also issued the third, and what he says is the final, 48-hour ultimatum to the rebels to surrender their weapons and turn themselves over to security forces (*al-Hayat*, February 18, 2007). Yet, like most of the previous mediation attempts and truce negotiations, this latest demand will likely be ignored.

[Original Publication: *Terrorism Focus* 4 (2) – February 21, 2007]

Yemen's Three Rebellions

By Brian O'Neill

Politics in Yemen has always been a violent affair. Two of its four presidents have died unnaturally – one in a hotel room surrounded by drugs and prostitutes; his successor, suddenly and absurdly, by an exploding briefcase. The next man to take office, a young tank commander named Ali Abdullah Saleh, was not expected to fare much better.

He did, though, and is approaching his thirtieth year in power. He survived and, through his intimate knowledge of Yemen's tribal politics, consolidated his rule. He oversaw the unification of his country with the formerly socialist South Yemen, and then crushed the south in a civil war. He never fully expanded his government's writ over the chaotic, tribal north, but he stayed in power and kept his country together better than anyone could have predicted.

President Saleh now faces three separate rebellions: A tribal, sectarian battle in the north, economic and social riots in the south, and a pervasive enemy in a younger and more brutal generation of al-Qaeda. These are happening while Yemen faces crushing demographic and natural pressures, from its exploding population to its dwindling water supplies to its aging leadership. Saleh has held his country together, but the fragile, violent quilt-work that makes Yemen is now threatening to come quickly apart.

The Shabab al-Muminin of the North

Tribal rebellions have never been rare in Yemen, but the al-Houthi rebellion, which started in 2004, seems to be a different, lingering animal. It has transformed itself from Saleh's persistent headache into a long and catastrophic war that has claimed thousands of lives and threatens the tribal and sectarian balance which the president has meticulously massaged over the years.

The rebellion started in 2004 when Hussein al-Houthi, a sheikh of the Zaidi sect of the Shiite branch, proclaimed that Saleh's government had become too aligned with the United States and Israel. Longing to reestablish the Zaidi Imamate (1918-1962), al-Houthi led his Shabab al-Muminin ("The Believing Youth") into battle. This came after government crackdowns on the sheikh's unlicensed mosques.

Sheikh Hussein al-Houthi was killed in September 2004 and was jointly replaced as commander by his son and son-in-law, while his father took the reins as spiritual leader. There were back-and-forth negotiations, stall tactics, ceasefires, and more battles over the years. The government accused the rebels of receiving aid and training from co-religionists in Iran, which may have been true or may have been a way for President Saleh to link his domestic concerns with the broader Arab fear of the emerging "Shiite Crescent" (and thus to obtain more outside assistance). None of these allegations have been proven.

Then, on May 2, 2008, a motorcycle-borne bomb exploded in a mosque in Saada, killing over a dozen people and wounding scores more (*Yemen Times*, May 5, 2008). Immediately, the violence began again as accusations flowed from both sides. More than 50 people were killed in a battle near the town of Dafaa (ArabianBusiness.com, May 5, 2008). Both sides in this war have accused the other of targeting non-combatants, with the Saada governor claiming the al-Houthis "kill innocent people and set fire to their farms" (*News Yemen*, May 5, 2008). This bombing, though, marked a new and spectacular level of violence.

Immediately, speculation rose as to the identity of the slaughter's architect. Abdul Malik al-Houthi – the brother of Hussein al-Houthi – was quoted as saying: "The renewed tension is due to the repeated aggressions of the army ... which is using tanks and other weapons in unjustified operations" (ArabianBusiness.com, May 5, 2008). While he stopped short of saying the government planted the bombs, his calls for a fair and legitimate investigation leads one to believe he is not discouraging that speculation.

But this rebellion has hurt the Saleh government, and renewed fighting is not in its interests. Cynically, one could say that a planted bomb that looks like an al-Houthi attack would hurt the rebellion, but Saleh knows his country. The north has never fully accepted the government of Sana'a, and continued fighting only helps further delegitimize his regime. This leaves a previously unknown faction or al-Qaeda as suspects in the attack. This would be a difficult but not impossible operation for al-Qaeda given the security in Saada. Their motivations for doing so will be dealt with below.

The Restless South

Civil wars rarely seem to happen along an east-west axis; similar climates help produce similar economies and ideas – it is typically when different regions are yoked together that violence is produced. So it is with Yemen. North and South

Yemen have had different histories, colonial experiences, and economies. Though it seems antithetical to the romantic idea of an ancient, eternal Yemeni state, it could be argued that having two separate countries made more sense.

Following the fall of the Soviet Union, the socialist south, known as the People's Democratic Republic of Yemen, was faced with a failed economy and little external support. It had also never recovered from a brutal internecine war of its own during the 1980s. So it turned toward the north, and unification with the Yemen Arab Republic.

Speeches of brotherhood were given; promises were made. But the speeches never translated into reality, as Saleh squeezed out southern politicians and attempted to make the south part of his extended patronage network. Eventually, in 1994, civil war broke out. Saleh used his superior army and, more importantly, veterans of the Afghan jihad to crush the godless south. Aden, which had been an open and secular city – where mini-skirts were far more popular than the hijab – fell under the harsh rule of victorious jihadis. It would be an exaggeration to say that Shari'a had been implemented, but the typical southern way of life had been disrupted [1].

Beside the difficulties of the new way of life, the south chafed in other ways. Its economy never improved and many blamed the north for lack of interest in helping out its rival. The influence of the jihadis was felt. Though it seems insignificant, the destruction of the city brewery marked a dramatic change of daily rhythm, and the buildings became cold and gray concrete hulks. More strikingly, terrorism began to hit the south, with both the al-Qaeda variety and homegrown groups such as the Aden-Abyan Islamic Army influenced by returning jihadis.

Commodity shortages have been hitting the south, including a severe diesel shortage (*News Yemen*, April 23, 2008). While these shortages intensified, dissatisfaction with a number of issues strengthened. In January 2008, citizens were killed during a riot protesting the lack of "rights and benefits" accorded to citizens of the south. The rally was held in Aden during the Forum for Forgiveness and Reconciliation, an attempt to get past the divisiveness of the civil war (al-Jazeera, January 13, 2008). Instead, it sharpened the divide. Youths complained they were not allowed into the army; army retirees claimed they were not getting their benefits (al-Jazeera, April 1, 2008). In April 2008, hundreds were detained following a massive protest two days after a government soldier was killed (*Yemen Times*, April 8, 2008).

Perhaps most threatening of all was the re-entrenchment of old players and the reopening of old wounds. On April 8, 2008, the *Yemen Times* reported that demonstrators were in "Al-Dahle's main street chanting 'Get out, Colonialization,' and 'Revolution, Revolution South.' " Ominously, a former president of the south, Ali Naser Mohammed, signaled his approval of the riots, demonstrations and discontent (*Yemen Observer*, April 5, 2008).

It seems clearer than ever that the tenuous grafting of north onto south never really fit. It is far from too late to fix the situation – a little more aid, a more just hiring procedure and a reining in of Islamist interference would make southerners feel less colonized in their own country.

The Pervasive Threat

In 2007-2008, a new generation of al-Qaeda has taken over from Yemen's old guard. This group has been hardened by the battles in Iraq and shared experiences in prison. The leaders and primary soldiers escaped from a Yemeni prison in 2006 (referred to as the Great Escape), and have since consolidated their own power while seeming driven to unravel President Saleh's.

Their first big blow was against Spanish tourists in July 2007. They have since attacked foreign and local interests, including the U.S. Embassy and the Customs Office (see *Terrorism Focus*, April 16, 2008). Al-Qaeda seems immune to the standard Yemeni tactic of negotiation and compromise that Saleh has used with the older generation. Though it seems contrary to ideas of justice to let the bombers of the U.S.S. Cole walk free, Saleh has to balance domestic concerns and local passions to avoid letting his country slip into the abyss.

But that seems to be the exact strategy of the hard new guard of al-Qaeda. They are working at undermining tourism revenue and shaking any faith people have in the government with attacks on foreigners and random violence against citizens. A recent statement proclaimed their desire to "control Yemen's waterways" by organizing attacks on "commercial, tourist and oil tankers" (*News Yemen*, April 30, 2008; *Terrorism Focus*, May 13, 2008). This will eat away at another source of revenue and further weaken Saleh.

In the Middle, Nearing the End

Ali Abdullah Saleh has held his country, and his office, for a staggeringly long time. But events seem to be swirling faster now. The history of Yemen is catching up with his efforts, and demography is working to accelerate these damning trends. Using jihadis to fight his secular war may have irretrievably poisoned unification. Buying time with northern tribal leaders allowed him to shift focus from sectarian discontent, which led to the al-Houthi rebellion. Making deals with al-Qaeda emboldened a new generation.

All of these decisions made sense at the time and even in retrospect one feels the hands of the government were tied. Governing Yemen is a series of ad hoc decisions, assuaging the immediate concern while punting other issues down the road. President Saleh is getting older, and a new generation of leaders is awaiting its turn. It is unknown whether new leaders will be able to save the waterless, booming population from fragmenting into a failed state. But now, near the end of his tenure, President Saleh has to make decisions to save his new/ancient country from both its short-term difficulties and the catastrophes that loom over the near horizon.

[Original Publication: *Terrorism Monitor* 6 (10) – May 15, 2008]

Notes

1. Joseph Kostiner, Yemen: *The Torturous Quest for Unity, 1990-94*, RIIA, London, 1996.

Iranian Leaders Weigh Support for the Houthi Rebellion in Yemen

By Babak Rahimi

The Houthi rebellion against the Yemeni regime, which erupted in 2004 and has intensified with the unleashing of "Operation Scorched Earth" by the Yemeni forces in the northern Saada governate, has brought various claims by Sunni-led Arab states of Iranian involvement (al-Jazeera, November 11, 2009; al-Arabiya, November 11, 2009). The allegations, most of which originate with the Yemeni elite led by President Ali Abdullah Saleh, accuse the Shiite Zaidi rebels of receiving financial and military support from Tehran. Yemeni authorities claim the Houthis are looking for patronage and arms (especially from Iran's Islamic Revolutionary Guards Corps) for their anti-government operations (al-Jazeera, August 18, 2009; al-Arabiya, November 11, 2009).

Zaidi Shi'ism is one of three main branches of the Shiite movement, together with Twelver Shi'ism and the Isma'ili branch. The adoption of the Sunni Hanafi school of Shari'a by the Arab Zaidis brings them theologically closer to their Sunni neighbors in Yemen than to the distant non-Arab Shiite Ayatollahs of Iran. The Houthist rebellion has its origins in the mid-1990s with the foundation of the *Shabab al-Muminin* ("The Believing Youth") by the late Hussein Badr al-Din al-Houthi, a Zaidi religious leader. Fighting between the Shabab al-Muminin (soon known as "Houthists") and the government broke out in 2004. The rebellion cannot easily be classified as a sectarian conflict since President Saleh and many political and military leaders in Yemen are themselves Zaidi Shiites (see *Terrorism Monitor*, May 10, 2005).

Sana'a condemned Tehran for "interference" in its domestic politics after the Iranian foreign minister, Manouchehr Mottaki, offered Iran's help in bringing security to Yemen (al-Arabiya, November 11, 2009; *Mehr*, October 17, 2009). In contrast to a united Arab front (with the exception of Syria) opposing any Iranian involvement, a debate is brewing in Iran between different political factions on how to deal with the Houthi conflict. The debate is exposing deep tensions within the Iranian political community and sheds new light on how Iranian foreign policy might be shifting on a regional scale in the post-election period. Meanwhile, the latest fighting between Houthi and Saudi forces along the northern borders of Yemen has transformed the local conflict into a regional crisis (*Yemen Times*, November 11, 2009; al-Arabiyah, November 11, 2009; *al-Alam*, November 16, 2009).

Ahmadinejad's administration has publicly denounced the military assault on the Houthis, but it has done so on a humanitarian basis, not because of any desire to support the rebels' aspirations for an autonomous state in north Yemen. In fact, Tehran has explicitly given its support to the territorial integrity of Yemen (IRNA, September 9, 2009). Tehran's opposition to the government's military attacks has largely centered on the "national rights" of Yemeni citizens, maintaining a consistent policy in backing state authority without giving up support for Yemen's Shiites (IRNA, September 22, 2009). This tactic is used mainly because Tehran faces its own separatist problems in Baluchistan and Kurdistan; therefore, overt support for the Shabab al-Muminin rebels could undermine Iran's own efforts to maintain central authority.

It is likely that the Iranian authorities desire a Houthist governorate in the north that would remain under the central authority of Sana'a. In this sense, Foreign Minister Mottaki's latest objection to the conflict was less about Saudis protecting their borders from foreign rebels and more about warning them against supporting "extremist and terrorist groups," such as militant Salafist Sunni factions in Yemen (*Hamshari*, November 13, 2009).

In reality, Tehran's greatest concern may in fact lie in the possible resurgence of al-Qaeda with the deepening of the Houthi conflict and the weakening of the Yemeni state authority in the course of the ongoing military conflict. Viewed in this way, ironically, Iran and Saudi Arabia may in fact share a common interest in Yemen, despite appearances of a "proxy war" between the two states.

As Tehran assesses its next move, the ideologically hard-line faction closely linked with those in power continues to object to the regime's lack of an aggressive diplomatic and military response to the situation in Yemen. On November 14, 2009, the hard-line *Keyhan* newspaper described the Houthi conflict as a "union of Arab reactionaries" inflicting the "slaughter of Shiites of Saada" (*Keyhan*, November 14, 2009). According to this view, the Wahhabist Saudis, with the support of other Gulf states like the United Arab Emirates, aim to crush the oppressed Shiite population primarily because of their sectarian goal of molding the Islamic world into the Wahhabi conception of Islam. The hardliners accuse the government of remaining silent about the Sunni slaughter of Shiite civilians in Yemen (*Tabnak*, November 12, 2009). The hardliners also condemn Iranian civic groups and religious authorities in the holy city of Qom, especially those who are not associated with the government, for their inaction against Saudi aggression (*Tabnak*, November 12, 2009).

In contrast to the hardliners, the clerical establishment in Qom has remained relatively silent, possibly because of a religious bias against the Houthis, as Zaidi Shiites are doctrinally closer to Sunnis than to Twelver Shi'ism – the largest branch of Shiite Islam and the one most commonly practiced in Iran. The most important cleric to object to the latest events in Yemen has been Grand Ayatollah Golpayegani. Just days after the Saudi military attack on the Houthis, Golpayegani vehemently denounced the strike, accusing the "Islamic world" of giving consent to a slaughter of innocent people at the hands of fellow Muslims (*Tabnak*, November 11, 2009). However, other Grand Ayatollahs, like Ali al-Sistani, prefer to remain silent, revealing the deep division over how to deal with the Houthi conflict within the clerical establishment. On the other hand, the reformists also appear to maintain a sense of ambiguity in regards to Yemen and Saudi Arabia's efforts to crush the rebels. While the reformists are disturbed by allegations that Tehran is shipping military equipment to the Shabab al-Muminin, the reformists are largely playing down the conflict by focusing more on Iran's internal problems, especially the post-election controversies that continue to haunt the hardliners in powers (*Etemad*, October 28, 2009).

In broad terms, the debate in Tehran reveals the emergence of a less boisterous and more cautious Iranian foreign policy in the region. Despite the hardliners' grab for power since the June 2009 elections, the Islamic Republic appears to be weaker as a regional force while facing outbreaks of violence inside and outside of its borders. On a rhetorical level, Tehran will show its support for the rebels as a sign of Shiite strength, but on a strategic level, it is highly unlikely that it will risk the eruption of a regional conflict with its neighboring Sunni states over a non-Twelver Shiite group in Yemen. With this new cautious regional policy, the level of violence in north Yemen could considerably diminish in the months to come. But much of this will depend on how the Saudis deal on a diplomatic and military level with a highly volatile situation that has the potential to drag the entire region into conflict.

[Original Publication: *Terrorism Monitor* 7 (35) – November 19, 2009]

Saudi Military Operations along the Yemen Border Repel Houthist Incursion

By Andrew McGregor

After a two-month Saudi military offensive along the Saudi Arabia-Yemen border, the Houthist rebels of northern Yemen appear ready to abandon their brief occupation of small areas of Saudi Arabia's Jizan province. In an audiotape message, the leader of Yemen's Zaidi Shiite rebels, Abdul Malik al-Houthi, offered a ceasefire and a withdrawal from Saudi territory. However, al-Houthi warned of consequences if his offer was ignored. "If [Saudi Arabia] insists on continuing its aggression after this initiative, this gives us the legitimacy to open new fronts and to wage an open war" (al-Jazeera, January 25, 2010).

Saudi Deputy Defense Minister Prince Khalid bin Sultan bin Abdul Aziz rejected the offer, however, suggesting the Houthists could not be trusted. "We must remember history when it comes to Abdul Malik al-Houthi and his people. They have gone to war with the Yemeni government on five occasions. They have also signed five agreements with the Yemeni Authorities. However, they broke those agreements after a year or two" (BBC, January 27, 2010). The Prince rejected the Houthist claim of a complete withdrawal, insisting the rebel fighters had been driven out of their positions by Saudi forces (al-Alam, January 26, 2010; BBC, January 27, 2010). Earlier this month Prince Khalid turned down a Houthist offer to withdraw on the condition that Saudis stop supporting the Sana'a government, saying, "We should not talk to infiltrators and subversives… Our talks must be with the Yemeni government" (Yemen Post, January 13, 2010).

Though Sana'a believes Iran is the main supporter of the six-year Houthi rebellion, Riyadh has been reluctant to join the Arab world's general condemnation of Iran as the secret hand behind the Houthist revolt. Though the claim is popular, little has been offered in the way of proof. The Saudis instead make an even more surprising claim: the Houthists are in league with al-Qaeda. According to Prince Khalid, "We have noticed it on the battlefield, but it is proven by various bodies that there are contacts and coordination between them, and that they have a common interest, which is sabotage" (Saudi Press Agency, January 23, 2010). Yemen's national security chief Ali Muhammad al-Ansi has similarly claimed that the Zaidi Shiites are working with the virulently anti-Shiite al-Qaeda organization, while simultaneously claiming the Houthists are supported "financially, politically and through the media" by Iran (*Asharq al-Awsat*, December 13, 2009; *Yemen Post*, December 15, 2009). Yemen's counterterrorism chief General Yahya Saleh has also stated "there is no doubt" Iran is supporting the Houthist rebellion (al-Jazeera, November 16, 2009). Yemen's Islamist leader Sheikh Abdul Majid al-Zindani insists that Iran is trying to "export the Shiite ideology by force" (al-Jazeera, October 5, 2009).

Houthist rebels crossed the border into southwest Saudi Arabia in November in retaliation for what they claimed was Saudi support of Yemeni military operations against the Houthists. Fighting began after the insurgents killed two Saudi border guards and occupied several villages along the Saudi side of the border. Though Saudi military officials said their orders were not to cross the border with Yemen, the Saudis admitted their intention of establishing a ten-kilometer deep buffer zone inside Yemen (Reuters, November 12, 2009).

Most of the fighting took place in the mountainous border region of Jizan, Saudi Arabia's smallest province. Fighting was especially heavy around Jabal Dukhan, where the conflict started. Saudi forces battled the army of Yemen's Imam Yahya in the same region in 1934. The terrain is well-designed for defensive warfare and the Saudis made several premature claims of victory before finally clearing the Houthists from their positions. Fighting was bitter, with 133 Saudi soldiers killed according to southern region commander General Ali Zaid al-Khawaji (*al-Riyadh*, January 21, 2010). Houthist losses are unknown, but are likely to have been significant in light of the Saudis' superior firepower. According to Prince Khalid, Saudi mountain troops have learned important lessons during the intense fighting (Saudi Press Agency, January 23, 2010). The Prince added that the slow pace of the Saudi offensive was deliberate. "Time is with us. There is no need to hurry. We could have controlled all the areas in a month, or two weeks, but we opted not to rush in order to preserve [civilian] souls" (*Arab News*, January 24, 2010).

Soon after hostilities began in November, the Saudi Royal Navy's French-built frigates imposed a blockade of Red Sea ports to prevent supplies from reaching the Houthists. The frigates belong to the Saudi navy's Western Fleet, operating out of Jeddah. Houthist forces made a desperate attempt to seize the Red Sea port of Maydi on Yemen's north coast in November 2009, but were repelled by the Yemeni army (*Asharq al-Awsat*, November 22, 2009). The Saudi frigates fired on two boats they suspected of smuggling arms to the Houthists in December 2009. After a chase with helicopters, the crews of both boats were reported to have been killed in massive explosions caused by the arms and ammunition they were carrying (*Arab News*, December 10, 2009). Shortly before the Houthist incursion into Saudi Arabia, ships of Yemen's navy announced the seizure of an Iranian ship (the Mahan-1) carrying anti-tank weapons to a port in northwest Yemen for distribution to Houthist rebels (al-Arabiya, October 26, 2009). Iran denied any official involvement (Fars News Agency, October 28, 2009).

The Houthists' main weapons are small arms and landmines. They have a small number of military vehicles captured from government forces, though many of these appear to have been destroyed in the fighting with the Saudis. When a single Katysusha rocket was fired at a Saudi military base, the movement felt the action worthy of an announcement (al-Arabiya, November 16, 2009). On the other side, Saudi artillery joined ground attack planes of the Royal Saudi Air Force in targeting Houthist positions and vehicles continuously throughout the conflict. In early December 2009, Saudi frontline forces received new Swiss-built Piranha III wheeled armored vehicles and U.S.-built Bradley infantry fighting vehicles (*Arab News*, December 10, 2009). Saudi paratroopers have played a leading role in the fighting since it began last November, though they have not participated in any airborne operations (*Saudi Gazette*, January 25, 2010).

The Houthists claimed Saudi warplanes dropped phosphorus bombs in night raids on villages as far as seven kilometers inside the Yemen side of the border, though Saudi authorities claimed what the rebels saw was merely flares (Hamsayeh.net, January 24, 2010; AFP, November 9, 2009; BBC, November 5, 2009). The rebels have also accused government forces of using phosphorus shells, though Sana'a says it does not have any such weapons in its arsenal (*Gulf News*, November 9, 2009). In January 2010, the Houthists claimed to have shot down a Saudi AH-64 Apache attack helicopter near the Saudi border town of al-Khouba, though this was denied by Saudi authorities (*Yemen Post*, January 16, 2010; Press TV [Tehran], January 16, 2010).

Iranian President Mahmoud Ahmadinejad recently condemned the Saudi role in Yemen, saying, "Saudi Arabia was expected to mediate in Yemen's internal conflict as an older brother and restore peace to the Muslim states, rather than launching military strikes and pounding bombs on Muslim civilians in the north of Yemen" (Press TV [Tehran], January 16, 2010). Saudi Foreign Minister Prince Sa'ud al-Faisal rejected Ahmadinejad's criticism and alleged Iran was responsible for the unrest in Yemen (Sana, January 14, 2010).

Though the Houthist rebels displayed tenacity and resilience in resisting over two months of attacks by Saudi Arabia's professional army and air force, the movement is incapable of resisting intensified attacks by Yemeni government forces engaged in "Operation Scorched Earth" while fighting off the Saudis in their rear.

[Original Publication: *Terrorism Monitor* 8 (4) – January 28, 2010]

Chapter Five

U.S.-Yemen Relations

Cooperation And Conflict: Analyzing The U.S.-Yemen Relationship

By Charles Schmitz

Although President Ali Abdullah Saleh condemned American military action against insurgents in Fallujah, saying that terror must be fought with persuasion and dialogue rather than anti-personnel bombs (*al-Motamar*, 2004), he welcomed the new U.S.-led Combined Joint Task Force-Horn of Africa (CJTF-HOA), based in Djibouti. Yemen has been balancing military operations with efforts to build stable political foundations for some time now, opening the door for those formerly associated with political extremism to reintegrate themselves into Yemeni politics after renouncing their past. Yemen has also promised speedy trials for those accused of terrorism. In the words of Yemeni Prime Minister Abdul Qader Bajammal, "They are all sons of Yemen" (*al-Hayat*, 2003). The U.S. focus on its military campaign to disrupt international terror networks contrasts with Yemen's approach, which sees the war on terror as a continuation of its previous efforts to stabilize domestic politics under the regime's auspices. Yemeni goals are long-term political aims whereas the American agenda focuses on short-term prosecution of military or law enforcement objectives. These goals are not necessarily contradictory, with each government recognizing that compromises and accommodations must be made, but their ambiguities create tense moments.

In December 2002, the White House ordered the release of a North Korean ship with SCUD missiles concealed under bags of cement to the Yemeni regime. Spanish warships had forcefully boarded the vessel under a U.S./NATO program for interdiction of illegal weapons at sea, but after conversations between then Vice President Cheney, then Secretary of State Powell, and President Saleh, the missiles were allowed to continue to port. The Yemeni government suffered equal embarrassment when its security forces killed a number of Yemeni citizens during protests against the American invasion of Iraq. Sana'a was also forced to defend its partnership with the U.S. after an American predator missile killed six people, five Yemeni citizens and one American citizen, in the desert of Marib. In both instances, the opposition press accused the regime of being an American puppet and demanded details on American involvement in Yemeni affairs (*al-Sahwanet*, 2002). However, these incidents have not deterred Sana'a from maintaining cooperation with the U.S. on security issues.

The American missile came from the CJTF-HOA base in Djibouti, whose mission is to "focus on denying safe havens, external support and material assistance for terrorist activity within The Horn of Africa region." The force was established to stop the reemergence of al-Qaeda in Somalia and Yemen, with a focus on the Red Sea and the possible emergence of a "seaborne Jihad" (*Lemarie*, 2003). The Spanish ships that boarded the Korean vessel were also working with the CJTF-HOA, when it was based on the carrier USS Whitney in the Gulf of Djibouti. Since then, the force has put a permanent land-base at Camp Lemonier.

Clearly designed to support special operations on land, sea and air and to provide assistance to local security forces, the CJTF-HOA has played an active role in Yemen. Last month, U.S. Coast Guard officials attended ceremonies in Aden marking the inauguration of the new Yemeni Coast Guard. The commander of the CJTF-HOA from Djibouti attended earlier ceremonies for the first graduates of an American training program for Yemeni crews. By late 2004, a full fleet, consisting of thirteen 44-foot "motor life boats" with American trained crews would patrol Yemen's long coastline. These forces are designed control Yemen's porous borders and to stop attacks like those against the MT Limburg and the U.S.S. Cole. There are similar efforts to build up Yemeni security on land. Yemen and Saudi Arabia are working jointly to secure their desert border, while the American embassy is helping train Yemeni personnel at border checkpoints (*Mukaram*, 2004). American trained Special Forces led by the son of the president himself are working to destroy paramilitary challenges to the state. These elite troops recently attacked the remnants of an infamous Afghan-Arab terrorist camp at al-Huttat, reportedly capturing fugitives accused of involvement in the attacks on the U.S.S. Cole and the Limburg (*al-Sahwanet*, 2004).

However, despite the fact that Yemen has welcomed the support of the CJTF-HOA, its participation in the American war on terrorism remains firmly rooted in the Yemeni regime's strategy for political survival in the post-Soviet world. In the last decade, the two overriding political objectives of the regime have been to cultivate an alliance with the United States for external support and stabilize domestic politics by eliminating the threat posed by former allies among the Islamic political movements. Yemen's economy and state are very dependent upon external sources of funding, therefore international alliances are extremely important. Internally, the regime's strategy for domestic security was initiated after the disruptions of Yemeni civil war of 1994, long before Americans heard anything about al-Qaeda.

In that war, the current president of Yemen led the remnants of a cold war alliance of conservative military-tribal leaders from the north and modern Islamic activists against the secessionist wing of the Yemeni Socialist Party in the south. This umbrella group received outside funding from the Saudis and retained a great deal of independence. During the early years of Yemeni unity from 1990 to 1994, Islamic groups, including returning Afghan-Arabs, harassed the socialist opponents of the regime. Similar to Washington's attitude towards Islamic militants fighting the Soviets in Afghanistan, Sana'a did not oppose these independent military and political groups while their guns and propaganda were trained on southern socialists. But following the demise of the Yemeni Socialist Party, the regime saw these independent groups as the main threat to their own power and sought to marginalize their political Islamic ideologies and neutralize any military threats by either incorporating them into the regular military or destroying them.

After the bombing of the U.S.S. Cole and the 9/11 attacks, the Yemeni regime accelerated its existing programs rather than launching new campaigns. The president publicly attacked the opposition Islah party for its alleged tolerance of extremist ideologies and support for terrorists. In the elections for parliament in 1997, and even more so in 2003, the president's party pressed hard to diminish Islah's influence in parliament, whereas prior to 1994, the two parties had coordinated their electoral strategies. The president forcefully repressed demonstrations against the American invasion of Iraq, and while acknowledging their right to express their opinions peacefully, directly accused opposition parties of endangering national security. The government began to regulate Imam's in mosques and to close the independent "Scientific Institutes" that had become the educational recruiting grounds for Islamists. The Institutes will be integrated into the regular public school system with a government-regulated curriculum. Yemeni security forces have also dealt harshly with those attempting to kidnap foreigners or attack the oil pipelines in the desert, and, as a result, these forms of violence have disappeared.

The government has relentlessly pursued paramilitary groups and training camps. The latest round of battles took place this spring at al-Huttat in Abyan province and then again in Lawdar. American trained Special Forces captured suspects in the bombing of the U.S.S. Cole that had earlier escaped from a prison in Aden. Reportedly an Egyptian, formerly the leader of the Jihad group, was captured and turned over to Egyptian authorities (al-Jazeera 2004; *al-Tawil,* 2004). Many people suspected of ties to extremist groups have been jailed, particularly in the aftermath of 9/11. Recently the Yemeni prime minister revealed a program to pay tribes in remote areas not to harbor fugitives of any sort. In poor tribal areas, foreign countries or organizations can buy influence from tribal leaders who will take payments from almost anyone who offers significant support. This has made Yemen a haven for anyone fleeing justice, hence the initiative. Similarly, in the negotiations for a final border settlement with the Saudi regime, the Yemeni president insisted that the Saudis stop their payments to tribes. These measures give the central government a bit more influence over remote regions. In short, Yemen has aggressively attacked extremist political ideologies, independent paramilitaries and those sowing chaos, not so much to cooperate with the U.S. campaign, as to fulfill their own domestic agenda. However, the two agendas have overlapped, with a few exceptions.

Since the American invasion of Iraq the regime has stressed its political independence and the sovereignty of Yemeni law in dealing with extremists, terrorists and Americans. The United States' apparent disregard for the conventions of international law has diminished the legitimacy of American requests for aid in the war on terror. President Saleh appointed a judge to head a ministry of dialogue with former Islamic extremists and after meeting with jailed suspects authorized the release of a large number of detainees considered "redeemed." Those remaining in prison were promised speedy trials. The FBI had long agitated in the case of the U.S.S. Cole bombing that suspects not be given speedy trials so that investigations could continue. Sana'a unsuccessfully fought the American extradition of Mohammed al-Muayyad from Germany on charges of financing terror, arguing that Yemeni citizens should face Yemeni law. When the United States announced it was freezing Abdul Majid al-Zindani's assets on charges of financing terror, the Yemeni government responded that any legal action against al-Zindani would take place in Yemeni courts and that Yemen

189

would never turn him over to the Americans. With the decline of support for the United States in the Arab world since the attack on Iraq, the Yemeni regime must respond to domestic criticism of its alliance with the U.S. Therefore, it has emphasized its own sovereignty and independence, and has refused requests by the Americans to set aside Yemeni law in the interests of American intelligence operations. These tensions will continue as Sana'a attempts to balance domestic and foreign pressures in an attempt to maintain power in Yemen.

[Original Publication: *Terrorism Monitor* 2 (10) – May 19, 2004]

Yemeni Cleric Moayad's Conviction Further Strains U.S.-Yemeni Relations

By Eric Watkins

Then German Chancellor Gerhard Schroeder's visit to Yemen in early March 2005 was well timed. Indeed, coinciding with the closing arguments in the New York terror trial of Yemeni cleric Mohammed Ali Hassan al-Moayad and his assistant, Mohammed Yahya Zayed, Schroeder's visit could easily be seen as support for President Ali Abdullah Saleh, as well as a means of blunting any criticism or retribution for Germany's role in the affair. After all, Germany had allowed the U.S. to use its territory for the sting operation which netted the two suspects, it turned them over to the U.S. for trial and – along the way – Schroeder even turned down personal pleas from Saleh for the return of Moayad and Zayed to Yemen.

Moayad was found guilty of both conspiring to support and attempting to support Palestinian suicide bombers and al-Qaeda. He was also convicted of actually supporting Hamas but acquitted of actually supporting al-Qaeda. Zayed was convicted of conspiring to support al-Qaeda and Hamas, and attempting to support Hamas. He was acquitted of attempting to support al-Qaeda. The jury returned the verdicts after carefully scrutinizing videotapes made secretly during a sting operation in Frankfurt in January 2003.

The videotapes were taken during the cleric's visit to Frankfurt in early January 2003. Moayad had been led to believe he would meet a wealthy American Muslim from New York interested in donating funds to charities that the Yemeni cleric oversaw in the Middle East. The man, actually a U.S. agent, introduced himself as Said Sharif bin Turi and appeared to be an American-born convert to Islam. Over the next three days the two men met several times to discuss money that the American might provide, some of which, he said, would go to Osama bin Laden's al-Qaeda network. Then, on the morning of January 10, 2005, as Moayad and two other Yemenis began prayers in his room, German police initiated a raid and arrested them.

That caused ructions in Yemen, where public demonstrations took place in support of the cleric. Moayad is a prominent figure in Sana'a, Yemen's capital. In 1998, he co-founded the Al-Ihsan Mosque and Community Center, which feeds about 9,000 poor families a day from its bakery and provides free education and

191

medical care to the indigent. He is also a respected religious scholar, a leading member of the Islamic/tribalist Islah party, a former legislator, and a senior consultant to the Ministry of Religious Guidance and Endowments. It was the reaction of the volatile Yemeni public that had everyone concerned, along with the possibility of violent retribution from Islamists. The Yemeni government, for its own self-preservation, could do little but appeal for the release of the two.

On a state visit to Germany in June 2003, Ali Abdullah Saleh met Gerhard Schroeder. According to German newspaper *Der Spiegel*, "despite all the global problems, what the head of state was particularly worried about was the issue of two prisoners in Weiterstadt, Hesse – two fellow citizens." The paper named them as Moayad and Zayid. It also said the Yemeni "president, who provided $50,000 from government coffers for the defense of the sheikh, had promised his people before he departed for Germany: 'I will not return without the two.'" *Der Spiegel*, however, observed that, "Saleh's final attempt of personally turning the situation around in Berlin was doomed to failure. Both Interior Minister Otto Schily and Justice Minister Brigitte Zypries, whom the president received at Hotel Palace in Berlin, referred to the independence of the judiciary. They told him that politicians must not interfere in such matters" (*Der Spiegel*, June 30, 2003).

The Yemeni government still did not give up the case. Its embassy in Berlin issued a statement in July 2003, saying that "Yemeni authorities will monitor developments in this case with care and would do all that was within their powers to render success to all the legal efforts being made by the highest German prosecution authorities and all the official, parliamentary and cross-party quarters to have them released" (Republic of Yemen Television, July 21, 2003). In November 2004, after a German court approved the extradition of Moayad and Zayed to the U.S., the Yemenis launched another high-level appeal. "Yemeni authorities are conducting contacts with the German government to prevent the extradition," said Foreign Minister Abu-Bakr al-Qerbi. He deplored the arrests as "illegal" and "not compatible with the human rights and international law." He even said Yemen "might take the case to the European Court of Human Rights" if the German government decided to send Moayad to the U.S. (Deutsche Press-Agentur, November 13, 2003).

From the outset of its investigation, the U.S. has viewed Moayad as a key player in connection with al-Qaeda. "Al-Moayad indicated that he worked directly for a high-ranking official in the Islah party of Yemen ... purchasing weapons for al-Qaeda," said FBI agent Robert Fuller in his arrest warrant application. But the DPA suggested that the U.S. case was weak: "Al-Moayad is known as a fund-raiser for the Palestinians, but his alleged links with al-Qaeda are not widely known in Yemen" (Deutsche Press-Agentur, November 13, 2003). Yemeni authorities tried to make matters even simpler. "Sheikh al-Moayad is a simple religious man, who is doing a lot of charity work," Mohy Dhabbi, Yemen's ambassador to Germany, told investigators according to court documents. "He is beloved by the people he is dealing with." But in the trial, Mohammed Alanssi, the star witness who lured Moayad to Frankfurt, said: "The charity work of Sheikh Moayad is a front and the money he gets is for mujahideen." Toward the end of the trial, the judge allowed evidence to be used showing that Moayad had supported the application of one fighter to a bin Laden training camp in Afghanistan. In the end, though, jurors were largely unconvinced about connections with al-Qaeda and convicted the two men largely for their support of Hamas – a crime in the U.S. but not in Yemen.

The arrest and trial of Moayad and Zayed clearly strained relations between the United States and Yemen, a U.S. ally in the war on terrorism. But Germany was equally involved in the fate of the two men. "This investigation has been a joint investigation with the Germans. This has been a cooperative effort from the start," said a Justice Department official at the time of Moayad's arrest. Gerhard Schroeder's visit to Yemen was thus well-timed to support Ali Abdullah Saleh and keep the peace among uneasy allies in the war on terror.

[Original Publication: *Terrorism Focus* 2 (6) – May 5, 2005]

Yemen's Enduring Challenges: An Interview with Jonathan Winer

Jonathan Winer was former U.S. Deputy Assistant Secretary of State for International Law Enforcement. Currently a partner at the firm of Alston and Bird LLP, he also serves as a Member of the Council of Foreign Relations Task Force on Terrorist Financing.

Jamestown Foundation: Have there been any positive developments recently in Yemen to counteract Yemen as a terrorist breeding ground?

Jonathan Winer: Prior to 9/11, Yemen was not thinking about Islamic terrorism, it was thinking only about tribal terrorism. Since 9/11, Yemen has been cooperating with the US on countering Islamic terrorism by detaining and expelling terrorists, and by conducting military operations. But its borders remain porous and it is still a sanctuary for al-Qaeda. [...] There is also the inheritance of Afghan Arabs who have come back to Yemen since the overthrow of the Taliban regime in Afghanistan post-9/11. These individuals are embedded in the security institutions in Yemen. The country is a good location for incubating terrorism, although recently the government has been more aggressive in combating it.

JF: Could you comment on terrorist financing as it relates specifically to Yemen, including any links with government officials?

JW: There are three or four main strands when it comes to this subject. One is the honey trade, with Abu Zubaidah and Khalil al Deek – both al-Qaeda members – who have been linked to the honey business. This is one sector.

The second sector involves the entities Osama bin Laden got going a decade ago in Yemen, including companies dealing with electrical appliances, ceramics, and publishing. These were operated through middle-men and were linked to certain tribes: the Sana'a, the Saada, and the Abayan. It is difficult to know a decade later to what extent these operations still exist.

There is also a huge amount of activity related to the Palestinians, especially Hamas, with the president of the country openly encouraging Yemenis to send arms and money to that group as recently as 2003. Charities and religious

194

institutions have also been linked to support for terrorism. [...] Another aspect of the problem is the *hawala dars* [informal network for money transfer], who are tied to narcotics traffickers. They also have links to money launderers in the US, especially in New York.

JF: Were there strong ties to Afghanistan prior to September 11?

JW: Yes, with the most prominent and important links being those involving Sheikh Abdul Majid al-Zindani, who has been very close to Osama bin Laden. Zindani is a major player in Yemeni politics and has likely been as significant a threat as has existed to Saleh's control of the country. He was the central figure sending Yemenis to Afghanistan to fight with the Taliban and the central figure training and recruiting them as well. Zindani was designated as a global terrorist by the U.S. Treasury in February 2005, and Yemen was asked to freeze all of his assets. Treasury has charged him with actively recruiting for al-Qaeda training camps and purchasing weapons on behalf of al-Qaeda and other terrorists. He was a leader of the Islamic Front, formed to channel Yemeni volunteers to the Afghan Jihad while enhancing Riyadh's influence in Yemen. The Islamic Front in turn evolved into the Islah party. Although Islah is part of the current government, it and Zindani also represent a major source of covert and overt opposition to Saleh's government.

JF: Were there strong ties between members of the Yemeni government and Al Qaeda prior to September 11?

JW: Yemen was a prime location for the building of al-Qaeda in the early 1990's with Zindani and his Al-Iman University playing a substantial role in recruitment. Yemen also housed a number of Osama bin Laden's business interests. It's difficult to determine from the outside how governmental and private business interests relating to al-Qaeda were intertwined in Yemen prior to September 11. The government of Yemen has been largely run by and for a small group close to the president of the country. Corruption is rampant in the private and public sector, extending to the higher levels and exemplified by government conferred monopolies and contracting and licensing abuses. So to the extent that bin Laden had businesses in Yemen, senior officials or friends of the government of Yemen likely played some facilitation role at least. Separately, it is also pretty clear that there was senior support for Osama bin Laden and al-Qaeda in Yemen's police, security and military services prior to September 11. Bin Laden

195

was not alone. The Yemeni government has reportedly allowed Hamas and Palestinian Islamic Jihad to maintain offices in Yemen, and members of Islamist terrorist groups from Algeria, Egypt, and Libya have also used Yemen as a haven.

JF: Regarding Hamas, are there any additional details you could provide about who – individuals and/or organizations – are supporting them with arms and funding? What impact does Yemen's support for Hamas have on its relations with Washington? Do you have an estimate for how much money flows from Yemen to Hamas?

JW: The President of Yemen has encouraged Yemenis to send weapons, men and money to the Palestinians to help their struggle in the West Bank. The President has supposedly met with a leader of Hamas (Khaled Mashaal, based out of Damascus) and has supported the organization with financial donations. This state-sponsored support for Palestinian terrorism by Yemen has continued since the September 11 attacks. On May 4, 2002, the Associated Press reported that the Yemeni president was making a donation of $10 million to the Palestinian Authority and to "active Palestinian forces" such as the militant groups Hamas and Islamic Jihad. This was later appended with a correction that stated that the donation had not come directly from the president's personal funds, but was "collected from Yemenis."

JF: Which do you think presents a greater security challenge for the U.S. – Saudi Arabia or Yemen?

JW: While Saudi Arabia may be of more national security significance for the U.S. given its size and wealth, Yemen may pose the greater security challenges. It is a much weaker state; much of the country is lawless and rural. Unless the president [Saleh] decides to go after someone, there is impunity. Yemen also has terrorist links with other places that have had terrorist problems such as Indonesia and Afghanistan. Also, there is no real regulation of the financial sector, which is another huge challenge. Then there is the ideological overlay, which continues to reveal itself through Yemen's treatment of the Palestinian problem. There is a culture of violence in Yemen as well as arms trafficking and overall poverty: 54% of the population is illiterate and half of the children are malnourished. Finally, the armed struggle between the tribes in Yemen is continuing. Their word for it is "thar" meaning on-going feuds between the

Yemeni versions of the Hatfields and McCoys, which leads to a lot of revenge killings.

JF: Do you see Yemen moving towards creating stronger institutions necessary to combat terrorism?

JW: Yemen is an incredibly poor country, one of the poorest in the world; it's in really rough shape. The government's difficulties are endless: smuggling, drug growing – the drug being qat [the leafy narcotic chewed by Yemenis, primarily in the north, as well as on the horn of Africa]. [...] Essentially the security forces are dedicated to protecting President Saleh and his tribal federation, the Hashids. They don't directly control security outside of these areas. When you have the level of poverty that exists in Yemen, it is easy to breed terrorism. The country needs a lot of help. In terms of its geography, there are similarities between Yemen and Afghanistan. The relationship between Yemen and Saudi Arabia and that between Afghanistan and Pakistan are similar. Both Yemen and Afghanistan are next to more prosperous countries, while they are more rural and ungoverned.

JF: In the aftermath of 9/11, there was some speculation that bin Laden might seek refuge in Yemen. Do you think this remains a possibility now?

JW: It is incredibly dangerous now for any country to knowingly house terrorists. Yemen has sought to oust al-Qaeda-related entities from the country. There are still some al-Qaeda related schools and other entities, but I do not believe that any area under government control would be a secure place for someone as notorious as Osama bin Laden.

JF: What direction do you think U.S. policy toward Yemen should take?

JW: We should focus on getting more foreign assistance and trying to develop Yemen's civil institutions. The more people from the Muslim world trying to develop it, the better. We should also help try to contain Yemen, in terms of those who travel from the country, and we should try to help it transform itself into an appropriate partner. Its political institutions, with the exception of their support for Palestinian terrorism, have shown themselves willing to work with us. We should also work on licensing the hawala system. But it is going to be a long struggle, so we should consider barriers to entry from Yemeni financial structures and individuals-or at least not before undergoing thorough background checks – before allowing them into the U.S. This problem will be with us for a long while.

[Original Publication: *Terrorism Monitor* 2 (7) – May 19, 2005]

Landscape of Shifting Alliances

By Eric Watkins

There can be little doubt that Yemen plays a key role in the U.S.-led war on al-Qaeda's terrorist network, but it is a role that the Arab country would have preferred not to take on. Indeed, had it not been for al-Qaeda's attack on the French oil tanker Limburg in October 2002, Yemen might well have continued the ambiguous posture it had long assumed toward the spectre of Islamist terrorism. The Limburg attack, unlike the October 2000 bombing of the U.S.S. Cole, threatened the government's oil revenues – almost its only source of income. Sana'a had little choice but to act decisively with Washington against al-Qaeda, reversing a policy begun by Yemen's President Ali Abdullah Saleh in 1980, following the invasion of Afghanistan by the Soviet Union.

The Yemeni president articulated his country's position towards what the U.S. described as "terrorists" in a speech at the private al-Iman University in Sana'a on April 17, 1999. "Our country does not sponsor violence. We sponsored our brothers who returned from Afghanistan. We and the entire world used to support Afghanistan, including the United States, the sponsor of the new world order. It supported the Islamic movements to go to Afghanistan to carry out jihad there and to confront Communism. After it dispensed with these mujahideen, it tried to brand them as terrorists. This is unacceptable. Many ulema and people know this. We said we welcome them in their country, Yemen, but we will not allow anyone to move in any direction against his country" [1]. President Saleh had supported the mujahideen from the outset of the Afghan war in 1980, this support translating into a willingness to provide them with sanctuary in Yemen. But the president likewise gave the so-called Afghan-Arabs, who later morphed into al-Qaeda, ample warning not to undertake any actions that would harm Yemen itself – actions such as the bombing of oil tankers like the Limburg.

Al-Qaeda's statement about the Limburg bombing said it carried out the attack "after the regime of treason and treachery in Yemen did all it could and could not do to hunt down, pursue, and arrest the Muslim mujahid youths in Yemen" [2]. Clearly suggesting that Yemen was being punished for its part in the US-led war on terrorism, the bombing seemed like retribution for Saleh's pursuit of al-Qaeda operatives then in the country. By that time, Yemen was under considerable pressure from the US to investigate terrorists such as Ramzi bin al-Shibh and Sinan Qa'id al-Harthi, who were suspected of involvement in the

199

bombing of the U.S.S. Cole as well as the attacks of September 11, 2001. Under such pressure, Sana'a had little choice but to bow to Washington's demands or face military reprisals or economic sanctions. Yet, as the al-Qaeda statement observed, the Limburg attack coincided "with the passage of a full year on the world Crusade against jihad and the mujahideen...and the passage of two full years on the destruction of the American destroyer U.S.S. Cole in the Yemeni port of Aden" [3]. In a word, the Yemeni government had come under counter pressure from al-Qaeda for exactly the same reasons chosen by the U.S. government.

More obliquely, by speaking of the regime of "treason and treachery" the al-Qaeda statement also referred to events farther back in time, when the Saleh government had forged an alliance with bin Laden's Afghan-Arabs. Like other Arab nations, Yemen supported the call for Islamic volunteers to fight against the Soviets in Afghanistan. But a large number of Yemen's contingent consisted of exiles from the former People's Democratic Republic of Yemen (South Yemen) driven out of the South by the Marxist take-over in 1967. Many had fled to Saudi Arabia where – together with earlier Yemeni émigrés such as the bin Laden family or the bin Mahfouz – they nurtured ideas of eventually returning home and expelling their political adversaries. That dream was not to be realized for at least two decades or more and it was President Ali Abdullah Saleh who provided the exiles with their opportunity for revenge.

In late 1989, as leader of the Arab Republic of Yemen (North Yemen), Saleh announced an agreement with the Southern leadership to merge the two countries into a single Republic of Yemen. Under terms of the agreement, power would be shared between the rulers of the two countries through a three-year transitional period leading to the full merger and democratic elections. But even as the merger was announced, Saleh undertook a separate and secret relationship with the fundamentalist al-Islah Party, aimed at securing the demise of his political partners from the South and giving him full control of the newly established state. Founded shortly after the unification of North and South Yemen in 1990, Islah was co-led by Sheikh Abdullah bin Hussein al-Ahmar, the hereditary leader of Yemen's largest confederation of tribes, the Hashed, and by Sheikh Abdul Majid al-Zindani, then head of Yemen's Muslim Brotherhood [4].

The two Islah leaders also worked with another exile from South Yemen named Sheikh Tariq al-Fadhli. A member of a former ruling family of South Yemen, Fadhli had taken up Islamist causes as a youth in Saudi Arabia and, funded by Osama bin Laden, he eventually "divided his time between Iran, the northern borders of Pakistan, and Afghanistan" [5]. In a word, Fadhli fought as a member of bin Laden's Afghan-Arabs against Soviet forces in Afghanistan. At the end of that war, he returned to Saudi Arabia, and with the continuing patronage of bin Laden, quietly filtered back into Yemen as head of its Islamic Jihad Organization with aims of exacting revenge on his Marxist adversaries then sharing power with President Saleh in the newly unified Yemen.

Islah and the Islamic Jihad Organization were discreet partners in Saleh's plan against South Yemen's ruling party, the Yemen Socialist Party (YSP). Forming the overt side of that relationship, Islah leaders frequently stated their distaste for working with the "godless" YSP. From the unification of the country to the civil war of 1994, Islah leaders repeatedly threatened jihad against the YSP. That threat and its apparent implementation first became evident in 1992 with debate in parliament over so-called scientific institutes founded by Zindani in the 1970s.

Funded by Saleh's government but operated by Islamist organizations, the institutes supposedly taught a Quranic curriculum. But the YSP discovered they were fronts for Islamic militants, used as staging posts and training facilities for a stream of mujahideen passing between Cairo and Kabul, with occasional stopovers in Khartoum, then home to Osama bin Laden and the Sudanese Islamist leader Hassan al-Turabi. As the Yemeni parliament began legislation to end government funding of the institutes, Ahmar threatened jihad. When the legislation passed, the home of the speaker of parliament – a member of the YSP – was attacked with rocket-propelled grenades [6]. As the covert side of the relationship, the Islamic Jihad Organization carried out a systematic campaign of terror and violence against the YSP that eventually led to the outbreak of the 1994 civil war. Members of the Islamic Jihad Organization, experienced by the war in Afghanistan and financed by bin Laden, even fought in the war on Saleh's behalf.

With the defeat of the southern leaders in July 1994, Saleh assumed full control over the unified Republic of Yemen. At the same time, and to the surprise of many in the Islamist cause, Fadhli disbanded the Islamic Jihad Organization, calling on former members to "get jobs in accordance with the legitimate framework" [7]. It is here that many Afghan-Arabs see Saleh's "treachery and treason". Unlike Fadhli, who regained hereditary lands owned by his family in the South, many Afghan-Arabs were not ready to join the establishment, expecting Saleh to grant them substantial political power in the new Yemeni state. Instead, they found they had been used by Saleh to dispose of his rivals, and were then being disposed of themselves. In effect, many of Afghan-Arabs were hoping to establish a theocracy that reflected their Islamist leanings.

Although denied this opportunity, the Arab-Afghans soon began to create their own economic structures in Yemen and by 1996 were "involved in 27 commercial ventures in the area of exports and who have at their disposal $20-$25 million... These firms are bankrolled by Osama bin Laden, who is adept at mixing commerce and ideology" [8].

Having made an enemy of bin Laden, Saleh has had to move cautiously over the years to maintain control over his country. At the same time, however, the Yemeni leader has had to move equally cautiously with the US – particularly after bin Laden's attacks on New York and Washington, DC. Clearly, Saleh has been treading a very narrow tightrope, and there can be little wonder of his need to tread cautiously in either direction. There can be even less wonder of his reluctance to make any move at all.

[Original Publication: *Terrorism Monitor* 2 (7) – May 19, 2005]

Notes

1. Yemen TV, April 17, 1999.
2. "al-Qaeda Statement Congratulates Yemenis on the Bombing of the French Tanker Off Yemen's Coast," London: *Al-Quds al-Arabi*, 16 October 16, 2002.
3. Ibid.
4. Both leaders had strong anti-Marxist credentials. According to files of the British Foreign & Commonwealth Office, Ahmar and his tribesmen came to the support of Saleh's government in its struggles against Marxist South Yemen in early 1979. As a result, Ahmar was appointed a member of Saleh's advisory council on its creation in May 1979, and by 1982 had become a member of the Permanent Committee of Saleh's ruling party, the General Peoples' Congress. Zindani had similar anti-Marxist propensities. Although born in North Yemen, Zindani received his early education in South Yemen under the British. He went onto Ain Shams University in Cairo where he initially studied chemistry and biology. But, under the influence of the early Islamist thinkers – Imam Hassan al-Banna and Sayyid Qutb – Zindani soon switched to Islamic studies. He returned to South Yemen in 1966, but had to flee in 1967 when the Marxists took control of the country. Like many other Yemeni exiles, he went to Saudi Arabia. There, he followed the teachings of the Saudi Mufti Abdul Aziz bin Baz and eventually became a senior official in the Islamic Call Organization. In 1970, Zindani returned to North Yemen where he was appointed advisor to the Ministry of Education and helped to found the Muslim Brothers.
5. *Al-Wassat*, pp 11-17, January 1993.
6. According to *al-Hayat*, January 8, 1993, the suspected attacker was a member of the Islamic Jihad Organization.
7. *Al-Hayat*, London: September 4, 1994.
8. *Al-Watan al-Arabi*, Paris: December 27, 1996.

U.S.-Yemen Relations and the War on Terror: A Portrait of Yemeni President Ali Abdullah Saleh

By Mark Katz

Colonel Ali Abdullah Saleh became president of North Yemen in 1978 and then of the Republic of Yemen after unification of the North with the former Marxist South in 1990. From 1978 through the 1991 Persian Gulf War, Saleh sought to gain leverage for his small nation by playing more powerful countries – including the United States – against one another. Although he pursued this strategy brilliantly at first, Saleh's plans backfired in 1990-91. Since that time he has concentrated on courting the United States, instead of trying to counterbalance its influence using other allies. This effort has been especially pronounced since the 2000 bombing of the U.S.S. Cole in Aden harbor and the events of September 11, 2001, which marked the beginning of Saleh's close cooperation with the United States. Despite a not altogether smooth relationship, Saleh's cooperative attitude is likely to continue in the foreseeable future.

President Saleh came to power at a time when North Yemen faced not only a threat from Soviet-backed South Yemen, but also contentious relations with neighboring Saudi Arabia. Though Saleh sought American military support against the South, he received less than he hoped for, as the United States tried to assuage Riyadh's concerns about populous but poor North Yemen potentially becoming a threat to the oil kingdom. So, in one of the more bizarre episodes of the Cold War, Saleh asked for – and received – arms from Moscow, using primarily Soviet-supplied weapons to quell a Marxist insurgency supported by Soviet-backed South Yemen.

The end of the Cold War and the withdrawal of the Soviet Union from the Third World allowed for the 1990 merger between North and South Yemen, Saleh becoming the predominant leader. But the end of the Cold War also eliminated Moscow as a source of support against American-backed Saudi Arabia, which had opposed Yemeni unification. It was the desire to replace the USSR with another powerful ally against Saudi Arabia that explains Saleh's tilt toward Iraq before and during the crisis over Kuwait. Had a stalemate ensued (as Saleh may have anticipated), Saleh would have been in a position to balance Washington/Riyadh against Baghdad just as he had previously done with Washington/Riyadh and Moscow. The plan collapsed, however, with

Washington and Riyadh cutting off assistance and isolating Yemen, while a defeated Iraq was in no position to help it.

Saleh's mighty efforts to restore normal relations with Washington and Riyadh after this episode were unsuccessful at first. In mid-1994, some of the southern leadership attempted to secede and reestablish the South's independence; Saudi Arabia supported the effort, the United States did not. A few weeks later, Saleh's army overran the South, ending the attempted secession with the help of northern tribesmen and Islamists [1]. It was from this point that Yemeni-American ties slowly began to improve. (Yemen's relations with the Kingdom also improved when a Saudi-Yemen border agreement was finally signed in 2000.)

In the late 1990s, U.S. naval vessels began refueling in Aden, southern Yemen's largest city, which had first served as a port for the British and later the Soviet navy. A suicide attack launched against the U.S.S. Cole in October of 2000, apparently orchestrated by Osama bin Laden and al-Qaeda affiliates, was claimed by the Aden-Abyan Islamic Army. The local group cited resentment of Northern dominance established over the South as a result of the 1994 civil war as their prime motivation [2]. Though Yemen responded more cooperatively to the FBI investigation of the U.S.S. Cole attack than the Saudi government had following the bombing of the Khobar towers, frictions developed when literally hundreds of U.S. government officials descended on Aden. Not only Yemenis, but also the then U.S. ambassador to Yemen, Barbara Bodine, complained of their intrusiveness [3].

With the investigation of September 11 attacks, it became increasingly clear that many Islamic terrorists came from and/or operated out of Yemen. Tribesmen, who control parts of the country not under the authority of the central government, sometimes provide shelter to these individuals for their own purposes. The tribes around Marib (a remote area east of Sana'a, near the desert border with the Kingdom) have long accepted support against the government from outsiders, including Marxist South Yemen, Ba'athist Iraq, conservative Saudi Arabia, and most recently, radical elements linked to al-Qaeda. The fact that the Yemeni army consists largely of insufficiently trained and equipped tribesmen complicates the situation further, as soldiers are often unwilling to fire upon other tribesmen and thus unleash more generalized tribal warfare. The typical government response to problematic tribes has been to attempt to meet some (if not all) of their demands. This reaction, unfortunately, has only encouraged tribes to continue seeking outside support, as doing so appeared to elicit a positive response from the Yemeni government.

Frustrated with the situation in Yemen, Washington reportedly contemplated unilateral military action inside Yemen against al-Qaeda in September 2002 [4]. Such action would have been extremely unpopular in Yemen, likely resulting in increasingly anti-American sentiment within the Yemeni public. However, Saleh also felt threatened by the rising strength of Islamists within Yemen and decided to cooperate more fully with the United States against them, thereby curtailing unilateral American intervention.

Small numbers of American troops have been providing training and support to Yemeni armed forces. In one spectacular example of joint cooperation, the Yemeni government gave its approval for the November 2002 American missile attack on an automobile carrying six Yemeni terrorists on an isolated stretch of highway. Although there was some angry reaction to this within Yemen, it was neither widespread nor long lasting [5]. When asked if Yemen would allow the United States to launch similar missile strikes, senior Saleh adviser and former Yemeni Prime Minister Dr. Abd Al-Karim Al-Iryani unhesitatingly responded, "Sure" [6].

Such quiet Yemen-U.S. cooperation has paid off: As of March 2004, there had been no terrorist attacks in Yemen for about two years [7]. There remain, however, important differences in the Yemeni and American approaches to terrorism. Then Deputy Secretary of Defense Paul Wolfowitz had stated that, "There are some things that we would like in terms of more aggressive detention of some of the terrorists that they hold and better access to some of them" [8]. The United States considered particularly risky the amnesty in 2003 of a number of prisoners who had renounced terrorism. Yemeni officials justified the release by pointing out that the men had been put into the custody of their families, who would lose their homes or businesses if terrorist activities were resumed. It is still too early to tell whether or not this program will work [9].

The principal difference between the Yemeni and American approaches to the war on terrorism was revealed in an exchange between Presidents Saleh and Bush during a visit by the former to Washington in late 2001. Saleh reportedly told Bush an Arab proverb: "If you put a cat into a cage, it can turn into a lion." Bush's response was: "This cat has rabies. The only way to cure the cat is to cut off its head" [10].

Notwithstanding a desire for even more cooperation, Washington seems obviously pleased at Saleh's cooperation with U.S. anti-terrorism efforts thus far. For his part, Saleh reaps not only the benefits of combating Islamic elements in Yemen (who are as much a threat to him as to the United States), but his cooperation serves four other purposes besides. First, Yemen's willingness to work with the United States has, for the first time ever, resulted in Washington favoring Yemen over Saudi Arabia in an issue of great importance to the United States. Second, increased Yemen-American cooperation in the war on terrorism has been accompanied by decreased U.S. interest in the lack of progress toward democratization in Yemen, despite Saleh's promises to the contrary. Third, the help Saleh receives from the United States to defeat Islamic terrorists also helps preserve his autocratic rule. Fourth, his cooperation with the United States in the war on terrorism reduces the prospect of unilateral American military action in Yemen, which could well undermine Saleh's rule. Saleh's ability to patch up relations with the United States demonstrates once again this astute politician's capacity for playing his hand right – for his own benefit.

[Original Publication: *Terrorism Monitor* 2 (7) – May 19, 2005]

Notes

1. Jamal S. Al-Suwaidi, ed., *The Yemeni War of 1994* (Saqi Books/The Emirates Center for Strategic Studies and Research, 1995).
2. Sheila Carapico, "Yemen and the Aden-Abyan Islamic Army," MERIP Middle East Report Online, October 18, 2000, (www.merip.org/mero/mero101800.html).
3. Danna Harman, "Yemen Slowly Warms to US," Christian Science Monitor/csmonitor.com, February 13, 2003, (www.csmonitor.com/2002/0213/p06s01-wome.html).
4. Robin Allen, Farhan Bokhari, and Mark Huband, "US 'Has Been Ready for Action inside Yemen,'" *Financial Times*, September 19, 2002.
5. Ibid.
6. Nora Boustany, "Yemeni Proclaims His Nation's Solidarity with US in Fight against Terrorism," *Washington Post*, November 27, 2002.
7. Eric Westervelt, "Efforts of Yemen in the War on Terror," Weekend Edition Sunday, National Public Radio, March 21, 2004.
8. Ibid.
9. Jonathan Schanzer, "Yemen's al-Qaeda Amnesty: Revolving Door or Evolving Strategy?" Policywatch #808, Washington Institute for Near East Policy, November 25, 2003.
10. Patrick E. Tyler, "Yemen, an Uneasy Ally, Proves Adept at Playing Off Old Rivals," *New York Times*, December 19, 2002.

Yemen and the United States: Different Approaches to the War on Terrorism

By Andrew McGregor

Following the introduction of a new two-year plan to eliminate religious-based political extremism in Yemen, President Ali Abdullah Saleh made an official visit to Washington from April 30, 2007 to May 3, 2007. While in the United States, President Saleh discussed security and counter-terrorism efforts with President Bush, FBI Director Robert Mueller, Secretary of State Condoleezza Rice, Secretary of Defense Robert Gates, CIA Director Michael Hayden and members of the House of Representatives Intelligence Committee. The visit marked an enormous change in U.S.-Yemeni relations since the dangerous days following the September 11 attacks, when a U.S. attack on Yemen seemed imminent. At the conclusion of his stay, President Saleh thanked the United States for its support of Yemen's counter-terrorism efforts, while President Bush spoke of Yemen's continuing cooperation in bringing "radicals and murderers" to justice. Nevertheless, while the sometimes-tempestuous U.S.-Yemeni alliance carries on, there are serious differences between the Yemeni and U.S. approaches to counter-terrorism.

Reforming Terrorists with Islam

The most unusual aspect of Yemen's counter-terrorist efforts is a broad effort to reform religious extremism (both Shiite and Sunni) and replace it with a moderate approach to Islam. This task (rooted in traditional Yemeni methods of conflict resolution) has been handed to Yemen's recently appointed minister for Endowments and Religious Guidance, Judge Hamoud al-Hattar, who states, "The strategy will be an important factor in treating their mistaken ideas" (*Yemen Observer*, April 30, 2007). As the leader of Yemen's Committee for Dialogue, al-Hattar developed a policy of confronting incarcerated militants in debates designed to expose their misinterpretations of Islamic doctrine and challenge the legitimacy of al-Qaeda-style jihadism. Using "mutual respect" as a basis for the discussions, al-Hattar points to numerous successes in reforming the views of extremist prisoners, some of whom later provided the security apparatus with important intelligence. Hundreds of terrorism suspects have passed through the program. Recidivism is untracked, however, and there are reports that some of

207

those released went to Iraq to fight U.S.-led coalition forces. The list of graduates is closely guarded, and ex-prisoners are warned not to discuss their participation in the dialogues, thus allowing a degree of deniability should graduates return to terrorism.

Within Yemen, al-Hattar is widely believed to be a member of the feared Political Security Organization (PSO). When 23 terrorism convicts escaped from a PSO prison in the national capital of Sana'a last year, their tunnel emerged in al-Hattar's mosque. The mass escape was clearly assisted by some PSO agents. The fact that the escapees included several convicted of bombing the U.S.S. Cole placed a severe strain on U.S.-Yemen relations.

For two years, the Ministry of Endowments and Religious Guidance has kept a close watch on unlicensed Quranic schools suspected of promoting political violence, although none have been closed so far. A corps of "religious guides" (both men and women) has been tasked with promoting "the noble values of Islam" and to establish the principles of moderation and tolerance in areas where the government fears extremism is feeding on a lack of religious knowledge (Saba News Agency, April 25, 2007). Saleh has challenged the country's religious scholars and preachers to "clarify the facts" of Islam for the Muslim community, especially in rebellious Saada province, where preachers have a "religious, moral and national duty" to eradicate sedition.

Steps Toward Disarmament

On April 24, 2007, Yemen's cabinet took the unusual measure of ordering the closure of Yemen's many arms shops and markets, finally acknowledging that the proliferation of weapons and their common use to resolve all types of disputes are continuing barriers to much-needed foreign investment. Heavy weapons are to be confiscated, while possession and sales of sidearms and assault rifles will be subject to licenses and registration. With some 50-60 million weapons in circulation in a country of 21 million people, the cabinet's order represents only a first step toward changing Yemen's ubiquitous arms culture. At the moment, there are 18 major arms markets and several hundred gun-shops in Yemen. Some shops will be allowed to reopen for the sale of personal arms under government control (IRIN, April 26, 2007). Yemen continues to be an important regional transit point for arms shipments of all types, a lucrative trade that benefits leading members of the regime.

Legislation to regulate the possession of arms continues to be opposed by a number of members of parliament who, like most of their constituents, regard holding one or more weapons as a traditional right. Some of the larger tribes possess stockpiles of heavy weapons that they will be reluctant to part with, given the 22 tribal clashes recorded last year alone. The tribes also regard their weaponry as a means of protecting themselves from government malfeasance.

Reforming the Security Apparatus

Apart from the military, Yemen's security is handled by three civilian agencies, at least two of which are believed to include Salafi and Ba'athist sympathizers at the highest levels. Most important of these is the PSO. A number of PSO officials have been dismissed in the last few years in an attempt to eliminate corruption and Islamist sympathizers from the organization as it is reshaped to take the lead in Yemen's counter-terrorism effort. The PSO reports directly to the president and its upper ranks are composed exclusively of former army officers. The Ministry of the Interior runs the Central Security Organization (CSO), a paramilitary force of 50,000 men, equipped with light weapons and armored personnel carriers. The smaller National Security Bureau (NSB), founded in 2002, reports directly to the president as well. The NSB may be designed to be in competition with the PSO. The United States currently offers counter-terrorist training to members of Yemen's security forces and is involved in helping build a new national Coast Guard (a project that also includes contributions from the United Kingdom and Australia).

The CSO's elite Counter-Terrorism Unit (CTU) is trained jointly by the United States and the United Kingdom. As a relatively new organization formed in 2003, the CTU is expected to apply innovative strategies to counter-terrorism work, while avoiding the corruption ingrained in more senior security groups. The Interior Ministry is also engaged in a campaign to decrease the size of both official and unofficial corps of bodyguards employed by public figures in Yemen. Some groups of bodyguards now approach the level of private militias, enforcing the will of local sheikhs and tribal leaders (*Yemen Observer*, April 24, 2007).

Arbitrary arrests and extended detentions without charge or trial continue to be preferred methods of the security services. The PSO, CSO and many tribal sheikhs operate their own extra-judicial detention centers. Relatives of militants are routinely imprisoned to put pressure on wanted individuals to surrender. At a recent judicial symposium, it was suggested that there are as many as 4,000 innocent citizens being held in the prisons of the security services (*Yemen Observer*, April 28, 2007). Regular use of torture in Yemen's prisons, as well as other judicial abuses have been documented in the U.S. Department of State's annual report on human rights (*Yemen Times*, March 14, 2007).

The ongoing rebellion in Saada province has the advantage, at least, of keeping the army busy while President Saleh attempts to repair relations with Washington. Many in the officer corps were trained in Ba'athist Iraq and deeply oppose the U.S.-led intervention there. Dissatisfaction in the ranks has not yet become disloyalty, however, and Saleh has placed a number of family members in crucial command roles to ensure that it stays that way. These include his son Ahmad Ali Abdullah Saleh (a possible presidential successor and presently commander of the Republican Guard and the Special Forces), his brother Ali Saleh al-Ahmar (commander of the Air Force) and half-brother Ali Mohsin al-Ahmar (commander of the northwest region and a long-time Salafi sympathizer). Two of the president's nephews serve as commanders of the CSO and the NSB.

U.S. diplomats in Yemen have frequently been targeted by Salafi extremists, although Yemen's security services have preempted several such operations. Typical of the "revolving door" approach to terrorism prosecutions that irks the United States is the case of two Yemenis convicted of trying to assassinate then U.S. Ambassador Edmund Hull (an important official in U.S. counter-terrorism efforts) in 2004. Only days after Saleh's return from Washington, the two convicts had their sentences reduced from five years to three on appeal (AFP, May 7, 2007).

Yemeni Prisoners in the United States

During his visit to Washington, President Saleh asked for the repatriation of Sheikh Muhammad Ali Hassan al-Moayad, a Yemeni religious scholar extradited from Germany to the United States (along with his assistant Muhammad Za'id), where he is serving a prison term after being convicted of supporting Hamas (but acquitted of supporting al-Qaeda). Yemeni human rights organizations are agitating for the sheikh's release on the grounds of declining health. The head of a national committee to free al-Moayad (who is popular in Yemen for his charitable work) notes that, since "Europe and the whole international community are (now) dealing with Hamas as an independent entity, why is it forbidden for al-Moayad?" (*Yemen Observer*, April 25, 2007).

Saleh also discussed the case of Yemeni citizens held in Guantanamo Bay. Although official Yemeni sources claim that Saleh requested the release of all the Yemeni Guantanamo Bay prisoners, there are signs that Yemen's government is not overeager for their repatriation. In a March 2007 visit to Yemen, Marc Falkoff, a lawyer for 17 of the Yemeni detainees, revealed that he had obtained documents from the Pentagon showing that many of the Yemeni prisoners had been eligible for repatriation as far back as June 2004. The Yemeni government justifies its inaction by claiming that the citizenship of some of the Yemeni detainees is under question. According to Falkoff, "Fully one-third of the Saudis are back in Saudi Arabia, more than half of the Afghanis are home with their families and every single European national has been released from Guantanamo. Yet, more than 100 Yemenis remain at the prison – sitting in solitary confinement on steel beds, deprived of books and newspapers, slowly going insane" (*Yemen Times*, March 11, 2007).

U.S. officials claim that there are 107 Yemeni prisoners at Guantanamo, while human rights activists cite as many as 150, but there is no doubt that Yemenis form the largest single group of foreign nationals detained at the facility. Although the government may be in no hurry for their return, reports of alleged torture practiced on Yemeni detainees in U.S.-run detention centers have inflamed anti-American sentiment in Yemen.

The Case of al-Zindani

Saleh also requested that the U.S. drop Yemen's controversial Sheikh Abdul Majid al-Zindani from its list of designated terrorists. Believed by U.S. intelligence services to be an important link to bin Laden and al-Qaeda, the sheikh's terrorist designation has been an unrelenting irritant to U.S.-Yemeni relations. The sheikh is a powerful member of the Islamist Islah Party and has close ties to Saleh's administration. Yemen's parliament recently rescinded a decision to join the International Criminal Court (ICC) system, largely because of the fear of Islah Party MPs that the ICC could be used as a tool to extradite and try al-Zindani on terrorism charges (*al-Thawri*, May 2, 2007). Apparently, Sheikh al-Zindani has lately joined the call for religious scholars to correct the mistakes in Islamic interpretation that promote dissension and political violence (*Yemen Observer*, May 2, 2007).

Conclusion

Security issues and concerns with government reforms led donor states to suspend economic aid to Yemen two years ago, but President Saleh's reform efforts appear to have regained the confidence of the international donor community. Despite the detention of political activists and opposition candidates during the 2006 election campaign, Saleh's new seven-year term as president is regarded as a sign of stability. European aid is flowing once again, and in February 2007 the Bush administration announced that Yemen was once more eligible to receive funds from the Millennium Challenge Account (MCA) (tied to progress in governance). Of the $94 million released by the MCA, $59 million is dedicated to the military and security sector (Saba News Agency, May 3, 2007). The aid represents vital assistance to Yemen's weak economy. Unemployment persists at about 40 percent, there is little development and Yemen's small petroleum industry does not enjoy the bountiful reserves found in its prosperous Arabian Peninsula neighbors.

While Saleh cannot ignore the general discontent within Yemen regarding U.S. foreign policy, he also recognizes that cooperation with the United States is the best method of ensuring the survival of his regime. Methods such as the "dialogue with extremists" and the "revolving door" of the judicial system allow Saleh to keep a lid on Sunni radicalism, while at the same time posing as a vital ally of the United States. Despite the apparent success of Saleh's visit to Washington, there is still much to concern the United States in its relationship with Yemen. Reforms to the security services have notably involved purges of al-Qaeda sympathizers at only the lowest levels. Yemeni extremists continue to join anti-coalition forces in Iraq and have been involved in terrorist operations in several countries as President Saleh continues his search for a "third option" in the war on terrorism.

[Original Publication: *Terrorism Monitor* 5 (9) – May 10, 2007]

Security Threats to Yemen Create Dilemma for United States

By Munir Mawari

Many American political analysts think that the problem the new American administration faces in Yemen relates mainly to the fate of the 100 Yemeni detainees presently incarcerated in Guantanamo Bay prison. Their homeland cannot guarantee that these individuals, if repatriated, will not become a renewed terrorist threat to America and others. In reality, Yemen's inability to deal effectively with this problem is just a small symptom of a much larger problem that faces President Obama and the West: Yemen's near future will undoubtedly witness a bloody resolution to the problem of the undemocratic nature of the present regime. The regional repercussions of this unavoidable event could be uncontrolled and widespread.

The regime that has held power in Yemen for over 30 years presents itself as democratic, yet Yemeni democracy has produced the same president in every election since July 17, 1978 (*al-Hisbah*, May 30, 2007). Although the constitution of Yemen sets a limit of two terms for a president, Ali Abdullah Saleh easily amends the constitution and resets the meter to start from zero every time his term reaches its end (*al-Hiwar*, February 25, 2007). It now appears that Saleh is grooming his son to succeed him when his current term expires in 2013. There is a belief held by some in Yemen that the policies and actions of the president have contributed to the development of an effective armed opposition (*Aram*, April 28, 2007). In consequence, President Saleh faces five major threats to his country's stability (*Sawt-Al-Yaman*, December 2008):

1. The Secessionist movement in the South: Saleh's Yemen did not always include the socialist South, which was independent until 1990. After a political unification, the leader of the South, Ali Salem al-Bied, was subjected to a series of calculated acts on the part of Saleh designed to marginalize him and his constituency, and to basically create a vassal state in the South (*Yemen Times*, May 26, 2003). This met with resistance, to which Saleh's reaction was an invasion of the south under the slogan "Unity or Death!" (Aleshteraki.net, March 31, 2008). After many deaths, Saleh won that war and achieved unity through military occupation. In his haste to neutralize the remaining southern forces, he disbanded both the southern army and security forces, sending more than 60,000 men in arms

213

packing and many jobless (Aleshteraki.net, April 6, 2008). This, of course, created a large reserve of anti-Saleh militants who were without positions but not without means. Over the course of the last 18 years, these people have reorganized themselves and now present a major threat to the "unity" of Yemen.

2. The Houthi Insurgency in the North: The Zaidi Shiite "Believing Youth" movement (also known as the *Shabab al-Muminin*) of northern Yemen was originally an organization supported as well as exploited by Saleh, who used it as a check against the spread of the Salafist movement in the North. Others, more cynically, suggested it was a means of occupying the energies of his cousin, Ali Muhsin al-Ahmar, the most powerful military man in Yemen (al-Arabiya, April 7, 2007, Nashwannews, May 11, 2009). This organization, however, grew out of its intended role and assumed its own agenda, holding its own in five rounds of serious armed conflict against Saleh (Nashwannews, May 11, 2009). A sixth round is not an unlikely event at this point, but it could very well spread from the provincial environment to larger areas, including even the capital of Sana'a (*Alahali*, April 7, 2009). The insurgency is named after the late Shiite cleric Hussein al-Houthi, who led the Believing Youth's first major military campaign against Sana'a in 2004.

3. Al-Qaeda and other militant Jihadist groups: The recent announcement by al-Qaeda's leader in Yemen, Nasir al-Wuhayshi that he is throwing his support behind the secessionist movement in the South received little approval in the jihadi forums (*Alboraq*, May 2009). Some political analysts believe the statement is an indication that Saleh is "engaging in dangerous games with the terrorists" (*Al-Majalis*, January 28, 2009). Al-Wuhayshi (transferred to Yemen by Iran in 2003) was one of the 23 al-Qaeda prisoners who "escaped" from a well-guarded Yemeni jail in 2006 (al-Jazeera, January 26, 2009). Since a public pronouncement of political support like this is not common al-Qaeda practice, it appears to be a transparent and manipulative act designed to mislead someone. The secessionist movement being socialist and secular, there is no apparent reason for al-Qaeda support to suddenly materialize.

Regional observers may conclude that none other than Saleh's political agents arranged the statement of support, using al-Qaeda operatives who owe him favors to create a political theater that can be presented to the West (al-Jazeera, May 14, 2009). The goal, of course, is to have the South aligned with inimical forces so they can be discredited by a gain in defensive allies for Saleh's regime. But this dangerous game could lead to actual war crimes being committed against Southern secessionist leaders, all in the name of "fighting terror" (Marebpress, May 3, 2009).

4. Popular grievances and grassroots movements: The U.S. Justice Department recently indicted Latin Node Communications Company, an American contractor accused of bribing one of President Saleh's sons and members of the Ministry of Telecommunications (*Yemen Post*, May 20, 2009). Latin Node eventually entered a guilty plea [1].

The news immediately plastered the front pages in Yemen, causing President Saleh to shut down eight independent newspapers, claiming they were guilty of "anti-unity" conduct. The origin of this retribution against the press is as follows: Saleh appointed a whole generation of his family members to high positions in the military and the government, placing them in control of the government's foreign investments committee (Bilakoyood, April 10, 2009; *al-Masdar*, April 14, 2009). These individuals, including his son, Ahmad Ali Abdullah Saleh, were charged with profiting from corrupt practices that used foreign investments for private gain by running fairly primitive "protection scams" wherein they were bribed to not do damage (*Al-Masdar*, April 28, 2009). While the president's son was cleared by the U.S. Justice Department, the general public in Yemen is not fooled by these corrupt practices, and as poverty levels and unemployment soar (both at 35% of the population) public resentment soars as well (*Yemen Times*, December 20, 2007; *Yemen Post*, April 25, 2009; May 7, 2009). The state of corruption in Yemen is not lost on the average citizen of Yemen who sees $80,000 Rolls Royce and Porsche automobiles being driven around the capital by clerks and mid-level personnel while he or she is commonly found standing in the bread line (Alhadath Yemen, April 24, 2009). The result has been a generalized and ever present anger within the population that could be galvanized in a form of an uprising, should some precipitating event come along.

5. Conflicts within the regime: Even within the regime, there are high-ranking members of the military or the ruling General People's Congress party who prefer their own candidacy for president to that of Saleh's son, Ahmad Ali Abdullah Saleh, leader of Yemen's Republican Guards and the Anti-Terrorism Special Forces. Many of these top officials are family members appointed by Saleh. Over the last decade a series of car accidents, helicopter crashes and illnesses have claimed the lives of many figures in Saleh's inner circle (Hadramut.net, March 3, 2006; Marebpress, April 30, 2008; *Yemen Times*, May 24, 2009). The frequency of fatal car crashes involving regime members and opposition figures (even in a country where 1,000 road fatalities a month is not uncommon) is a matter of public comment and has led to anxiety at the highest levels of the national leadership (Marebpress, April 30, 2008).

Conclusion

The policies and actions of the Saleh Regime have, in the course of 31 years, led to a critical situation that can be resolved by the Yemeni people only if Saleh is not supported by outside forces. A factor that does not often find its way into the press in this country – that the ordinary Yemeni citizen is armed – is of enormous importance in assessing the near future of Yemen. Among a population of 22 million, there are between 40 to 50 million weapons (*Asharq al-Awsat*, January 9, 2007). No matter who supports or opposes Saleh, he still lives in the middle of an armed camp. Saleh's hope is that his son takes over for him, not simply to consolidate power within his family, but also to prevent the opening of countless files about the methods used to ensure his 31 years in control. In the meantime he may find that the many armed camps within Yemen are unwilling to agree to this plan.

[Original Publication: *Terrorism Monitor* 7 (15) – June 4, 2009]

Notes

1. "Latin Node Inc., Pleads Guilty to Foreign Corrupt Practices Act Violation and Agrees to Pay $2 Million Criminal Fine," usdoj.gov. April 7, 2009; Department of Justice Press Release, Miami.fbi.gov., April 7, 2009.

Chapter Six

Economic Challenges to Stability

Yemen's Dangerous Addiction to Qat

By Michael Horton

Yemen faces an abundance of complex and interrelated social, economic, and environmental problems. Yemen's many challenges are compounded by the country's addiction to qat. Yemen is a country where large parts of its society and economy are organized around the consumption and production of the stimulant qat.

Qat consists of the tender leaves and shoots of the tree: *catha edulis*, which contain the amphetamine cathinone. Qat must be consumed soon after being harvested because the cathinone begins breaking down after twenty-four hours. When chewed, qat brings about a state of mild euphoria in the user, often followed by insomnia. Qat is considered a class 1 drug in the US and is illegal [1]. It is grown and consumed in Kenya, Ethiopia, and Yemen. While Somalia and Djibouti both import and consume qat, Yemen is the largest net consumer of qat with more than seventy percent of Yemeni households reporting at least one user [2].

There is much routine and ritual surrounding the chewing of qat. Before lunch, the earlier the better, Yemenis make their way to the qat markets that are found throughout the country to purchase a bundle or bag of qat that ranges in cost from three to as much as sixty dollars. Then after lunch Yemeni men (Yemeni women also chew qat though the number of women chewing is thought to be considerably less) gather in each other's homes to chew. A qat session often lasts more than six hours.

Changing Habits

The tradition of qat chewing in Yemen goes back at least five-hundred years. There is some question as to whether the plant originated in Ethiopia or Yemen. Historically, qat chews only took place one day a week and qat consumption was

217

limited to the wealthy and those who made up the *sayyid* and *qadi* classes, or those who were descended from the prophet and those who were members of the educated elite. This pattern of consumption began to change in the 1970s with the expansion of the Yemeni economy. In the 1970s and continuing up to the first Gulf War, Yemen's economy benefited from the millions of dollars in remittances sent back by Yemenis working primarily in Saudi Arabia. The growing economy resulted in the increased consumption of qat by lower and middle class Yemenis along with a dramatic increase in qat cultivation. When the current Yemeni regime led by President Ali Abdullah Saleh decided not to back the U.S. led coalition in the first Gulf War, Saudi Arabia canceled the visas of Yemeni workers which resulted in the return of eight-hundred thousand Yemenis [3]. Despite the loss of revenue from remittances and the subsequent decline in the Yemeni economy, throughout the nineties and continuing to the present, qat consumption and cultivation have continued to increase.

Effects on the Economy

While accurate economic statistics regarding qat are hard to come by, it is generally thought that the production and sale of qat accounts for twenty-five percent of the Yemeni economy; twenty- percent of national employment is related to the production and sale of qat. A recent report produced by the Yemeni Ministry of Agriculture estimates that Yemenis spend 1.2 billion dollars on qat annually. Qat has long since replaced coffee as Yemen's primary cash crop, the production of which has steadily declined since the 1960s (*Yemen Today*, November 21, 2009). In addition to declining coffee production, land where drought resistant grains and cereals were traditionally grown is increasingly being planted with qat. The Yemeni Ministry of Agriculture estimates that qat production is expanding at a rate of between four and six thousand hectares every year. Yemeni farmers can make up to five times more growing qat. The income from qat has therefore had a positive effect on some highland villages because the villages control both the means of production and sale. However, this is more the exception than the rule. Most of the qat trade is controlled by syndicates who buy qat from the farmers and then distribute the qat to a network of dealers and middlemen across the country. As a result, most of any real economic gain is limited to the few who have the means to market the qat.

The Yemeni governorates levy a tax on qat (26sep.net, March 14, 2010). The tax is collected from the dealers who pass through the governorate checkpoints as they take the qat to market. Figures regarding how much of a tax is imposed and how much is collected are almost impossible to come by. However, government sources in Sana'a suggest that the amount collected nationwide exceeds twenty million dollars. However, the same sources suggested that only a small percentage of this tax revenue makes its way into the official government budget. The majority of the revenue is lost due to corruption [4].

In addition to the legal trade in qat, there exists a lucrative illegal market that provides high quality qat to buyers in Saudi Arabia. Qat is illegal in Saudi Arabia but there is considerable demand for the expensive and potent Shami qat grown near the Saudi border in the Yemeni governorate of Hajjah (*Saba*, March 20, 2010). It is not known how much money the cross border trade in qat generates. However, sources in Sana'a estimated that smuggled qat generates revenues in excess of thirty million dollars a year [5].

Environmental Pressures

While qat trees are moderately drought resistant, yield increases three or four fold if the trees are irrigated. As a result, the number of wells dug throughout the highlands has increased dramatically [6]. The vast majority of these wells are unregulated: of an estimated 55,000 wells in operation only a small percentage are state owned or regulated. This and the pressure of a high population growth rate have resulted in a severe water shortage (*Yemen Observer*, February 16, 2010; *Yemen Post*, June 28, 2009). According to the United Nations Development Program (UNDP), the Yemeni population will exceed forty-million by 2025. Yemen has one of the world's lowest freshwater availability rates and one of the highest agricultural consumption rates for water. The Yemeni Ministry of Agriculture estimates that thirty-percent of Yemen's available water is being used for the irrigation of qat trees. A source within the General Authority for Rural Development estimated that the percentage was considerably higher than the official estimates.

The water shortage is particularly acute in Sana'a where the UNDP estimates that the extraction rate from the aquifer that supplies Sana'a is 2.5 times the replenishment rate. Recent studies estimate that the aquifer that provides water for Sana'a could run dry by 2017 [7]. The growth of the urban centers of Sana'a, Ta'iz, and to a lesser extent Ibb is placing increasing pressure on the important agricultural belts that surround all three of these cities. It is common for private tanker companies to raid unregulated wells just outside the cities so that they can provide their customers in the cities with water. In Sana'a, almost every house either has a private well or a tank to which water deliveries are made. The pressure being put on the surrounding rural areas has already led to a number of violent confrontations in all three areas.

Social Problems

It is estimated that the average Yemeni household spends over ten-percent of its income on qat. In some estimates the expenditure exceeds thirty-percent. This would be a problem in any country, but the problem is particularly acute in Yemen where the gross national income does not exceed nine-hundred dollars. In a traditional society such as the one that predominates in Yemen, men most often control the family's income. Many men place more importance on the day's qat purchase than on the needs of the family. This leads to much familial discord.

The amount of time spent buying and chewing qat every day also takes a toll on the country's productivity. In the 1960s, the Marxist government of what was then South Yemen estimated that more than four billion work hours were lost due to the consumption of qat. While at the time this was clearly more propaganda than fact, now this estimate may not be much of an exaggeration.

The effect of qat on users' health is a matter of some dispute. Most experts agree that while not physiologically addictive, qat does have a number of side effects. Among these are insomnia, paranoia, hypertension, cavities, and a tenuous link with some oral cancers. There is growing concern among Yemen's doctors over the use of qat by children. It is not uncommon to see boys as young as eleven or twelve chewing qat. Some doctors believe that the side-effects of qat chewing are more pronounced in the young.

Controlling Qat Usage and Production?

The Yemeni government has made no real effort to control the consumption of qat. Some efforts have been made to control or limit usage within the armed services. However, even this effort has been largely confined to certain elite forces. A number of private organizations have launched campaigns against qat but these have met with limited or no success. Much of the government's unwillingness to confront the issue of qat arises from the fact that it is now a crucial part of the Yemeni economy. If qat were made illegal or even if it were heavily regulated, the already fragile Yemeni economy would unravel. The short-term shock would be unsustainable and there would likely be a countrywide revolt. Many of the highland villages, home to some of the most powerful tribes, are now largely dependent on the money generated by the sale of qat. These villages and communities function as mini-states and often possess arsenals worthy of mini-states. The Yemeni government does not seem to have any short or long term plans to counter the increasing consumption and production of qat. A recent program to restrict the planting of more qat tress in the governorate of Dhamar has not resulted in any measurable reductions in qat production (*Yemen Times*, March 5, 2010) [8]. The poor rains of 2009 and increasing cost of water have driven qat prices higher thereby encouraging farmers to continue to produce qat and in many cases expand production.

Conclusion

The Yemeni government faces a plethora of serious challenges both short and long term. It is unlikely that it will at any point be able to tackle the country's addiction to qat. The Saleh regime is currently facing multiple separatist movements as well as the perennial threat posed by Islamic extremists. Given qat's popularity throughout the country, any attempts to tax or prohibit qat would result in further problems for the Saleh regime. Increasing food and water insecurity will likely lead to slow and sporadic measures undertaken at the local level to replace qat with food crops. These measures will almost certainly be driven by necessity rather than any governmental authority.

[Original Publication: *Terrorism Monitor* – April 15, 2010]

Notes

1. Kennedy, J.G., *The Flower of Paradise: The Institutionalized Use of the Drug Qat in North Yemen* (New York: Springer, 1987), p. 10-15.
2. Milanovic, Branko, "Qat Expenditures in Yemen and Djibouti: An Empirical Analysis," World Bank January 2007.
3. Dresch, Paul, *A History of Modern Yemen* (Cambridge: Cambridge University Press, 2000), p. 186.
4. Author interview in Yemen (November 2009).
5. Author interview in Yemen (December 2009).
6. Milich, Leonard; Al-Sabry, Mohammed, "The 'Rational Peasant' vs. Sustainable Livelihoods: The Case of Qat in Yemen," Society for International Development, 1995.
7. Author interview in Yemen (December 2009) – also see: "Human Development Report: Yemen 2009," United Nations Development Fund.
8. Oudah, Abdul Aziz, "Qat Absorbs More than Yemen's Depleting Water," *Yemen Observer*, Feb. 16, 2010.

Food and Water Security in Yemen

By Mohammed al-Maitami

Food and water security are very complex and multidimensional issues that cannot be reduced to simple formula and measures. Rather, food and water security are determined by the interaction of a range of economic, social, political, demographic, environmental, and biological factors. In this article, I will briefly focus on just three major, but interrelated, dimensions of food and water security in Yemen: the production and consumption of food, the availability and use of water resources, and the macro-economic determinants of food and water security.

The Prevalence of Food and Water Insecurity

Yemen has experienced three major famines in the 20th century (in 1944, 1958, and 1970/71) and again in the contemporary period Yemen faces such enormous economic challenges that the prospect of famine is very real. Thus the World Bank views Yemen "the single most significant development challenge in the Middle East" [1]. The challenges facing Yemen are sobering and while Yemen's human history is long and steeped in tradition, today that history and tradition are partly an obstacle to change and progress.

The Challenge of Poverty

Yemen is the poorest country of the Middle East, surrounded by relatively stable countries with great wealth and prosperity, which seems only to accentuate Yemen's relative poverty. Yemeni per capita income today is barely US$965 [2], and over 40 percent of the population lives below the national poverty line [3]. A full third of Yemeni households are food insecure, and the open unemployment rate is 17 percent. Yemen is also the most populous country in the Arabian Peninsula. At 23 million, Yemen's population is nearly equal to the population of the GCC combined (discounting immigrant labor). The Yemeni population is youthful, with about 50 percent of the population under the age of 15. The population is expected to more than double in the next twenty years. To make matters worse, Yemen suffers from acute water shortages, with per capita share of water at 2% of the international average and 10% of the Middle Eastern average. The water situation is so critical that homes in some major cities, such as Taiz, the second largest city, which gets its water for just a few hours every other week. Water reserves for Sana'a, the capital city, are expected to be depleted in twenty years. Finally, depletion of oil reserves, scarcity of arable land (3% of the total area) and internal and external shocks that the country has suffered and continues to suffer aggravate these challenges.

Poverty and Food Security

The recent global food and financial and economic crises has been particularly damaging for Yemen, especially in terms of poverty and food security. The gains in poverty reduction that had been achieved between 1998/99 and 2005/06 have been reversed. According to IFPRI's and MOPIC findings, poverty in Yemen has increased by 8 points over the past five years, from a national prevalence of 34.8% in 2005/06 to 42.8% in 2010. The increase has been particularly acute in the urban areas, which have seen a 40.0% increase in poverty as compared to a 19.8% increase in the rural areas. The country's Millennium Development Goal is to decrease poverty to 10% by 2025, a goal that is increasingly distant.

Poverty is highly correlated with food insecurity, as poverty rates increase when food insecurity goes up. The percentage of the population that are identified as 'food insecure' (those who do not have enough food) has increased from 13.2% in 2005 to 32.2% in 2010, reflecting the deterioration in food security over the past five years. The absolute number of food-insecure is five times greater in rural areas than in urban areas. The Poverty Reduction Strategy (2003-2005) interpreted this increase as a result of modest economic growth, which averaged about 4% per annum during the period 2005-2010. The World Bank and other international institutions view economic growth as the single most important factor in food security. Unfortunately, Yemen has not been able to achieve a sustainable program of economic growth. None of the last three five-year economic plans have achieved their goals and in order to achieve the Millennium Development Goals, the Yemeni economy must grow at an average annual rate of 8 percent. Such growth rates require far higher levels of investment. Sustained high levels of economic growth will also require intensive efforts to attract foreign direct investment, including comprehensive political reforms, establishment of the rule of law and stabilizing the security situation. However, recent results seem to indicate that even sustained economic growth may not suffice to solve Yemen's problem of poverty. In my calculation, only 2-3% of the total share of recent economic growth went to the benefit of the poorest

20th percentile, and about 50% went to the benefit of the richest 20th of population. Clearly, economic growth in Yemen has not been to the satisfactory of the poor, and has not had any positive impact on poverty reduction. Quite the contrary, the number of poor has grown and the severity of poverty has deepened.

Macroeconomic Instability and the Agricultural Sector

Moreover, Yemen's macroeconomic stability is threatened by declining hydrocarbon revenue – Yemen is expected to become a net oil importer by 2015, and Yemen's balance of payments has deteriorated as a result. From comfortable surpluses in the middle of the decade, the current account now faces deepening deficits. This will have a severe impact on the government budget and more importantly on ability of the country to import food for its population, as oil constitutes about 70% of government revenues. In the face of these macroeconomic shocks, accelerating economic growth, even growth that benefits the poor, will still be insufficient to solve Yemen's economic challenges. Yemen will need to implement additional policies aimed at restructuring the economy. The agricultural sector still employs more than 50% of labor force and is considered a source of livelihood for 75% of the population, though in terms of the larger economy, agriculture plays a small and declining role: its share in GDP is little more than 13 percent. However, in terms of food and water security, the agricultural sector plays a much more important role and contributor. Its importance to the water crisis stems from the fact that it utilizes between 90% and 93% of total water resources in Yemen. And the marked discrepancy between the low contribution of agriculture to GDP and the large percentage of the labor force employed, points to the persistent problem of low labor productivity – a critical factor in low incomes and poor standards of living for workers employed in the sector.

Agricultural Production, Macroeconomic Instability, and Food Insecurity

Wheat and other cereal products are the dominant elements in meeting food requirements for Yemeni households and the majority of Yemen's staples are imported. Imports of food cost 466.4 YR billion in 2008 ($2.33 billion USD) [4], and cereals make up 60% of total food imports. Local cereal production is mainly for subsistence and it supplies only about 21% of total demand. The vast majority of Yemen's food needs are met through imports. Hence, food insecurity is possibly greater today than ever in Yemeni history because of the growing deficits in Yemen's balance of payments. Yemen's foreign reserves are declining rapidly as a result of falling oil revenues.

There are prospects for expansion of domestic cereal production and, with the current rise in international and domestic prices, there can be a sizable benefit from such expansion for many key players. But there are serious constrains to agricultural expansion and the development of food security in Yemen. The most important are the following:

1. Water scarcity and poor performance in irrigation
2. Severe scarcity of arable land and the continuing fragmentation of land holdings
3. Inequity in land tenancy and water rights
4. Expansion of Qat production
5. Hostile environment for the private sector

Water Scarcity and Qat Production

Yemen is facing a severe water crisis. In 1995, total water consumption was estimated at about 3.2 billion cubic meters (m³), while the annual renewable fresh water resources were stable at 2.5 billion m³ of which surface and groundwater contribute a billion m³ and 1.5 billion m³ respectively. This means that Yemen had a water deficit of 700 million m³ in 1995. In 2006 this deficit had more than doubled and it was estimated to be 1.6 billion m³ [5]. Yemen's per capita water use is 75 times less than the international average. Using an analogy for per capita water consumption, if the average international per capita water consumption is a one liter bottle of water, Yemen's per capita consumption is a teaspoon of water. Ten years from now, even that teaspoon will be dry if water consumption continues at the current rate.

The problem of water scarcity is compounded by the expansion of Qat production. Qat production depends heavily on underground water extracted through the use of wells and pumps (80 percent of production). The rapid expansion of Qat production is a major challenge facing Yemen. While Qat production and the Qat trade contribute significantly to GDP (about 9 percent), it causes serious social and economic problems for the country. The area under Qat cultivation today is estimated at about 147 thousand hectares [6], which is about 11% of the agricultural land in Yemen. Land under Qat cultivation has increased 18 fold over the last four decades, which translates into an annual rate of increase of 7.5% between 1970 and 2008. The rapidly expansion of Qat cultivation is exhausting underground water resources due to excessive pumping. The total water consumption for Qat production increased from 670 million m^3 in 1996 to 840 million m^3 in 2000, or around 23% of the total use and about 25% of the total water consumption for the agricultural sector. This means that every bundle of Qat (about 100 grams, which is the average daily Qat consumption per individual) uses almost 535 liters of water. This is enough to secure the household water needs of an average Yemeni family for almost 3 days.

It is true that Qat is an important source of income for a large part of the rural economy; nevertheless, Qat consumption threatens the food and water security of Yemen. The World Bank estimated that Qat consumption absorbed 11% of the average household budget in Yemen, and the expenditure on Qat and complementary items consumed significantly, reduced the savings capacity of most families. If all Qat expenditure were reallocated to other uses such as food and clothing, the incidence of poverty would decrease by 6.2 percent. Qat cultivation poses a difficult dilemma for policy-makers because it represents such a lucrative crop for the relatively poor agricultural sector, yet at the same time, its production threatens food and water security. Today, that dilemma is even greater.

Notes

1. إستراتيجية المساعدة القطرية ، وثيقة البنك الدولي ، تقرير رقم 36014 ، 17 مايو 2006..

2. التقرير الأقتصادي السنوي 2007. وزارة التخطيط والتنمية ، الجمهورية اليمنية ، صنعاء ، 2008م.

3. Country Assistance Strategy for the Republic of Yemen," Document of the World Bank, February 24, 2009.
4. Statistical Year Book 2008, CSO, Sana'a, July 2009.
5. Qat production in Yemen, Ministry of planning and FAO, September 2008.
6. Agricultural Statistics Year Book 2008, Ministry of Agriculture, Sana'a, March 2009.

Yemen On The Brink
Implications for U.S. Security Interests in the Horn of Africa

Jamestown Foundation Conference
April 15, 2010

held at the

Carnegie Endowement for International Peace
Washington, DC

<u>Keynote Speakers</u>

Ambassador Daniel Benjamin
&
Bruce Riedel

AMBASSADOR DANIEL BENJAMIN
Coordinator for Counterterrorism,
U.S. Department of State

Good morning. I want to thank Jamestown for holding this important conference and Glen Howard for inviting me back to address it. I take this as a vote of some confidence since it was just last December that I was honored to deliver the keynote at your annual conference. Well, I guess I'll have to take it as a vote of confidence because if someone is pulling a fast one they've certainly gotten it past me.

In any case, I'm pleased to have been asked back to speak about Yemen, one of the foremost challenges we face in foreign policy and in counterterrorism more specifically.

Let me start by talking about the circumstances we face today arose in Yemen. Then I'll turn to the Obama administration's strategy for the country, which aims to help the Yemeni government to both confront the immediate security concern of al-Qaeda and mitigate the serious political, economic, and governance issues that the country faces over the long term.

In terms of public perception of the shifting geographic focal points of contemporary terrorism, one might argue that no place in the last year has received as much attention as Yemen. The failed December 25th bombing was a stark reminder that un- or under-governed spaces can serve as an incubator for extremism.

Furthermore, that conspiracy demonstrated that at least one al-Qaeda affiliate has developed not just the desire but also the capability to launch strikes against the United States itself. We can no longer count on AQ affiliates to be focused exclusively on the near enemy – the governments in their own countries – or American facilities in their immediate surroundings.

Having said that, we also need some perspective. Contrary to some recent and overblown media accounts of al-Qaeda in Yemen, the country did not turn into an al-Qaeda safe haven overnight. In fact, Yemen was arguably the very first front. Al-Qaeda has had a presence in Yemen since well before the United States had even identified the group or recognized that it posed a significant threat. The December 1992 al-Qaeda attempt to bomb a hotel in Aden where American military personnel were staying was probably the first genuine al-Qaeda attack. Those troops, you may recall, were in en route to Somalia to support the UN

228

mission there – this was almost eight years before the U.S.S. Cole attack in 2000. Al-Qaeda has always had a foothold in Yemen, and it's always been a major concern for the United States.

In the 1990s, a series of major conspiracies were based in Yemen, most of them aimed at Saudi Arabia. Following the attack on the U.S.S. Cole in 2000, the Yemeni government, with support from the United States, dealt significant blows to al-Qaeda's presence in Yemen through military operations and arrests of key leaders.

After that period of collaboration, however, the Government of Yemen became distracted by other domestic security concerns, and our bilateral cooperation experienced setbacks. In the wake of the May 2003 al-Qaeda attacks in Saudi Arabia, the Government of Saudi Arabia dramatically improved its counterterrorism efforts. That forced many violent extremists to flee Saudi Arabia for Yemen, joining other fighters who had returned from Afghanistan and Pakistan. As you may recall, a group of senior al-Qaeda leaders escaped from a Yemeni prison in 2006, further strengthening the organization's presence in the country.

For the last five years, these terrorists have carried out multiple attacks against Yemenis, Americans, and citizens of other countries. In the last two years, this al-Qaeda franchise has carried out a string of attacks, including an attack on the U.S. Embassy in September 2008, kidnapping of several groups of foreign tourists, and attempts to terrorize Yemen's own security services. Then in January 2009, the leader of al-Qaeda in Yemen (AQY), Nasir al-Wuhayshi, announced that Yemeni and Saudi al-Qaeda operatives were now working together under the banner of al-Qaeda in the Arabian Peninsula (AQAP).

Yemen, of course, does not exist in a vacuum. The stability of the country is essential to the broader Gulf region and global security, and delegitimizing AQAP also requires addressing Yemen's own shortcomings to break the cycle of radicalization. A key part of our work to "disrupt, dismantle, and defeat" al-Qaeda is to understand that Yemen's future is tied to its neighbors and others in the global community. AQAP has already shown itself to be a formidable threat to Yemen's internal security, with attacks on the Yemeni security services, as well as a threat to Saudi Arabia, with an August 2009 failed assassination attempt against the head of counterterrorism in Saudi Arabia, Prince Mohammed Bin Nayif. Similarly, we must also be mindful of the regional dimension of the AQAP threat, including its ties with Somalia. The freedom of movement and the large refugee population from Somalia amplify the historic ties between these two nations, and we know that the vast majority of these connections are not only related to terrorism. The extremist threat coming from Somalia in the form of al-Shabaab is different from AQAP in Yemen, but we recognize a source of common threat and we are concerned about the possibility that they'll operate jointly.

Now I'd like to turn to the administration's strategy as a whole for Yemen and its approach to countering and constraining AQAP. What I can say, definitively, is that the dangerousness of AQAP was clear to the Obama administration from day one, and it has been focused on Yemen since the outset. Let me put this in personal terms: Quite literally, on my first day at the State Department – in fact, the day I was sworn in – Deputy Secretary of State Steinberg said to me, "Here are some of the priorities you need to be looking at," and right at the top of the list was Yemen.

In the spring of 2009, the administration initiated a full-scale review of our Yemen policy. The review has led to a new, whole-of-government approach to Yemen that aims to coordinate our efforts with those of other international actors. Our new strategy seeks to address the root causes of instability and improve governance. Central to this approach is building the capacity of Yemen's government to exercise its authority and deliver security and services to its people.

To advance this strategy, we've engaged consistently and intensively with our Yemeni counterparts. Senior administration civilian and military officials – including Deputy National Security Advisor Brennan, Assistant Secretary of State for Near Eastern Affairs Jeffrey Feltman, General David Petraeus, and myself – visited Yemen to discuss how we can jointly confront the threat of al-Qaeda. The result has been a significant – and we hope enduring – turn by the government in taking on AQAP. Those actions, it is important to emphasize, began before the December 25th plot, and have continued ever since.

Now, Yemen has conducted multiple operations designed to disrupt AQAP's operational planning and deprive its leadership of safe haven within Yemeni territory.

But there is more to this story. As I mentioned at the beginning of my speech, the administration's strategy toward Yemen is two-fold: to strengthen the Government of Yemen's ability to promote security and minimize the threat from violent extremists; and to bolster its capacity to provide basic services and good governance. Al-Qaeda in the Arabian Peninsula takes advantage of insecurity in various regions of Yemen, which is worsened by internal conflicts and competition for governance by tribal and non-state actors. This is why we, if we are going to succeed, we must address the problem of terrorism in Yemen from a comprehensive, long-term perspective. The logic behind this strategy is that while we work with the Yemeni government to constrain and dismantle AQAP, we will also assist the Yemeni people in building more durable, responsive institutions and a more hopeful future, which in turn will go far in reducing the appeal of violent extremism.

Real security and sustainable development – the two are inextricably connected. And they can be achieved when the Yemeni government takes the lead. The United States will provide assistance and support, but Yemen is a sovereign nation, and we respect its responsibility for its own development and security. So what we are doing in Yemen is one of the cornerstones of our counterterrorism policy – capacity building. Both on the security side and the economic and governance side of things, we are helping to address the state insufficiencies that terrorism thrives on, and we are helping invest the Government of Yemen to more effectively confront the threat.

On the security front, the Departments of State and Defense provide training and assistance to Yemen's key counterterrorism units. We provide training to security forces in the Ministry of Interior, including the Yemeni Coast Guard and the Counterterrorism Unit (CTU) as well as assisting the Central Security Forces. The training includes border control management, crime scene investigation, fraudulent document recognition, surveillance detection, crisis management, and a comprehensive airport security/screening consultation and assessment. We also see additional opportunities to increase our training and capacity-building programs for Yemeni law enforcement. We are working with the Department of Defense to coordinate closely in planning and implementing assistance programs.

All of this will help strengthen the Government of Yemen's ability to promote security and minimize the threat from violent extremists. But as I mentioned earlier, this strategy will only succeed if we also strengthen Yemen's capacity to provide basic services and good governance. Yemen is grappling with serious poverty. As you all know, it is the poorest country in the Arab world and it complicates governance across a country that is larger than Iraq. Its per capita income of $930 ranks it 166th out of 174 countries. Yemen's oil production is steadily decreasing. Water resources are fast being depleted. With over half of its people living in poverty and the population growing at an unsustainable 3.2 percent per year, economic conditions threaten to worsen and further tax the government's already limited capacity. Furthermore, endemic corruption further impedes the ability of the Yemeni government to provide essential services.

Therefore, the U.S. is providing development assistance to improve governance and help to meet pressing socio-economic challenges. Excluding counterterrorism funding, U.S. development and security assistance have increased in Yemen from $17.2 million in FY2008, to $40.3 million in FY2009, and we expect total FY 2010 assistance to be as much as $63 million. Priorities for U.S. assistance include political and fiscal reforms; reducing corruption and implementing civil service reform; and economic diversification to generate employment. Additionally, USAID is working to build the capacity of Yemen's government ministries to deliver services more effectively, efficiently, and responsively. And the Middle East Partnership Initiative (MEPI) works with Yemeni civil society to empower Yemenis to build a more peaceful and prosperous future.

The challenges in Yemen are obviously large. So appropriately, our efforts in the country are part of a global partnership to enhance security and improve governance. Many nations share our concern about Yemen and want to assist. We are working with all of Yemen's international partners to better coordinate foreign assistance and to make sure that it has an impact on the ground. Through the Friends of Yemen process, the United States is engaged with international partners, especially regional states, in working with the Government of Yemen to help address the multitude of problems. The United States is mindful of the fact that although we are a major donor to Yemen we are not the only one. The United Kingdom, Germany, the Netherlands, and others contribute large amounts of aid every year, and Saudi Arabia, the UAE and other Gulf states play an extremely important role in supporting Yemen.

We are also working internationally to prevent funds from getting to al-Qaeda in the Arabian Peninsula. As soon as it announced its formation, we began gathering evidence to build international consensus behind designating it under UN Security Council Resolution 1267. After our designation of AQAP as a Foreign Terrorist Organization and its senior leaders as designated terrorists, the UN announced the designation of AQAP as well as al-Wuhayshi and al-Shihri on the consolidated list. This requires all UN member states to implement an assets freeze, a travel ban, and an arms embargo against these entities.

In order to succeed in Yemen, it is also vital that we understand how recruits are radicalized; what their motivations are; and how we can address the drivers of radicalization so that we can begin to turn the tide against violent extremism.

Some of our aid programs will help address underlying conditions for at-risk populations. Reducing corruption and building legitimate institutions with our assistance will also reduce the appeal of extremism. And we will continue to build positive people-to-people engagement with the people of Yemen, through educational and cultural exchanges. Exchange programs have a multiplying effect as participants return to Yemen and convey to friends and family the realities of American culture and society, dispelling damaging but persistent stereotypes. These initiatives contribute to the long-term health of our bilateral relationship and help allay suspicion and misunderstanding.

In addition to such global initiatives, we are committed to supporting internal peace within Yemen. The violent conflict in the Saada governorate of northern Yemen between the central government and Houthi rebels, and the protest movement in the South, which has led to riots and sporadic outbreaks of violence, are fueled by long-standing grievances. The United States is encouraging the Yemeni government to seek a lasting peace in Saada as well as to allow for the provision of humanitarian and development assistance there, and is asking Yemen's Gulf neighbors and other partners to do so as well.

The United States is very encouraged that the recent ceasefire has ended armed conflict. This ceasefire will only hold if both sides address the political problems that underlie the conflict. Recent efforts to release prisoners and allow international aid into Saada show promise for the future. The United States, along with international partners, will continue to press for peace by requesting that the Government of Yemen grant aid agencies access to the Sa'ada governorate to provide assistance to displaced persons and facilitate their return. To assist those displaced by the conflict, USAID's Office of Food for Peace has donated $7.5 million in emergency food aid and the Office of Foreign Disaster Assistance has contributed $3 million to relief efforts.

The U.S. strategy in Yemen recognizes that Yemen has not always had the political will or focused attention to address its problems. We are working hard with our international partners to address Yemen's security and other challenges. We are encouraged because President Saleh and his government have shown more resolve than ever before to confront AQAP and to engage with the international community on domestic non-security issues. The United States commends Yemen on its counterterrorism operations and we are committed to continuing support for security initiatives and economic-development initiatives.

As I conclude, I'd like to stress that we don't claim to have all the answers. Given the difficult political, economic, social, security, and governance challenges besetting Yemen, it is important that we recognize progress will not come easily. We are involved in a number of different, rather difficult undertakings; this is a beginning and not an end.

I'd also like to reiterate that our approach to the problem of terrorism in Yemen must be comprehensive and sustained, taking into account a wide range of political, cultural, and socio-economic factors. Ultimately, the goal of U.S. and international efforts is a stable, secure, and effectively governed Yemen. As the Government of Yemen grows more transparent and responsive to the requirements of its citizens, the seeds of extremism and violence will find less fertile ground and a more positive and productive dynamic will begin to prevail.

I invite your questions.

BRUCE RIEDEL
Senior Fellow
Saban Center for Middle East Policy,
Brookings Institution

Thank you Glen for that very, very kind introduction. Thank you for inviting me back to Jamestown.

Twelve years ago Osama bin Laden, Ayman Zawahiri, and three other men declared war on the United States of America in the city of Khost in Eastern Afghanistan. Ten Years ago an al-Qaeda cell in Yemen came close to sinking an American destroyer, the U.S.S. Cole, and inflicted catastrophic damage on it in the port of Aden. Today al-Qaeda has rampaged around the world from New York to Bali, from Virginia to virtually every city in the Islamic world. Today al-Qaeda is the world's first truly global terrorist network. With cells throughout the Muslim diasporas, with franchises throughout the Muslim world and with the headquarters and CEO operating somewhere in South Asia. Al-Qaeda has demonstrated over the last decade it is a remarkably dynamic, adaptive and agile organization. What I would like to do over the course of the next half hour or so is set the stage here a little bit for the very important conference that you are having here today.

And talk about first al-Qaeda and then al-Qaeda in the Arabian Peninsula (AQAP). We now see that al-Qaeda has what I would like to say one and a half major hubs today. The one major hub is of course the headquarters in Pakistan and Afghanistan, which is today facing unprecedented pressure upon it. Pressure that it has not seen anything like since early 2002. There is an emerging second center—what I call the half hub in Yemen. How dangerous is that half hub? How serious is it going to be for the future of the global Islamic jihad? What role does it play in the decision-making process of al-Qaeda? Those are I think some of the central questions for today, for this conference, and for the United States to understand.

Let me begin with a brief overview of the state of al-Qaeda the global organization today, to set the stage for talking about AQAP over the course of the day. I would like to make 5 points about the state of al-Qaeda today. Five what I would call facets of the organizational structure.

First is of course the senior leadership. The man who declared war on the United States 12 years ago. They are alive; they are still plotting. They are under tremendous pressure but they are deeply involved in plans to strike at the United States of America. We have two recent, very interesting pieces of evidence that underscore this. First is the guilty plea brought in by David Headley last month in Chicago, where he pleaded guilty to six charges of murder involved in the attack on Mumbai in November of 2008.

For those of you who have not followed the David Headley case, let me set the stage for a minute. David Headley is a Pakistani-American who began working for Lashkar-e-Taiba (LeT) in 2002. Over the course of three years, he was trained extensively in their camps in Pakistan. In 2005, he was assigned the mission of being the scout for what would become the attack on Mumbai in November 2008. He made five trips to Mumbai [inaudible] every single one of the targets in minute detail. After the attack, he was sent on another mission to do scouting for an al-Qaeda attack in Copenhagen, Denmark. In the course of that operation, he met twice with senior al-Qaeda officials in Waziristan and was told the al-Qaeda elders were personally involved in overseeing his activities. In other words, Osama bin Laden, Ayman Zawahiri, deeply involved in a major attack on a major European city. The senior leadership active and involved.

The second piece of information we have, new data, comes from the interview with the Jordanian triple agent who attacked the CIA's forward operating base in Khost on the 30th of December of last year. I will use his nomme de guerre Mr. Kharassani. In his martyrdom video, which if you have not looked at, it's one of the most chilling I've ever seen, he describes how in a few hours he's going to go kill people. But he says in his video that he is being guided in this attack by al-Qaeda's top Shura Council. Once again, the senior leadership still active, still involved, still setting overall strategy and still involved in the tactics of individual attacks. This is remarkable. Osama bin Laden and Ayman Zawahiri are the two most wanted men in history. They are the target of the largest manhunt ever in human history. We think they are in Pakistan, but the honest truth is we don't have a clue where they are. They could be sitting in the back row of this meeting for all we really know. Wherever they are, they are under pressure today in a way they have not been before. But they are still active, and still involved. This second point I would make is the al-Qaeda senior leadership in Pakistan is embedded in a multi-layered syndicate of terror that is extraordinarily complex and adaptive. Al-Qaeda itself may be relatively small. You will see in the newspapers senior

American officials telling you there is two or three hundred of them in Pakistan. Do not believe it. We do not have a clue how many people are in AQ. If we knew how many were in, we could answer the question, where is Osama bin Laden? But let's assume it numbers somewhere in the hundreds or few thousands. It is embedded in a much larger syndicate of terrorist groups like LeT; like the Pakistan Taliban; like the Afghan Taliban. Not a monolith; not a single agenda; not a single leader but operationally connected more and more cohesive. The Headley case is the perfect illustration of that. LeT actually transfers its operative from its control to al-Qaeda's control. The Kharassani example is another good example. Kharassani worked for al-Qaeda, but sitting next to him in his martyrdom video was the head of the Pakistan Taliban. And just last week, Haqqani Network – the Afghan Taliban – claimed credit for bringing him to the target site.

Third, there are of course the franchises. Al-Qaeda in the Arabian Peninsula is by far the most active today and the only one, which has taken on a role on the global level. Al-Qaeda in Iraq, formerly the premier star of al-Qaeda has been in eclipse but I suspect it's on the rebound. Al-Qaeda in the Islamic Maghreb (AQIM) is expanding its network south into the Sahel and into northern Nigeria. The different franchises all vary in lethality and in how they are doing at any time.

Think again of the corporate model. Sometimes you are a distributor, and North America is doing well, sometimes not so well. What is most important to bear in mind about the franchises is, none of them so far has been truly effectively destroyed. The franchise in Indonesia is the one that comes closest. But every time we have said a franchise is finished, we see it come back a few years later.

The fourth aspect of al-Qaeda's structure today is the cells throughout the Muslim disapora. This, of course from the counter-terrorism perspective and defense of the homeland, is the most dangerous element of al-Qaeda today. For example, the case of Najibullah Zazi who pleaded guilty recently to a plot to attack the New York City metro. The targets were Grand Central Station and Times Square station. The timing was to be on the anniversary of 9/11 last fall. Mr. Zazi, an Afghan-American, had gone to Pakistan to join the Taliban. The Taliban saw that they had an extraordinary prize. They were not going to waste him in the Hindu Kush. They trained him in how to use explosives, just like those used in the attack on the London underground in 2005 and then came back to this country with the mission to create carnage on the anniversary of 9/11.

The British government has recently released a report in which it says her Majesty's government arrested in 2009 some 200 militants in the United Kingdom connected to al-Qaeda. The report also says 200 more were arrested throughout the rest of Western Europe in 2009 connected to al-Qaeda. Even if only one half or a quarter of those arrested were serious al-Qaeda operatives, that remains a dangerous threat.

The fifth element of al-Qaeda today and perhaps the single most important is the idea of al-Qaeda. Al-Qaeda has evolved from a terrorist cell to an idea.

The idea of global Islamic jihad. This idea motivates self-motivating extremists around the world. People like Major Nidal Hasan at Fort Hood who connected with the global Islamic jihad on his laptop.

Some of these people are probably never going to be a danger to anyone. Jihad Jane was I think more of a danger to herself than she was to anybody else. Some will be extremely dangerous. But the idea is more than just something that fuels a few extremists. It's an idea that pushes the entire spectrum of Islamic militancy toward the al-Qaeda narrative and ideology. What was once a very small movement is now gradually seeping into many, many other movements, which initially resisted the idea of global Islamic jihad.

Lashkar-e-Taiba is the perfect example. LeT began as a movement focused on India and Kashmir. But in Mumbai in November of 2008, it attacked the targets of the global Islamic jihad. Yes Indians, but also Americans and other crusaders in the city, and above all the Israeli target. The al-Qaeda senior leadership clearly sets the broad strategy for the overall organization. It dictates the priorities. It sets the target stage. But it leaves tactics and it leaves local initiative in the hands of its emirs.

It is smart enough to know that you cannot run a global terrorist organization clandestinely from somewhere in Pakistan. We saw this clearly, for example, in the statement that announced the creation of al-Qaeda in the Arabian Peninsula, the merger of al-Qaeda in Yemen and al-Qaeda in Saudi Arabia in January 2009. The affirmation of who is in charge, let me quote to you from it:

We affirm to our leaders and sheikhs, Sheikh Osama bin Laden, and Sheikh Ayman al-Zawahiri, that we are abiding by our pledge to them to carry out jihad.

Clear definition of who is in charge and who sets strategy. If you read the statement carefully, it also underscores AQAP's commitment to the long-term goals of al-Qaeda as laid out by Dr. Ayman Zawahiri in dozens of audio and video tapes since September 11th.

The first priority is to attack the crusaders; to attack the far enemy. This will lead to the overthrow of the quisling apostate regimes, set the stage for the recreation of the caliphate, and set the stage for the final and climactic battle to destroy Israel.

Again, if you go back to the merger statement, it quotes Abu Musab al-Zarqawi, the late commander of al-Qaeda in Iraq as saying: "We fight in Iraq while our eyes are always looking to Jerusalem."

This statement of who is in charge, who sets the tone was also clear in the statements of responsibility for the Christmas Day attack on northwest flight 253 into Detroit. AQAP went out of its way to give credit to Osama bin Laden for inspiring the operation. And in his two statements in which he took responsibility, he in turn placed it in the strategic framework of al-Qaeda's priorities. These raids – this raid on Detroit – was in his eyes just the latest culmination of the long series of raids since September 11th with the intention of punishing the United States of America for continuing to support apostate regimes and above all, for continuing to support Israel.

It is no surprise that Osama bin Laden would place such a high priority on AQAP. Yemen has always been at the heart of many of his designs. Of course, there is the family connection: the origins of the bin Laden family in South Yemen in the Hadhramout. But there is more than that. After 1989, when bin Laden felt that he had personally helped defeat the Soviet Union in Afghanistan through the creation of what became the potale of al-Qaeda, he wanted to take his war to South Yemen. To overthrow the People's Democratic Republic of Yemen, and give the Soviet Union another defeat.

What he did not recognize was that South Yemen was toppling on its own and that the Soviet Union was in such a difficult situation, it didn't need any further pushes. In any case, the Saudi authorities vetoed the idea, saying we have other plans for South Yemen.

Aden may have also been the scene of the first tack of violence, first use of violence of a group under bin Laden's control. The attack on the Movenpick Hotel in 1992. To underscore again, the importance that Yemen has in his worldview: on the eve of 9/11, he married a Yemeni.

Now Yemen seems to fit in a much larger grand strategy in several ways. Yemen is first of all for al-Qaeda a foothold on the Arabian Peninsula. The Arabian Peninsula has always been, for obvious reasons, high on the list of al-Qaeda's priorities for de-stabilization and terrorism. Osama bin Laden prematurely ordered al-Qaeda in Saudi Arabia to begin an uprising in 2003 and 2004. In order to put pressure on the West as the West was moving into Iraq. It was premature because al-Qaeda in Saudi Arabia wasn't ready. Its leaders told him that. But he exercises authority in the organization and they went forward.

He clearly also was a major player behind the scenes in masterminding the merger of the weakened al-Qaeda in Saudi Arabia, which desperately needed a refuge from the Saudi authorities, with al-Qaeda in Yemen. It looks that he predicted accurately the merger of the two would be a force-multiplier for both of them.

It is no accident of course that the first serious and significant target of AQAP was the Saudi Deputy Minister of the Interior Mohammed bin Nayef, the man who had destroyed al-Qaeda in Saudi Arabia. Through luck, the man tripped at the last minute, the prince survived. But it was an awesome wake up call that al-Qaeda was still coming after the house of Saud.

Secondly, al-Qaeda in the Arabian Peninsula offers an opportunity for the al-Qaeda senior leadership to stretch the global battlefield against the United States at a time when they are realize they are increasingly in the crosshairs of the United States.

The pressure I alluded to before on al-Qaeda in Pakistan has grown enormously over the last several years. In 2007, there were two drone attacks on al-Qaeda's leadership in Pakistan. I am sorry; in 2007, there were seven attacks. We missed all seven times. In 2008 there were 20 attacks and we began to have influence. In 2009, there were 53 drone attacks. And in 2010, we are now at a pace which will probably triple that before the end of the year. We are close to a drone attack now on al-Qaeda in Pakistan almost every 72 hours. And it is having an impact. We saw that on December 30 when al-Qaeda struck back.

One of the key players in al-Qaeda's attack on the CIA's forward operating base was a Yemeni, whose nomme de guerre Hussein al-Yemeni was killed in a drone attack last month. We know that because al-Qaeda published his martyrdom statements.

Yemen in this sense offers a chance to try to draw some of the pressure away. This is a classic al-Qaeda tactic. We played into their hands in 2003 precisely by invading Iraq and they were ready to draw us away from Pakistan then. They'd love to do it again in Yemen. Al-Qaeda's best case scenario, the United States would be enticed to move into Yemen on a large scale, to put boots on the ground, to create what al-Qaeda has referred to as a "bleeding war." To recreate in essence what al-Qaeda believes it did to the Soviet Union in Afghanistan in the 1980s. The formative experience in the life of Osama bin Laden and Ayman Zawahiri.

For them, Yemen is the perfect role model and they look back to the Egyptian intervention in Yemen in the 1960s when 70,000 Egyptian soldiers armed with chemical weapons were unable to curb the Yemeni insurgency. For its part, AQAP also clearly sees Yemen as the perfect place to bleed America. Let me read to you from one of their statements in 2009, talking about the history of their country.

Invaders have always been crushed on the rocks of Yemen's mountains, starting from the invasions of Portugal and Britain, and later the Ottomans and the Egyptians in modern times. This while the rest of the lands of the peninsula are a flat desert which do not provide strategic options for fighting.

The Obama administration has rightly chosen not to fall into the trap. Instead it has chosen to do the right thing in Yemen, in my judgment, which is to work with the Yemenis to try to develop their capacities in order to deal with AQAP. The days of unilateral American military intervention as the solution to al-Qaeda's threats, I hope, are coming to an end.

Whether the government of Yemen is up to the challenge is of course the subject for discussion later on today. AQAP also has larger and somewhat grandiose strategic designs for what it can do. It makes a great deal of Yemen's strategic location on the maritime choke points of the Bab-el-Mandeb. It makes a great deal of alliances with Somalia and Somalia insurgents on the other side of the Gulf of Yemen. Whether these are realistic fears and threats that America should think about is another subject for conversation and debate today.

No one can deny however that the events of the last several months have once again put Yemen very much into the center of the debate about the future of al-Qaeda, the threat it poses and the global Islamic jihad. Thank you very much for your attention.

ABOUT THE AUTHORS

Rafid Fadhil Ali is an Iraqi journalist, writer and researcher, and currently a senior broadcast journalist at the BBC World Service in London. From 2003 to 2007, he covered the Iraq war and the events that followed. Working for different Iraqi, pan-Arab and foreign media organizations as a TV reporter, Mr. Ali is an expert in Iraqi politics and militant groups in the Middle East. He writes frequently in Arabic and English for publications such as *Terrorism Monitor* of The Jamestown Foundation, and the daily *al-Hayat* Arabic newspaper.

Abdul Hameed Bakier is an intelligence expert on counter-terrorism, crisis management and terrorist-hostage negotiations. Since 2006, he has monitored Iraqi Jihadist websites and written on insurgent tactics and techniques for The Jamestown Foundation. He is based in Jordan.

Daniel Benjamin was sworn in as Coordinator for Counterterrorism at the Department of State with the rank of Ambassador-at-Large on May 28, 2009. Prior to his appointment, Ambassador Benjamin was Director of the Center on the United States and Europe and a Senior Fellow in Foreign Policy Studies at the Brookings Institution from December 2006 to May 2009. He spent six years as a Senior Fellow in the International Security Program at the Center for Strategic and International Studies. From 1994 to 1999, Mr. Benjamin served on the National Security Council staff. In 1998-1999, he was Director for Counterterrorism in the Office of Transnational Threats. In 1994-1997, he served as foreign policy speechwriter and special assistant to President Clinton. Before entering the government, Mr. Benjamin was a foreign correspondent for *TIME Magazine* and *The Wall Street Journal*. He has co-written two books. *The Age of Sacred Terror* was published by Random House in 2002 and documents the rise of religiously motivated terrorism and American efforts to combat it. *The Age of Sacred Terror* was named a *New York Times* Notable Books of 2002 and was given the Arthur Ross Book Award of the Council on Foreign Relations. *The Next Attack: The Failure of the War on Terror and a Strategy for Getting it Right*, was published by Holt/Times Books in 2005 and named a *Washington Post* "Best Book" of 2005. He also edited *America and the World in the Age of Terror: A New Landscape of International Relations* (CSIS, 2005). He has published numerous articles in the *New York Times, Washington Post, Slate, TIME Magazine*, the *Los*

Angeles Times, and other publications. Mr. Benjamin holds degrees from Harvard and Oxford, where he was a Marshall Scholar.

Christopher Heffelfinger is a Washington, DC-based specialist on militant Islam and Islamist ideology and radicalization. He was a consultant to the Combating Terrorism Center (CTC) at the U.S. Military Academy at West Point, where he served as a FBI fellow providing counterterrorism training and instruction for the FBI and Joint Terrorism Task Forces. He has also lectured publicly, and to other government agencies, about radical Islam and terrorism. Mr. Heffelfinger is author of *Radical Islam in America: Salafism's Journey from Arabia to the West* (Potomac Books Inc, Forthcoming, 2010). He is also editor of *Unmasking Terror: A Global Review of Terrorist Activities* (Vol I and II, The Jamestown Foundation).

Michael Horton is an independent analyst who specializes in Yemen and the Horn of Africa. He writes for *Jane's Intelligence Review, Intelligence Digest, Islamic Affairs Analyst*, and the *Christian Science Monitor*.

Gregory D. Johnsen is a Ph.D. candidate in Near Eastern Studies at Princeton University. He was a former Fulbright Fellow in Yemen.

Mark N. Katz is a Professor of Government and Politics at George Mason University. He writes on Russian foreign policy, the international relations of the Middle East, and transnational revolutionary movements. Before starting to teach at George Mason University in 1988, he was a research fellow at the Brookings Institution (1980-81), held a temporary appointment as a Soviet affairs analyst at the U.S. Department of State (1982), was a Rockefeller Foundation international relations fellow (1982-84), and was both a Kennan Institute research scholar (1985) and research associate (1985-87). He has also received a U.S. Institute of Peace fellowship (1989-90) and grant (1994-95), and several Earhart Foundation fellowship research grants. He was a visiting scholar at the Hokkaido University Slavic Research Center (June-July 2007), and at the Kennan Institute (January 2008). He received his Ph.D. in political science from MIT.

Mohammed Al-Maitami, Ph.D., is Professor of economics at Sana'a University in Yemen, where he as served since 1988. He has also served as a visiting scholar, professor, and researcher at many academic international institutions, such as the Institute for Research Studies for the Arab and Muslim World in France, UC Berkeley, and Georgetown University. He is also the founder and member of many Yemeni NGOs, one of which is the Institute of Yemeni Democracy in Washington, D.C. Professor Al-Maitami is also a Silatech Senior Country Representative for Yemen, Vice Chairman on Non-governmental Counsel of Advisors for the President of the Republic of Yemen, Vice Chancellor of the International University of Technology Twintech, Yemen Branch, Sana'a, since 2009, a founder and member of the board of trustees and the Board of Directors of Sheba Center of Strategic Studies in Sana'a, and a member and affiliate of many international academic and business institutions including the Economic Research Forum, Global Development Network, and others. Professor Al-Maitami has published extensively in Arabic, English and French and in academic journals and newspapers both in and outside of Yemen.

Munir Mawari is a Yemeni-American journalist and native speaker of Arabic. Currently a freelance writer, he has worked previously for al-Jazeera TV, Voice of America, and *Asharq al-Awsat*. He appears frequently on the BBC Arabic service and other satellite TV channels.

Andrew McGregor is Director of Toronto-based Aberfoyle International Security and Managing Editor of the Jamestown Foundation's Global Terrorism Analysis publications. He received a Ph.D. from the University of Toronto's Department of Near and Middle Eastern Civilizations in 2000 and is a former Research Associate of the Canadian Institute of International Affairs. He has worked as a consultant to New Scotland Yard's SO15 Counter Terrorism Command and provided expert witness for the UK's Crown Prosecution Service. His latest book is *A Military History of Modern Egypt*, published by Praeger Security International in 2006. Dr. McGregor has written over 300 articles on international security issues for organizations including Jane's Intelligence, the Royal Institute of International Affairs and the Canadian Institute of Strategic Studies. He is the author of an archaeological history of Darfur published by Cambridge University in 2001 and provides frequent commentary on military and security issues for international newspapers, radio and television, including the *New York Times*, *Financial Times*, and the BBC.

Brian O'Neill is a former writer and editor at the *Yemen Observer*. Currently a freelance analyst based out of Chicago, he has published extensively on Yemen, with a focus on the relationship between Yemen's history, politics, economics, and security. With Gregory Johnsen, he currently runs the Yemen-focused blog *Waq al-Waq*, and also blog at *Always Judged Guilty*.

Shaun Overton is an independent analyst specializing in the Arab World. He spent nine months conducting research in Yemen.

Sarah Phillips lectures at the Centre for International Security Studies at Sydney University. She lived and worked in Yemen for nearly four years and specializes in Middle Eastern politics and the politics of state-building. Her recent book, *Yemen's Democracy Experiment in Regional Perspective* (2008) was published by Palgrave Macmillan. She can be contacted at sarphil@gmail.com.

Babak Rahimi is Assistant Professor at the Department of Literature, Program for the Study of Religion, at the University of California - San Diego. From 2005-2006, he was a Senior Fellow at the United States Institute of Peace, where he conducted research on Grand Ayatollah Ali al-Sistani and Shi'a politics in post-Ba'athist Iraq. From 2000-2001, he was also a Visiting Fellow at the Department of Anthropology at the London School of Economics and Political Science. Dr. Rahami holds a B.A. from the University of California – San Diego, M.A. in Ancient and Medieval Philosophy from the University of Nottingham, and a Ph.D. from the European University Institute in Florence, Italy.

Bruce Riedel is a Senior Fellow in the Saban Center for Middle East Policy at the Brookings Institution. He retired in 2006 after 30 years of service at the Central Intelligence Agency including postings overseas. He was a senior advisor on South Asia and the Middle East to four Presidents of the United States in the staff of the National Security Council at the White House. He was a negotiator at several Arab-Israeli peace summits including at Camp David and Wye River. He was also Deputy Assistant Secretary of Defense for the Near East and South Asia at the Pentagon and a senior advisor at the North Atlantic Treaty Organization in Brussels. In January 2009 President Barack Obama asked him to chair a review of American policy towards Afghanistan and Pakistan the results of which the President announced in a speech on March 27, 2009. He is the author of *The Search for al Qaeda: Its Leadership, Ideology and Future* (2008), published by Brookings Press. He teaches at Georgetown University and SAIS.

Michael W. S. Ryan is an independent consultant and researcher on Middle Eastern security issues and a Senior Research Associate at the Jamestown Foundation. Dr. Ryan has served as the Vice President of the Middle East Institute as well as Vice President at the Millennium Challenge Corporation (2007-2008), and as a Political-Military and foreign assistance specialist for the Departments of Defense and State with an emphasis on Middle East and North Africa (1979-1997). He is a former Fulbright Fellow at the American Research Center in Egypt. Dr. Ryan received his B.A. from St. John's College and a Ph.D. from Harvard University.

Michael Scheuer served in the Central Intelligence Agency for 22 years before resigning in 2004. He served as the Chief of the bin Laden Unit at the Counterterrorist Center from 1996 to 1999. He is the once anonymous author of *Imperial Hubris: Why the West is Losing the War on Terror*. His other book also includes *Marching Toward Hell: America and Islam After Iraq*. Dr. Scheuer is a former Senior Fellow at The Jamestown Foundation.

Charles Schmitz is an Assocaite Professor and a specialist on Yemen and Arab political economy at Towson University, Baltimore, MD. His interests include the political economy of development and development policy in the Arab world, international law and the war on terror, contemporary geopolitics and the issue of the "failing state," Arab politics, and cross cultural understanding and communication. He received his Ph.D. in geography from the University of California – Berkeley.

Murad Batal al-Shishani is a London-based analyst on Islamic groups and terrorism. He is also a specialist on Islamic movements in Chechnya and in the Middle East. Al-Shishani is a regular contributor to several publications in both Arabic and English such as The Jamestown Foundation's *Terrorism Monitor* and the London-based *al-Hayat*. His weekly column is published at the Jordanian daily *al-Ghad* every Wednesday. He is also the author of the books, *The Islamic Movement in Chechnya* (2002) and the *Chechen-Russian Conflict 1990-2000*, and also *Iraqi Resistance: National Liberation vs. Terrorism: A Quantitative Study* (2005).

John Solomon is Global Head of Terrorism Research at World-Check. Currently on attachment at the United Kingdom's National Fraud Intelligence Bureau with the City of London Police's Overseas Anti-Corruption Unit, he is pursuing his doctorate in the Department of War Studies, King's College London.

Michael Taarnby is an independent terrorism researcher and consultant based in Denmark. He was a research fellow at the Danish Institute for International Studies with a specialization in political and militant Islamism.

Stephen Ulph is a Senior Fellow at The Jamestown Foundation. One of the preeminent analysts of the Islamic world, Mr. Ulph specializes in the economic and political developments of the Middle East and North Africa. He is the founder and former editor of the *Terrorism Security Monitor* and former editor and analyst of Islamic Affairs for Jane's Information Group.

Eric Watkins is the first Western person ever allowed to reside in Yemen as a foreign correspondent. Altogether, he lived some 20 years in the Red Sea region, including Saudi Arabia (1981-88), Yemen (1989-94) and Cyprus (2000-04). On the recommendation of the desert explorer Wilfred Thesiger, Watkins was elected a Fellow of the Royal Geographical Society in 1989 for his contributions to knowledge of the Arabian Peninsula. Watkins holds a Ph.D. in Comparative Literature from the University of California at San Diego, and is writing a book documenting the impact of trade on Yemeni history.

Chris Zambelis is an Associate with Helios Global, Inc., a risk analysis firm based in the Washington, DC area. The opinions expressed here are the author's alone and do not necessarily reflect the position of Helios Global, Inc.

ABOUT THE EDITOR

Ramzy Mardini joined the Jamestown Foundation in 2007 as a Middle East Analyst. Prior to joining, Mr. Mardini had served at the Executive Office of the President and as Iraq Desk Officer for Political Affairs at the U.S. Department of State, where he handled the office portfolio on intelligence for the Director of Iraq Affairs. Proficient in Arabic, he has traveled extensively to the Middle East and had also served as a Research Analyst on Iran at the Center for Strategic Studies at the University of Jordan. Mr. Mardini graduated *summa cum laude* with *research distinction* in political science from Ohio State University, and received an honors M.A. in international relations from the University of Chicago.

INDEX